Ritual and Language

T0373808

While ritual is often associated with phenomena such as ceremonies, cursing and etiquette, it actually encompasses something much more important: it includes all instances of communally oriented language use. As such, ritual manifests itself in many forms in our daily lives, such as politeness, swearing and humour, and in many different life situations, spanning trash talk in sports events, through market bargaining, to conventional social pleasantries. This pioneering book provides an introduction to ritual language use by presenting a cutting-edge, language-anchored and replicable framework applicable for the study of ritual in different datatypes and languages. The framework is illustrated with a wealth of case studies drawn from Chinese and Anglophone rituals which demonstrate how to use it effectively. The book is essential reading for both academics and students, and is relevant to pragmatics, applied linguistics and other fields.

DÁNIEL Z. KÁDÁR is Chair Professor at Dalian University of Foreign Languages, China, Research Professor at HUN-REN Hungarian Research Centre for Linguistics, Hungary, and Professor of English Linguistics at University of Maribor, Slovenia. He is Ordinary Member of Academia Europaea. He has research interests in pragmatics, linguistic politeness, interaction ritual and applied linguistics.

Ritual and Language

Dániel Z. Kádár

Dalian University of Foreign Languages
HUN-REN Hungarian Research Centre for Linguistics
University of Maribor

CAMBRIDGE
UNIVERSITY PRESS

Shaftesbury Road, Cambridge CB2 8EA, United Kingdom

One Liberty Plaza, 20th Floor, New York, NY 10006, USA

477 Williamstown Road, Port Melbourne, VIC 3207, Australia

314–321, 3rd Floor, Plot 3, Splend or Forum, Jasola District Centre,
New Delhi – 110025, India

103 Penang Road, #05–06/07, Visioncrest Commercial, Singapore 238467

Cambridge University Press is part of Cambridge University Press & Assessment,
a department of the University of Cambridge.

We share the University's mission to contribute to society through the pursuit of
education, learning and research at the highest international levels of excellence.

www.cambridge.org
Information on this title: www.cambridge.org/9781108472968

DOI: 10.1017/9781108624909

First published 2024

A catalogue record for this publication is available from the British Library.

Library of Congress Cataloging-in-Publication Data
Names: Kádár, Dániel Z., 1979– author.
Title: Ritual and language / Dániel Z. Kádár, Dalian University of Foreign
Languages; HUN-REN Hungarian Research Centre for Linguistics; University of
Maribor.
Description: Cambridge ; New York, NY : Cambridge University Press, 2024. |
Includes bibliographical references and index.
Identifiers: LCCN 2023026048 | ISBN 9781108472968 (hardback) | ISBN
9781108460828 (paperback) | ISBN 9781108624909 (ebook)
Subjects: LCSH: Pragmatics. | Ritual language (Linguistics) | Interpersonal
communication.
Classification: LCC P99.4.P72 K23 2024 | DDC 394.01/41–dc23/eng/20230919
LC record available at https://lccn.loc.gov/2023026048

ISBN 978-1-108-47296-8 Hardback
ISBN 978-1-108-46082-8 Paperback

Contents

Figures

Tables

Acknowledgements

First of all, I would like to express my heartfelt gratitude to my dear friend Juliane House, to whom this book is dedicated. Juliane's and her late husband Willis Edmondson's thoughts have deeply influenced my view of ritual and language, and I would have never been able to finish this book without all the support and care I have received from Juliane over those five years during which the manuscript of this book was being prepared. Juliane and I spent many hours online where we not only discussed serious work but also madly laughed and quarrelled – and having such a time made it real fun to formulate the ideas of this book!

I am also grateful to the various Reviewers and the Clearance Reader who helped me enormously to improve the quality of the present manuscript. I am indebted to Helen Barton at Cambridge University Press who is the best Editor one can ever wish for. I am also grateful to Isabel Collins at Cambridge University Press for all her support. I would also like to say thank you to all those colleagues at Dalian University of Foreign Languages who contributed to the birth of this book, including Emily Fengguang Liu, as well as various of my previous and present PhD students, including (in alphabetical order) Lin Jiao, Shiyu Liu, Wenrui Shi, Yulong Song, Zongfeng Xia and Sen Zhang. I am also grateful to Tamás Váradi and Réka Dodé at the HUN-REN Hungarian Research Centre for Linguistics for all their support.

On an institutional level, I would like to acknowledge the funding of the National Excellence Programme of the National Research, Development and Innovation Office of Hungary (grant number: TKP2021-NKTA-02). This grant, which is the continuation of another one (Momentum Grant of the Hungarian Academy of Sciences, grant number LP2017/5) provided funding to conduct the present research. The above grants have been hosted by the HUN-REN Hungarian Research Centre for Linguistics.

Last but definitely not the least, I am indebted to my family: Keiko, Naoka, Zita, András and Eszter, as well as Koma. Thank you all for bearing with me while I spent those many hours in front of my computer.

Foreword

This book covers an important phenomenon of language usage: interaction ritual. When pragmatics gained momentum at the beginning of my academic career in the 1970s, everyone in the circle of academics I worked with, my late husband Willis Edmondson, my friends Shoshana Blum-Kulka and Gabriele Kasper, and many others in our research group had an interest in ritual in one way or another, and we mentioned ritual in different contexts in various of our studies. Interestingly and regretfully, the study of ritual then largely faded in the 1990s, along with the early pragma-linguistic criteria that Willis Edmondson and myself always advocated: the necessity of using a strictly language-anchored and bottom–up approach to language use where one only employs linguistic pragmatic units of analysis. This is why it is so refreshing to see the present book: the author Dániel Z. Kádár not only provides a ground-breaking theory of ritual – he also proposes a strictly language-anchored and bottom–up pragmatic framework which is replicable for the study of ritual phenomena across various languages and different types of data.

I knew this book was on the way because Dániel is a dear friend with whom I have now collaborated on a daily basis for half of a decade, and I have also contributed to the research presented in various chapters. When he reached out to me to write this foreword, I initially felt that this may not be a good idea because it is difficult to be objective when one comments on one's friend's work which includes one's own academic input. However, I nevertheless accepted Dániel's request because he wanted me to tell the reader why a language-anchored and bottom–up pragmatic framework is so important for present day pragmatic inquiries.

In the 1980s, the circle of scholars with whom I conducted the renowned Speech Act Realization (CCSARP) Project profited a lot from the earlier work by Edmondson and myself on a pedagogic interactional grammar which also included a radically minimal and finite typology of speech acts that enabled us to interpret interaction in a replicable way across many different languages and datatypes. Our goal was to avoid falling into the trap of claiming pragmatic universals, and instead we worked towards methodological replicability and rigour which meant that we created categories which could be used to describe phenomena across various languages, without claiming that these phenomena are the same across various languages.

While the work by the CCSARP group has had a large influence through cross-cultural pragmatics from the 1990s to the mid-2010s, it had been mainly replicated in the form of 'applied' research – many scholars worldwide used this methodology to study language use in Chinese, Japanese, Arabic and various European languages to this day. It was in the mid-2010s that Dániel reached out to me through what he called 'a crazy email' in which he proposed that he and myself should engage in a cross-generation collaboration. He said he wanted to go back to what we were doing in the 1980s, and renew it by cross-fertilising it with more recent views on language use, as well as his own work on ritual. In the years to come, we produced together many studies in which we breezed new life into cross-cultural pragmatics, and meanwhile Dániel prepared the present book, which is now finally ready.

Why is it important that Dániel Kádár's framework, the first of its kind, captures ritual – which is arguably the most ancient form of interpersonal interactional phenomenon – in a bottom–up way? The answer to this question is that the present framework allows us to have a clear vision of what 'ritual' involves from a linguist's point of view, and also how this phenomenon is realised in many different linguacultural contexts. A key problem since the beginning of pragmatics has been that ritual is such a broad phenomenon that we often use it either in a simple way to describe social symbolic communication, or in a vague manner to describe ceremonies. The present book creates an order in the fuzzy world of ritual, without oversimplifying it – in fact, it successfully shows how complex ritual phenomena can be from a linguist's point of view, while at the same time providing a rigorous academic framework through which the reader never feels at loss. I expect this book to become a must-read, not only in pragmatics but also in other areas of linguistics and other fields where ritual is studied.

Juliane House (University of Hamburg)
31 January 2023, Hamburg

1   Introduction

1.1   Objectives

The aim of this book is to provide a pragmatically anchored framework of ritual. Pragmatics is a field focusing on the study of language use. It started to develop in the mid-twentieth century, and it gained momentum with the work of the language philosophers John Austin and John Searle who proposed to look at language as a means to get things done.[1]

'Ritual' can mean different things to different people, such as ceremonies, religious practices, curses, conventionalised patterns of civility and so on. The study of ritual has its roots in anthropology, and anthropologists provided more than just one definition of ritual.[2] In linguistic pragmatics, the term 'ritual' has also been used in many different ways, including stylised and formalised language,[3] ceremonial and performative aspects of language use,[4] a sense of façade,[5] in-group interactional practices which are often meaningless to group outsiders,[6] and many other aspects of language use. In the pragmatic jargon influenced by sociology in general and the seminal work of the sociologist Erving Goffman in particular (see more in Chapter 2),[7] ritualists[8] also distinguish various types of ritual, such as 'presentational rituals', i.e., rituals through which the individual makes specific attestations to the recipient, versus 'avoidance rituals' through which the speaker expresses deference to the other (Goffman 1967: 57–76). The word 'ritual' and its equivalents also have different meanings across languages, as Chapter 2 will show. Finally, 'ritual' can also mean different things in the language use of an individual. For example, while I define myself as a ritual pragmatician – an assertion which could imply that I somehow apply the word 'ritual' in a more expert way than 'lay' people – I nevertheless often use the expression 'That's only a ritual' in daily interaction to indicate that a particular form of language use is meaningless.

Due to its many meanings and uses, 'ritual' is a difficult phenomenon for the linguist to pin down. A simple working definition for this phenomenon is the following: ritual encompasses communally oriented language use through which social structures reproduce themselves. 'Communal orientation' means that ritual should be viewed as conventionalised language use, which serves a social grouping primarily and the individual only secondarily, and which therefore needs to be observed through rights and obligations holding for a particular context.[9] However, this simple definition is already problematic to a certain degree because the 'reproduction' of social structures is not so much a linguistic but rather an anthropological and sociological concept.[10] More importantly, such a definition cannot capture all the facets of ritual in interaction. In spite of such definitional difficulties, ritual phenomena need to be pinned down in pragmatic theory for various reasons:

- As this book will show, ritual is such a primordial and essential part of language use that it simply must be studied if our goal is to understand why people use language by following certain conventionalised patterns.
- Ritual encompasses a wide variety of phenomena of language use, such as politeness, impoliteness, sarcasm, humour and so on, through which language users build up and maintain relationships. Ritual is not an umbrella term for these sociopragmatic[11] phenomena but rather it represents communally oriented language use in which such phenomena manifest themselves in conventionalised and contextually expected forms. As such, ritual is broader than perhaps any other sociopragmatic phenomena, which accords with the fact that from an evolutionary point of view ritual is perhaps the most primordial form of interpersonal pragmatic behaviour, as Bax (2010) has shown in his ground-breaking research.
- Ritual represents the realm of conventionalised and contextually expected language use, and so its study allows the scholar to examine language use in a rigorous and replicable way, beyond idiosyncrasies. While idiosyncratic language use has its own role in ritual, as Chapter 3 will show, ultimately idiosyncratic behaviour which violates the flow of a ritual tends to be sanctioned. The conventionalised nature of ritual also makes it a prime phenomenon to study in contrastive pragmatics (see House & Kádár 2021a). Furthermore, ritual research provides insight into various noteworthy aspects of language use, such as the relationship between language, context and morality.
- Finally, ritual manifests itself in all the three key units of language use, i.e., expressions, speech acts and discourse, as the present book will show. This, in turn, makes the pragmatic study of ritual particularly intriguing and productive from a methodological point of view.

Chapter 2 will describe ritual in more detail, by arguing that instead of simply relying on a working definition like the one provided above, the best practice for the pragmatician is to define ritual primarily through its main characteristics. It is important to note already at this point that ritual language use is not identical with conventionalised language use. While all rituals are conventionalised, they also have many spontaneous elements, as this book will show (see also Mahmood 2001). Further, convention is a much broader concept than ritual: it encompasses all the recurrent ways through which conveying and interpreting a message is organised (see e.g., Marmor 2009). For example, it is a pragmatic convention to use requests when the speaker wants the recipient to do something for him, it is also a convention to formulate a requestive utterance indirectly in certain interpersonal contexts, and also the interpretation of such a formulation tends to be conventionalised (see the phenomenon of conventionalised implicature). Ritual is something much more specific than this. To stick to the example of the speech act Request, it can be said that certain ritual contexts conventionally require one or more of the participants to formulate requestive utterances in certain conventionalised ways. For instance, in diplomatic protocols the speech act Request needs to be realised in certain ritual ways, in order for the participants to avoid breaching the protocol.[12] Also, a speech act like Request can become such a main constituent of certain rituals, like a religious act, that in turn the whole act will be centred on the particular speech act.[13] Finally, a ritual context may prompt a particular speech act like Request to manifest itself in the form of chains, or by following preset sequential patterns.[14] In summary, ritual and convention are two different pragmatic phenomena, but ultimately convention is always in the focus of the pragmatic study of ritual because all ritual contexts and practices have their conventions as regards how utterances need to be formulated.

While previous pragmatic research has addressed various aspects of ritual language use, to the best of my knowledge no book has been devoted to the comprehensive study of ritual and language for its own sake. Many pragmaticians, including myself, have attempted to capture ritual through the lens of linguistic politeness research – i.e., the study of how language users express that they care about the other – a field which has gained momentum through the seminal work of Brown and Levinson (1987) (see more in Chapter 2). Because of this, in pragmatic research, ritual has had a somewhat 'subordinated' role to politeness. This book aims to challenge this view. As part of attempting to provide a pragmatic account of ritual language use, I will follow a decidedly bottom–up and corpus-based view on ritual. Such a view is fundamental if one wants to avoid watering down the linguistic pragmatic study of ritual, by talking about cultural and psychological notions like 'sensitivity' and 'values'.[15] While culture studies have their own important role in ritual research, there is so much yet to be said about ritual from a pragmatic point of view that it is simply not advisable to attempt to venture beyond the boundaries of pragmatics in this book.

In filling the above-outlined knowledge gap, this book will propose a ritual view on language use, by arguing that many pragmatic phenomena can be best captured if we look at them through the lens of ritual. This view will be positioned against what I will refer to as the 'politeness perspective'.

As already noted, politeness is a very important pragmatic phenomenon, and the present book is by no means an attempt to criticise the validity of politeness studies. However, politeness has become interpreted in such an overly broad way over the past few years that now the terms 'politeness' and 'impoliteness' tend to describe literally all aspects of interpersonal behaviour. I believe that such a view is problematic, if for nothing else, because it compromises the analytic force of 'politeness' itself. The ritual perspective of language use allows us to disentangle ritual, including ritualised politeness, from non-ritualistic aspects of polite, impolite, humorous, etc. language use, without 'pitting' ritual and politeness against each other.

A further goal of this book is to provide a pragmatically comprehensive overview of ritual. In order to achieve this goal, the book follows a tripartite structure, to cover the following areas:

- Part I focuses on the general pragmatic features of ritual. Here the book will discuss all those pragmatic features which make ritual a founding element of interpersonal interaction, beyond the scope of perhaps any other pragmatic phenomenon. This part of the book will also provide an overview of the conceptual repertoire of the pragmatic study of ritual, and it will also propose a typology through which the pragmatician can examine different uses of ritual. Most importantly, the chapters in this part will show why and how a pragmatic framework of ritual can help us observe many seemingly *ad hoc* and confusing, and other seemingly robotic and uninteresting manifestations of language use in a replicable and meaningful way.
- Part II studies three features which characterise pragmatically complex rituals, including mimesis, (self-)display and liminality. While none of these features are unheard of in pragmatic inquiries, they have been rarely studied jointly in previous pragmatic research. However, as the book will show, they are important to talk about as part of a systematic ritual view on language use, in particular if our goal is to understand why people use language often in seemingly 'unreasonable' ways.
- Finally, in Part III, the present book discusses key methodological issues of the pragmatic study of ritual. Here the main focus is on how one can study interaction rituals in two general methodological routes, and by focusing on the three units of pragmatic analysis, including expressions, speech acts and discourse.

Ultimately, I hope that the present book will invigorate the pragmatic study of ritual. As Chapter 2 will show, while ritual has been on the agenda of pragmaticians since the 1980s, the ritual perspective has remained unduly backgrounded in recent pragmatic inquiries.

1.2   Conventions

In the following, I outline the conventions of this book.

While most technical terms will be introduced when they first occur, there is a small set of basic terms which will be used throughout the book, and which should be introduced right at this point. Perhaps the most important one of these terms is 'ritual frame'. Simply put, ritual frame describes the (often invisible) rights and obligations and the related moral and interactional order which a ritual imposes on the participants. The ritual frame is such an important concept that it will be treated as a foundation of all the methodologies of the pragmatic study of ritual.

Following my joint work with Juliane House, I use the term 'linguaculture' to describe culture manifested through patterns of language use (see House & Kádár 2021a). This term is particularly useful in pragmatic research like the current one, which aims to consider pragmatic issues through the lens of language rather than culture. In the study of certain linguaculturally embedded phenomena, I will refrain from using wording that would attribute them to a particular culture. For example, instead of talking about 'a Chinese rite of passage' it is more productive to talk about 'rites of passage in Chinese'.

I use the technical term 'expression', representing the lowest unit of analysis, instead of 'word'. This is because 'expression' describes a pragmatic unit, which may include forms of varying size. Another central concept is speech act, which is an utterance considered as an action. Typical speech acts are Request and Apologise. Following the convention of Edmondson and House (1981), speech acts are indicated in capital letters, and also I will not use the word 'of' in the designation of speech acts, e.g., I will use 'speech act Apologise' instead of 'speech act of apology'. When a ritual is not analysed from a speech act point of view, I normally do not apply the above convention. For instance, 'public apology' as a phenomenon is referred to in small letters whenever the focus is not exactly on how the speech act Apologise is used in this ritual.

Along with conceptual conventions, the present book follows various ethical conventions. In each naturally occurring example and other data involving participants whose language use I observed, the participants are anonymised. As part of collecting data, the various teams of researchers who contributed collecting data for this book followed the standard ethical procedure of asking the consent of the participants and storing data safely.[16] Also, as an ethical consideration and in the spirit of gender equality, I use both the feminine and the masculine pronouns in the manuscript in a rather arbitrary fashion.

The present book was written for both academics and advanced student readers. To help this latter group of readers, chapters onwards from Chapter 3 include a case study, and also all chapters provide a recommended reading.

Furthermore, I will refrain from overwhelming the reader with technical terms – while using some technical jargon is unavoidable in an academic book of the present scope, I will limit the number of technical terms to the possible lowest number. Finally, this book includes many visualisations of the proposed analytic procedures, in order to make these procedures as accessible as possible.

The reader will note later on that Chinese language plays a prominent role in the case studies of this book. This is partly because I work in a Chinese university as an academic and in this role (and also as a speaker of Chinese myself) I had an opportunity to gain some insight into the fascinating world of rituals in the Chinese linguaculture. More importantly, I believe that while Chinese has gradually gained importance in pragmatic inquiries, still more work needs to be done to promote academic research on Chinese pragmatics. Yet, it is important to repeat at this point that the aim of this book is to present a replicable pragmatic framework of ritual language use, and so rituals in Chinese are merely used as case studies instead of being studied for their own sake.

1.3   Contents

The chapters in this book are organised according to the tripartite structure outlined above. Part I includes three chapters, which introduce the reader to the basics of ritual and language.

Chapter 2 positions ritual in pragmatics. The chapter first provides an overview of previous pragmatic research on ritual and discusses why Goffman's term 'interaction ritual' is particularly useful to describe what ritual is from the pragmatician's point of view. The chapter then considers why ritual offers a powerful perspective through which one can approach and interpret language use across different linguacultures and context types. At that point I outline the aforementioned notion of ritual perspective in more detail. Finally, the chapter defines the key pragmatic features of ritual as elements of a pragmatic approach to ritual and language. Interpreting ritual through this cluster of pragmatic features allows the researcher to venture beyond any single working definition, like the one provided in the present chapter.

Chapters 3 and 4 illustrate how the ritual perspective can be put to practice in the study of interactionally complex rituals. These chapters also show how and why a pragmatic typology of ritual allows one to observe seemingly very different types of pragmatic behaviour – such as mediatised aggression and protocols of public communication – as different manifestations of ritual. The chapters will also point out why it is useful to observe certain phenomena through the lens of ritual rather than politeness and impoliteness. Chapter 3 discusses the ways in which the ritual perspective can help the researcher to systematically describe seemingly *ad hoc* interactional events, such as mediated ritual aggression.[17] Here the expression 'ritual aggression' is used differently from behavioural sciences:[18] I interpret it in the sense of Labov (1972) to describe aggressive language use which follows ritual patterns. Ritual aggression can be a challenging phenomenon to study for two reasons. Firstly, in-group ritual aggression often appears to be 'violent' and, more importantly, 'unreasonable' for group outsiders. While all manifestations of ritual aggression have their own conventions, the pragmatic conventions of in-group ritual aggression may be very different from what other social groups find normative and acceptable. For instance, Chapter 2 will touch on intensive ritual cursing, which is normative for certain ethnic groups but may sound menacing for members of other groups, often leading to racist stereotypes and prejudices. A clear advantage of the ritual perspective is that it allows the researcher to describe the exact pragmatic conventions of such rituals in a rigorous and replicable way, and on a par with rites of civility, by moving beyond stereotypes and prejudices. Secondly, other less 'exotic' aggressive interaction rituals – which do not 'belong' to one particular group but rather 'the whole' of a society, or at least one of its major subgroups – also often manifest themselves in forms that one may describe as 'violent' and 'unreasonable'. The ritual perspective also helps the scholar to capture the pragmatic conventions and dynamics of these social rituals, which are the focus of Chapter 3. As a case study, the chapter examines language use before, during and after a 'grudge match' in a Mixed Martial Arts event, representing a present-day aggressive ritual which is watched (and participated) by many due to its mediatised nature.

Chapter 4 brings the reader into yet another area where the ritual perspective can provide a particularly accurate view on language use: the study of social protocols in public discourse, representing the realm of 'overly' ordinary language use. The term 'public discourse' includes both monologues and dialogues that take place in public, often through mediatised events or written (online) pieces which are available for, or even addressed to, members of the public. 'Social protocols' describe forms of language use associated with 'politeness' in public discourse specifically, where 'politeness' in the interpersonal sense is hardly needed, i.e., such forms at first sight may seem to be entirely 'superfluous' if not 'redundant'. Because of this, while social protocols and mediatised public aggression may appear to have little in common, interestingly both of them have an 'unreasonable' element. This sense of unreasonableness however dissolves once one looks at such forms of language use through the ritual perspective. As a case study, Chapter 4 examines the ritual conventions of social protocols in a corpus of Chinese public announcements made in the wake of a major crisis.

Part II of this book includes three chapters, which introduce the reader into those phenomena which one can usually witness when a ritual becomes interactionally complex: mimesis, (self-)displaying behaviour and liminality. Chapter 5 focuses on the phenomenon of mimesis. All rituals are mimetic because ritual language use triggers replication and reciprocation. However, Chapter 5 will show that in various interactionally complex rituals, including both ceremonies and certain types of institutional discourse, one can observe a specific mimetic phenomenon – 'performative mimesis' – which has not received sufficient attention in the study of language use, and which is worth exploring if one wants to understand why in certain ritual contexts language users play 'roles'. Simply put, the concept of 'performative mimesis' refers to contrived interactional performance whereby the performer sustains mimicking a predated interactional schema, just like an actor in a theatre manages a performance on stage by enacting a role. Performative mimesis is a particularly interesting phenomenon to consider because the participants of a ritual which necessitates such mimetic behaviour follow often invisible and uncodified scripts. Chapter 5 includes a case study which describes performative mimesis in Chinese university military training courses, representing an understudied ritual drawn from the realm of higher education in China.

Chapter 6 investigates the ritual phenomenon of (self-)display. Any instance of ritual language use implies a sense of displaying: the participants of a ritual tend to display their awareness of the rights and obligations and related conventions holding for the context which necessitates the given ritual. For example, by 'properly' greeting someone, one unavoidably displays one's awareness of the convention that the speech act Greet is due in the particular context. However, in certain ritual scenarios, especially if a ritual is competitive, display transforms into self-display, i.e., through following – and often excessively over-doing – the pragmatic conventions of the ritual, one may as much display one's awareness of these conventions and related skills like expressing 'politeness' or 'impoliteness' to the other. Since ritual (self-) displaying behaviour has been only touched on in a limited number of pragmatic studies, Chapter 6 attempts to introduce this phenomenon in a diversified way, by considering how different degrees of self-displaying behaviour can be distinguished from one another. As a case study, I investigate a corpus of historical Chinese letters written by an epistolary expert Gong Weizhai to various recipients, including both 'ordinary' recipients such as patrons, family members, lovers and so on, and fellow epistolary expert friends representing 'professional' recipients. With this latter audience, Gong engaged in a playful self-displaying competition as to who can be 'more' intricately deferential and humorous to the other.

Chapter 7 discusses the phenomenon of liminality from a pragmatic point of view. All interactionally complex rituals take the participants through a threshold to some degree, in that the rights and obligations and related conventions of pragmatic behaviour holding for rituals tend to differ from

their counterparts in 'ordinary' life. For example, the above-mentioned phenomenon of ritual (self-)display in letters can be said to be liminal simply
because outside of the ritual such a phenomenon might not manifest itself in the
same form, or even not occur at all. Yet, such a liminality is temporal rather than
permanent,[19] and it is relevant for the ritualist to study fully-fledged liminal
rituals with a sense of irreversibility. For example, ritual public apologies are
liminal in the fully-fledged sense because the person who realises such ritual
apologies passes a threshold with no return. Liminal rituals come together with
strong metapragmatic awareness: if the frame of the ritual and the related moral
order are violated, both the participants and the observers tend to become
alerted and engage in intensive metapragmatic reflections. Chapter 7 will
present a case study focusing on the liminal rite of workplace dismissal. Such
dismissals represent typical liminal rituals in the very sense of the word: they
change the life of the recipient and as such they are very meaningful and
irreversible. Because of this, perceived 'errors' in the realisation of the rite of
workplace dismissal trigger particularly intensive metapragmatic reflections
and evaluations.

Part III includes four chapters focusing on methodological issues in the
pragmatic study of ritual. As noted above, I propose two major methodological
takes on interaction ritual. In the first one, the analyst sets out to study ritual by
looking at the pragmatic units of expressions and speech acts. In this methodological take, therefore, one departs from pinning down ritual as a form, i.e.,
either as an expression or a conventionalised realisation of speech act through
which ritual comes to life. Yet, associating ritual with a form of language use
has its problems because expressions and speech acts tend to gain a ritual
pragmatic function in actual ritual frames rather than having a ritual value
per se, and one can only study their ritual function in a rigorous and replicable
way if one considers their conventional use(s) in interaction. Because of this,
both Chapters 8 and 9 propose replicable methodologies by means of which
one can study in a bottom–up way how expressions and speech act relate to
ritual. Chapter 8 considers the relationship between expressions, the smallest
unit of pragmatic analysis, and ritual. The chapter will provide a bottom–up,
corpus-based and replicable approach through which expressions associated
with structurally or functionally ritual speech acts are used to indicate awareness of the different ritual frame. Structurally ritual speech acts include speech
acts like Greet and Leave-Take which occur in ritual phases of an interaction
like Opening and Closing, while functionally ritual speech acts encompass
speech acts like Request and Apologise which tend to be realised in a ritual way
in many contexts. The chapter points out that the relationship between expressions
and interaction ritual can be best captured through a contrastive pragmatic lens
because the contrastive view allows the researcher to consider how strongly
a pragmatically important expression tends to indicate a functionally or structurally

ritual speech act and the related ritual frame when pitted against a comparable expression in another – preferably typologically distant – linguaculture. The chapter provides a case study of Chinese and English expressions associated with the speech act Apologise.

Chapter 9 examines how speech acts associated with ritual can be examined in a replicable way. The chapter makes an argument against 'identifying' new so-called 'ritual speech acts' *ad libitum* because such a procedure shuts the door on studying speech acts through which ritual is realised in a replicable way. Instead, it is a more productive practice to identify and describe one's subject of analysis with the aid of a finite typology of speech acts. The next task is to consider how this speech act is realised in a particular ritual frame. Chapter 9 provides a case study of the ritual phenomenon of 'admonishing' in a corpus of ancient Chinese texts. Admonishing represents a ritual realisation type of the Attitudinal speech act category Suggest (do-x)/(not-to-do-x).

The second methodological take on ritual proposed in Part III provides a solution for the study of interactionally complex ritual phenomena, by systematically breaking them down into replicable pragmatic units of analysis. As noted already, the complexity of a ritual phenomenon can either mean that a phenomenon is too broad to be discussed as a single ritual, i.e., it represents a form of ritual behaviour which spans across many different ritual contexts, or it represents a particular context and related ritual frame which triggers ritual behaviour but cannot be subsumed under a single ritual heading from the pragmatician's point of view. Chapter 10 focuses on the first of these cases: it explores the ritual phenomenon of self-denigration in Chinese. Self-denigration occurs in many different contexts of Chinese ritual practices and ceremonies, and if one attempts to describe its pragmatic features by relying on data drawn from a single context one unavoidably risks oversimplifying it. Rather, in the study of such a ritual phenomenon one should consider how it is used in different interpersonal scenarios with varying power and intimacy and in different phases of an interaction.

Chapter 11 focuses on the second type of difficulty: it proposes a discourse-analytic approach through which seemingly *ad hoc* and erratic interactional ritual behaviour in a single complex ritual frame can be studied in a replicable way. As a case study, the chapter will examine ritual bargaining in Chinese markets. While bargaining is a ritual in the popular sense of the word, it is problematic from the pragmatician's point of view to describe bargaining as a grand ritual, without considering how it can be systematically broken down into recurrent patterns of ritual language use.

Finally, Chapter 12 summarises the contents of the present book and proposes future areas of research.

Part I

The Language of Ritual: Foundations

Synopsis

Chapter 2 positions interaction ritual in pragmatics and defines its key pragmatic features. The chapter first provides an overview of previous pragmatic research on ritual and discusses why the renowned sociologist Erving Goffman's term 'interaction ritual' is particularly relevant for describing different types of ritual from the pragmatician's point of view. The chapter then discusses why ritual offers a powerful perspective through which one can systematically approach and interpret many seemingly very different manifestations of conventionalised and communally oriented language use across various linguacultures and context types. Finally, the chapter provides a definition of the basic pragmatic characteristics of interaction ritual. Chapters 3 and 4 show how the ritual perspective presented in Chapter 2 can be put to practice in the study of different types of communally oriented language use, by capturing them as different manifestations of ritual. Chapter 3 discusses how and why the concept of ritual can help us to systematically study seemingly *ad hoc* and interactionally intensive events, such as mediated ritual aggression. The chapter shows that many such events can be described through the very same pragmatic features of ritual as ordinary 'civil' rituals. Chapter 4 examines public political monologues where seemingly nothing 'interesting' is happening. The analysis shows that such monologues transpire to have intriguing ritual features once one observes them through a ritual lens. In summary, the analyses in Chapters 3 and 4 illustrate that seemingly very different manifestations of language use such as mediated aggression and political monologues operate according to similar ritual principles.

2   Interaction Ritual: The Basics

2.1   Introduction

This chapter provides a departure point for the academic journey in the rest of this book, by positioning ritual in pragmatics and defining its key pragmatic features.

The relationship between language use and ritual is far from being simple. Ritual practices appear in the whole spectrum of human interaction, including forms of behaviour which are polar opposites, such as highly formalised and institutionalised interaction[1] versus socially controversial ritual insults and aggression.[2] Further, 'ritual' has many popular meanings and interpretations, spanning ceremonies, through religious practices and in-group interactional habits, to manifestations of daily civility. Also, there is significant variation across linguacultures with regard to the degree of importance dedicated to ritual in its fully-fledged, ceremonial interpretation and the meaning of 'ritual'. For instance, in Japanese, the word *gishiki* 儀式 is almost inseparable from conventional ceremonies and has an essentially positive meaning,[3] while as Muir (2005) argues, in 'Western' linguacultures influenced by Latin, the word 'ritual' has a much broader semantic scope and it has a potentially negative connotation. At the same time, ritualists like Staal (1982) argue that humans are 'addicted' to ritual activity, i.e., ritual seems to equally prevail in any linguaculture irrespective of the connotation of the actual meaning of 'ritual' and comparable expressions. Due to such complexities, it may ever be a futile attempt to try capturing the relationship between ritual and language by relying on any popular definition of 'ritual'. Instead, in the rest of this book I will use 'ritual' as a technical term, and I will often refer to ritual with the collective term 'interaction ritual', which is to be introduced in more detail in Section 2.2 of this chapter. Such a detailed definition is needed because, as was noted in Chapter 1, it may be problematic even to rely on a single academic working definition of 'ritual'.

Ritual has a massive interface with many other pragmatic phenomena, in particular linguistic politeness, i.e., the ways in which language users build up and maintain their relationships, and impoliteness, i.e., the ways in which interactants disrupt and destruct their relationships. This is most likely the main reason why experts in the pragmatics of ritual have been reluctant to provide a single comprehensive definition of ritual.[4] For instance, in historical pragmatic research in which ritual has been broadly studied, the concept of 'ritual' has remained vaguely defined from a pragmatic point of view (see e.g., Arnovick 1984; Bax 1999). The difficulty of defining ritual in pragmatics may also relate to the fact that ritual research has its roots in anthropology and sociology rather than linguistics. As an example, one may consider the ritual framework of Émile Durkheim (1912 [1954]), which has had an enormous influence on anthropology and sociology, and even on anthropological linguistics, but has had a limited impact on pragmatics. Of course, there are various important intersections between anthropology, sociology and pragmatics, but as far as mainstream pragmatics is concerned, such intersections have limited influence, and therefore so has ritual itself. For instance, Durkheim described ritual as a cluster of practices organised around sacred objects, by means of which communities are bound together and socially reproduce themselves. 'Social reproduction' is straightforward to interpret from a pragmatic viewpoint, even though it is not a linguistic concept, and it is not a coincidence that the working definition in Chapter 1 included this notion. However, while the Durkheimian notion of 'sacred' has been implanted into pragmatic thought through Goffman's (1967) concept of 'face', sacredness in its fully-fledged ritual tribal/historical (non-urban) meaning is not a phenomenon that pragmaticians would normally study.

Such cross-disciplinary differences have terminological implications. Take the concept of 'liminality' as an example (see also Section 2.4). Liminality is a ritual term that describes the mental or relational changes that ritual triggers. 'Liminality' was introduced by the anthropologists Arnold van Gennep (1960) and Victor Turner (1969) into ritual research. Although 'liminal' is not unheard of in pragmatics, it has primarily been used by scholars such as Alexander (2004) working on the interface between pragmatics and sociology. While Senft and his colleagues (e.g., Senft & Basso 2009), as well as Bax (2003a) carried out invaluable work enriching pragmatics with the terminological inventory of ritual research, their work has remained relatively marginalised in pragmatics. This does not imply that ritual terminology has been entirely ignored in the field. 'Ritual' has been featured as a simple concept in such important works as Austin (1962) and Brown and Levinson (1987). Further, notions such as rights and obligations – which is essential to ritual and which received impetus from the Wittgensteinian philosophy, most notably Wittgenstein's notion of 'language games' – have been important in pragmatic inquiries.[5] However, ritual terminology in its own right has been neglected in the mainstream of the field of pragmatics.

The aim of this chapter is to fill this knowledge gap by positioning and defining ritual from the pragmatician's point of view, and also to provide an overview of the key terms of ritual research. The structure of the chapter is as follows. Section 2.2 provides a synopsis of how ritual has been seen in pragmatics, by describing the two main ways in which pragmaticians interpreted ritual phenomena. Here I also discuss the value of Goffman's notion 'interaction ritual', which encompasses the above-outlined two major pragmatic views on ritual. Section 2.3 presents the concept of 'ritual perspective', that is, the idea that interaction ritual offers a powerful perspective through which one can approach and interpret language use across many linguacultures and context types. Finally, Section 2.4 provides a definition of the key pragmatic features of interaction ritual, followed by a conclusion in Section 2.5.

2.2   Pragmatic Views on Ritual

In the following, let us discuss how previous pragmatic research has interpreted ritual and why a Goffmanian view helps us to interconnect these interpretations.

2.2.1   Interpretations of Ritual in Pragmatics

In pragmatics, 'ritual' has been interpreted in two different albeit closely interrelated ways: in a literal and an abstract sense. According to the first 'literal' definition, ritual encompasses a wide variety of behaviours, spanning ceremonies, through cursing, to manifestation of daily civil language such as Small Talk. Ritual in this sense includes both very 'meaningful' rites such as prayers, and 'meaningless' ones such as social niceties. 'Meaningless' here is borrowed from Edmondson's (1981) seminal work, describing the lack of referential message, which however does not correlate with a lack of social message. For instance, the remark 'It's nice weather, isn't it' is a typical ritual utterance, which does not say anything 'actual' but at the same time conveys an important social meaning. In the second more abstract sense, ritual encompasses any conventionalised interaction in contexts where rights and obligations are set and the interaction is communally oriented. For instance, 'You are fired' uttered by a manager is an Informative speech act which is typically ritual because it animates the voice of an institution, uttered by a speaker who is both a ratified 'principal' and 'animator' in Goffman's (1979) sense, endowed with a right to produce this utterance. Figure 2.1 illustrates the above-outlined two definitions of ritual in pragmatics:

| Literal definition: Variety of forms (e.g., ceremonies, cursing, daily civilities), including both 'meaningful' and 'meaningless' ones (but consider social meaning!) | Abstract definition: Variety of contexts in which rights and obligations are important and where the interaction is communally oriented |

Figure 2.1 Definitions of ritual in pragmatics.

The boxes in Figure 2.1 have dashed lines because the two above-outlined definitions are not in contradiction: they simply interpret ritual from different angles, i.e., either through form (of behaviour) or context. Also, some phenomena such as 'apology' can simultaneously be interpreted in both these senses, e.g., as a form (speech act) realised in a ritual context and as a ritual context and a related activity which triggers some expected form of behaviour. As this book will show, these definitions of ritual trigger different data analytic procedures. The double-headed arrow in Figure 2.1 indicates that these definitions of ritual can – and are advised to – be used in combination.

I will consider how such combined research can be carried out in more detail later in this section. Yet, before so doing, let us discuss the trajectory of these two different but closely related interpretations of ritual in pragmatic research. In early pragmatic work in the 1980s, the concept of ritual emerged in studies on routinised language use, speech acts, politeness and discourse. Representatives of such research are Coulmas (1981), Edmondson (1981) and Edmondson and House (1981) who all used ritual to discuss seemingly 'empty' but socially meaningful (and often ceremonial) communication. In their renowned framework of linguistic politeness, Brown and Levinson (1987) used the concept of ritual to capture ceremonial aspects of language use. For Brown and Levinson, ritual as a ceremonial phenomenon was such an important phenomenon that they opened their work with a reference to the seminal research of Durkheim. The following excerpt represents how ritual is typically used by Brown and Levinson:

Greetings and farewells, and in general rituals of beginning and terminating encounters often contain . . . bald-on-record commands. In Tzeltal we have:

. . . (43)   *ban.* (farewell)
         Go.

     (44)   *naklan.* (offer to visitor)
         Sit down.

     (45)   *solan.* (trail greeting)
         Pass.   (Brown & Levinson 1987: 99)

Brown and Levinson included both macro–social and micro–in-group rituals in their discussion of the ceremonial aspects of politeness. For example, they drew attention to

a parallel between interpersonal ritual and institutionalized rites . . . [which helped them forming their] ideas about typical dyadic rituals of interpersonal communication [and which] suggest a startlingly simple theory of a *symbolism* of exchange. (Brown & Levinson 1987: 45)

Ritual also played an important role in later criticisms of the Brown and Levinsonian paradigm. In particular, East Asian critiques of Brown and Levinson – such as Ide (1989) and Gu (1990) – used ritual data to argue against the validity of Brown and Levinson's framework. For example, Ide used the following example to argue why, according to her, Brown and Levinson's universalistic approach to politeness as a strategic form of behaviour is wrong:

#Sensei-wa kore o yonda
'The professor read this.'

*Sensei-wa kore o **o-yomi-ni-natta***
'The professor read this.' (Ide 1989: 227)

According to Ide, talking about a lecturer in Japanese triggers a ceremonial ritual style, and so speakers of Japanese are not free to 'strategically' use politeness as argued by Brown and Levinson (1987). In other words, Ide argued that certain ritual contexts preclude the use of strategic or *ad hoc* language use. Yet, as Kádár and Mills (2013) pointed out, East Asian critiques of Brown and Levinson did not attempt to systematically integrate their arguments into ritual theory, even though they used examples like the one above of a clearly ceremonial and ritual nature. Along with politeness researchers like Brown and Levinson, experts of various other pragmatic areas such as historical pragmatics (e.g., Bax 2001, 2010; Reichl 2003) and second language (L2) pragmatics (e.g., Keshavarz et al. 2006; Bruti 2018) also often defined ritual in a literal way, i.e., as a ceremony of some kind. For the ritual pragmatician, such studies represent a fundamental academic background because they show that the ceremonial and routinised aspects of interpersonal interaction are at least as important as free-flowing and often idiosyncratic conversation.

Pragmatics has also witnessed the development of another body of research on ritual where ritual tends to be interpreted in a more abstract sense – i.e., as a cluster of conventionalised practices – beyond what a lay person normally understands when using the word 'ritual'. To the best of my knowledge, such research in pragmatics started with the seminal study of House who developed a ritual line of analysis and an essentially ritual concept – 'standard situation' (House 1989) – to distinguish normative behaviour from politeness behaviour, without however explicitly pursuing interest in ritual. As House (1989) pointed out, in standard situations, the interactants are bound by rights and obligations to produce and respond to utterances in certain preset ways. For example, a policeman is likely to produce the speech act Request 'Please move your car' to reprimand a driver parking in the wrong place, and the driver is likely to utter 'Yes' in response (instead of e.g., the Request for information 'Why'). As

House argues, such behaviour is very little (if at all) related to politeness but rather it is somehow preset and normative (i.e., ritual as now we would say) – an argument which was well ahead of its time! Later on, the above-outlined interest in context triggering ritual language use has gained momentum in North American pragmatic research on civility, in particular the work of Jeffrey Alexander and his colleagues (e.g., Alexander 2004; Alexander et al. 2006). Recently, Mervyn Horgan (2019, 2020) made a fundamental contribution to this line of research, by examining how breaches of civility indicate language user's awareness of ritual contexts in their daily lives. Juliane House and myself pursued a somewhat different but closely related line of research as we examined how language use, in particular the choice of certain pragmatically loaded expressions, indicate awareness of the ritual frame and related contextual rights and obligations (e.g., Kádár & House 2020a; see also Chapter 8). Through this research we could identify how context triggers instances of language use which may not be called 'ritual' in the popular sense of the word, but which has all the key pragmatic features of ritual.

One may argue that pragmatic research not only encompasses but also encourages the co-existence of these two complementary views on ritual. Let us revisit here the previously mentioned 'crossovers' in the pragmatic study of ritual. Pragmatics has witnessed a surge of interest in aggressive ritual behaviour, starting with Labov's (1972) seminal sociolinguistic work on 'rude' rituals. Typically, in such research scholars have examined rude (or at least 'rough') forms of pragmatic behaviour which may be described as ritual by some, but which may be too erratic and 'mundane' to be described as ritual in comparison to, for example, ceremonies or rites of civility. Also, unlike ceremonies, such rituals only gain a ritual function in specific contexts, which trigger ritual behavior, and so they are examples *par excellence* for a crossover between ritual as a form and ritual as a context. Let us provide some examples here. Rampton (1995) studied manifestations of 'crossing'. 'Crossing'

involves code alternation by people who are not accepted of the group associated with the second language they are using code switching into varieties that are not generally thought to belong to them. (Rampton 1995: 485)

Many forms of crossing are ritual: a typical example includes cases when students realise in-group ritual humour by mimicking a disliked lecturer's manner of speech. In the study of such a case of language use, one may examine the 'rite of crossing' as a context, while one also needs to examine how certain forms of language use – which in themselves may not be ritual – operate in this context. In a similar vein, I also examined how seemingly erratic and aggressive language behaviour such as heckling in stand-up comedy and political speeches can be captured as a context and form of ritual if it is interpreted as part of a broader ritual contextual frame (see Kádár 2017). Various other scholars followed the same train of thought in other related areas, such as the study of aggressive ritual socialisation both as a frame and as a form of behaviour (e.g., Blum-Kulka 1990; Kádár & Szalai 2020).

2.2.2   *The Goffmanian View: Interaction Ritual*

We may contend at this point that pragmatics affords various definitions of ritual in a rather liberal way. Indeed, one can witness very little academic debate between pragmatic experts of ritual as regards the accuracy of their ritual definitions. This liberal attitude is different from how scholars of many other pragmatic phenomena have approached their object of research – as an example, one may refer here to fierce definitional discussions in linguistic politeness research (see e.g., Eelen 2001). The reason why ritual pragmaticians have rarely (if at all) debated about the validity of their definitions may be partly due to the above-outlined lack of contradiction between various views on ritual, and partly due to the fact that the pragmatic worldview has been heavily influenced by Goffman's ground-breaking work on ritual. In other disciplines, ritual theory is often attributed to the work of Durkheim (1912 [1954]), and Goffman himself was influenced by Durkheim.[6] However, Durkheim's work has only had a limited impact on pragmatics (but see Senft and Basso 2009 cited above).[7] Goffman (1967, 1974, 1983) demonstrated that rituals are not limited to sacred ceremonies, even though ceremonies are also very important parts of our modern life (consider, for instance, Collins's 2004 discussion on ceremonial smoking!). Rather, they include both 'demarcated' (Staal 1979) ceremonial events, originally studied in anthropology, and many seemingly 'insignificant' mundane events in urban lives, with more relevance for sociologists like Goffman himself. As Goffman (1983: 10) argues:

If we think of ceremonials as narrative-like enactments, more or less extensive and more or less insulated from mundane routines, then we can contrast these complex performances with 'contact rituals', namely, perfunctory, brief expressions occurring incidental to everyday action – in passing as it were – the most frequent case involving but two individuals.

With the diversity of ritual in mind, Goffman coined the term 'interaction ritual', which includes ritual both in a literal and an abstract sense, which are both present in many contexts in industrialised societies. I believe that Goffman's term is particularly useful because it captures ritual as an interactional process, and also it describes ritual both as a form and as a context. Thus, the way in which 'ritual' is interpreted in this book is largely aligned to the Goffmanian worldview, even though I use ritual in a more specific sense than Goffman by attempting to pin it down through its pragmatic characteristics (see more below). For Goffman, ritual is broader than simple language use: it includes all routines of our daily lives including, for example, 'addressing a person by name, making eye contact, [and] respecting someone's space' (see Swidler 2001: 98).

Similar to Durkheim, Goffman argued that the essence of interaction ritual is that it helps social structures to reproduce themselves (see also the working definition of this book in Chapter 1). Social groups conventionalise a wide variety of interactional practices to create an interactional order, underlied by an invisible moral order. In this book I define 'moral order' in the sense of Wuthnow (1987: 14) who argued that moral order involves 'what is proper to do and reasonable to expect', i.e., it is a cluster of unwritten social mores and conventions which serve to maintain the interactional and broader societal order. Unlike the term 'convention' in pragmatics which is neutral, 'moral order' has an important judgmental facet. This definition of the moral order is essentially discourse analytic, and it differs from how this notion has been interpreted in conversation analysis.[8]

The fact that Goffman defined ritual as a highly variable phenomenon is logical if one considers that:

social ritual is not an expression of structural arrangements in any simple sense; at best it is an expression advanced in regard to these arrangements. Social structures don't 'determine' culturally standard displays, merely help select from the available repertoire of them. (Goffman 1983: 11)

In sum, Goffman's view provides a powerful foundation to study ritual. Further, building on Goffman allows us to develop a ritual perspective on language use. Goffman developed a range of concepts such as 'face', 'demeanour' and 'deference' which became the foundations of politeness theory (see Haugh 2013: 50). Yet, Goffman did not use the concept of 'politeness', and in the following I will discuss why viewing many instances of interaction as forms of ritual rather than politeness – i.e., adopting a ritual perspective in pragmatic research – is important.

2.3   The Ritual Perspective

Following Goffman's above-outlined definition of interaction ritual, it is safe to argue that ritual is a phenomenon which is so relevant to our daily interactions that it provides a specific perspective for the scholar to look at language use itself. Adopting such a perspective is important because very many aspects of language use are ritual, even though language users themselves do not always realise that they are acting in a ritual way. While perhaps few pragmaticians would disagree with this claim *per se*, it is not without controversy because in pragmatic research ritual tends to be perceived as the 'little brother' of the much broadly studied phenomenon of politeness (and impoliteness).[9] For example, Brown and Levinson (1987) have left the relationship between politeness and ritual largely intact beyond arguing that certain routinised manifestations of politeness are ritual. Many other scholars could be listed here – including both early and recent work such as Ferguson (1976), Haverkate (1988), Fraser (1990), Kerbrat-Orecchioni (2006), Traverso (2006), Ghezzi and Molinelli (2019) and many others – but the main point is that ritual has been subordinated to politeness by practically all politeness researchers who discussed ritual phenomena. This is also valid to experts who focused on ritual in their work, such as Bax (2001, 2010), Held (1992, 2010), Ohashi (2008), Paternoster (2022), Kádár and Bax (2013), Kádár and Paternoster (2015) and others. I also followed a low-key approach to the relationship between ritual and politeness in my previous work (Kádár 2017): instead of considering how ritual and politeness *differ* from each other, I tried to identify how certain aspects of politeness and impoliteness can be described as ritual.

2.3.1   Why Not Subordinate Ritual to Politeness?

Relating politeness and ritual is no doubt important because through considering this relationship one can gain insight into various issues surrounding politeness. An eminent example may be the study of Leech (2005; see also 2007), who attempted to capture what brings together politeness in 'Eastern' and 'Western' linguacultures by proposing 'a Grand Strategy of Politeness'. In explicating this concept, Leech used highly ritual examples, like the following:

Asymmetries of politeness: Politeness often shows up in opposite strategies of treating S and H in dialogue. Whereas conveying a highly favourable evaluation of H is polite, conveying the same evaluation of S is impolite. Conversely, while conveying an unfavourable evaluation of S is polite, giving the same evaluation of H is impolite. . . .

   Almost as a technical term, I use the phrase courteous belief for an attribution of some positive value to H or of some negative value to S, whereas a discourteous belief is an attribution of some positive value to S or some negative value H. Compare, for example, the courteousness of (a) and the discourteousness of (b):

(a) You're coming to have dinner with us next week. I insist!
(b) I'm coming to have dinner with you next week. I insist!

There are such asymmetries in Chinese and Japanese honorific usage:

Bìxìng wáng, nín guìxìng? 敝姓王, 您贵姓?
(My surname is Wang, your surname?)

(Namae wa) Buraun desu. O-namae wa?
(My name is Brown. And your name?) (Leech 2005: 8–9)

What strikes the ritualist is that all the examples which Leech uses here are highly ritual, and while he does not mention the concept 'ritual' in his study, his examples show that ritual may be used as a phenomenon which interconnects pragmatic behaviour in typologically distant linguacultures.

Notwithstanding the importance of studying ritual through the lens of politeness, and politeness through the lens on ritual, in this book I take a different route because I believe that interaction ritual is potentially *much more important* than any other interpersonal pragmatic phenomena, including politeness. Therefore, in the following I focus on the benefits of an interaction ritual perspective on language use in comparison to the politeness perspective – without, however, arguing that these perspectives are incompatible. On the contrary, I believe that the ritual and politeness views are both important and complementary to each other, but the ritual view needs to receive more attention in pragmatics. Why is this so?

Consider the following utterance:

Example 2.1   It gives me a great pleasure to welcome here as our guest this evening Professor Quatsch from the University of Minnesota Junior.

(Quoted from Edmondson & House 1981: 193)

One may argue that here we have a polite utterance in hand. Although any utterance, including this welcoming, may be used in an idiosyncratic way as discursive politeness scholars such as Eelen (2001) argued, most would agree that Example 2.1 occurs in a formal public event, and this public interpersonal scenario largely precludes any other use and interpretation of language than a default polite one.[10] The speaker who utters the above welcoming may attempt to play on prosody or use other pragmatic phenomena to express that she actually dislikes the welcomed person, which then would be an idiosyncratic realisation of the welcoming.[11] However, any such move would likely become salient and could potentially harm the speaker's own face and reputation. So, when one encounters an utterance such as Example 2.1 uttered in an ordinary way, the question may ultimately emerge: is politeness a matter of interest *at all* when the speaker is socially dutybound to be polite (or impolite in other occasions)?

This is a rhetorical question, and the answer is meant to be 'no'. This is why politeness research conventionally prefers studying data with a sense of individuality and *ad hoc*-ness rather than communal orientation, even when it comes to highly conventionalised phenomena, as otherwise there would be very little for the politeness scholar to look at. This is of course a rather oversimplified statement. While in the so-called 'discursive' research (see e.g., Mills 2003) politeness has been interpreted on a strictly individual level, various politeness scholars such as Blum-Kulka (1987), Terkourafi (2001), Culpeper and Demmen (2011), Hultgren (2017) and others have studied conventionalised aspects of polite language usage. Also, many experts of politeness research considered communal aspects of politeness and impoliteness behaviour, including Culpeper (2005, 2011) who considered such behaviour in 'activity types' and 'frames', Terkourafi (2001) who discussed 'frames', and Garcés-Conejos Blitvich (2010) who distinguished 'genres'. However, even in such research, communally oriented behaviour has often been subordinated to individual behaviour, simply due to the focus on politeness. In other words, the aforementioned studies had more interest in 'trends or preferences in the way people speak in different situations' (Culpeper & Terkourafi 2017: 18) than in studying why and how certain practices and contexts through which social structures reproduce themselves *prompt* or even *force* people to follow certain tendencies of producing and evaluating language – a question which relates to the ritual view on language use. Accordingly, recent politeness inquiries considered the role of pragmatic conventions in language use, without however foregrounding the cohesion between these conventions, which is reasonable if one considers that the primary focus of politeness research is the language use of the individual.

One could argue that ritual has many shared characteristics with notions such as 'activity type', which was proposed by Levinson (1979) and which has been used in some work in politeness research. However, this is certainly not the case for various reasons. Activity type describes conventions of pragmatic behaviour holding for one particular context. Ritual, on the other hand, has many general pragmatic features which will be introduced later on in this chapter, and which characterise all ritual contexts and manifestations of ritual, i.e., ritual encompasses a much broader phenomenon than activity type.[12] Furthermore, the fully-fledged study of ritual often assumes a bottom–up view on data, as this book will show, that is, one often first looks at ritual language use to identify various ritual contexts in which such language use occurs. This is different from how activity type has been used as a notion to capture language use in one particular context. Further, since activity type is chosen by the researcher, politeness scholars who used activity type often pursued interest in polite and impolite behaviour in incidents or case studies which are, for one reason or another, interesting for the researcher and salient for the participants, while there has been little appetite to study instances of 'boring' language use such as Example 2.1. To provide a single example here, Watts (2003: 27–28) used activity type to consider the conventional dynamics of incidents like the following one:

Imagine yourself standing in a queue at the booking office of a coach station. It is your turn next, but before you can even begin to order your ticket, someone pushes in front of you and asks the official behind the counter for a single ticket to Birmingham.

Fortunately, this sort of thing is not a daily occurrence, but when it does happen, we are likely to feel somewhat annoyed. The least we could have expected is some kind of excuse on the part of the person for her/his action. . . . If we were asked to comment on the incident afterwards, we would probably suggest that the pusher-in had behaved *impolitely*, even *rudely*, to those in the queue. We might not consider his behaviour to have been rude towards the official, but we would have certainly expected the official to point out the 'rules of the game' and to refuse to serve her/him.

This fictional situation is recognisable as a public service encounter in which none of the participants is expected to know any of the others (although, of course, they may). As a social activity type it is subject to a so-called *interaction order*, i.e., the politic behaviour of waiting to be served in a queue involves the participant in certain types of behaviour which take place at certain sequentially ordered points in the interaction.

While such an analysis is certainly relevant from a ritual point of view, the ritual view would prompt one to also look at the scenario of standing in a queue at the booking office of a coach station from other angles than the impoliteness-relevant phenomenon of a breach of civility. For example, it would be note-worthy to study ritual conventions of waiting – including pragmatic phenomena such as Small Talk during the waiting time – as well as cases when seemingly 'nothing is happening' but people in the public scene nevertheless invisibly communicate with one another by pretending not to notice others, i.e., the phenomenon of 'civil inattention' (Goffman 1963).

2.3.2   Differences Between the Ritual and the Politeness Perspectives

Returning to Example 2.1, it can be argued that it is not particularly relevant for politeness research because it lacks individuality and *ad hoc*-ness as far as it is realised in a default way. A seeming solution to make this example politeness-relevant would be to argue that welcoming someone is a 'polite speech act', and an individual may make this utterance 'more or less polite' by playing on its style. However, such an argument would be false for two reasons: Firstly, rigorous research on speech acts, in particular House (1989), pointed out very early on that there is no straightforward relationship between politeness and speech acts, i.e., illocutions such as Welcome, Request, Apologise and so on are only potentially (if at all) related to politeness. Secondly, if welcoming someone in a public event is meant to be realised in a strictly conventionalised manner – e.g., 'great pleasure' in Example 2.1 is a phrase we may hear even if the speaker does not feel such a great pleasure! – ultimately individual preferences for how the speech act in question should be realised are normally overruled by pragmatic conventions (see also Ide's 1989 above-mentioned study). In the case of Example 2.1, such conventions may prevent the individual from 'tampering' with the expected style of the speech act because normally an audience expects a public welcoming to have a positive tone.

The second-best option to keep Example 2.1 relevant for politeness research would be then to provide and examine plenty of contextual information behind the utterance, e.g., consider the identities of the speaker, the recipient and the broader ratified audience, the background and trajectory of the public welcoming, the location where the utterance takes place, etc. For such a discursive analysis, it would be a piece of cake if there was an anomaly in the welcoming – something which is however missing from Example 2.1 if it is uttered in a default way. Discursive politeness scholars such as Watts (2003), Mills (2003) and many others (including the author of this book in his early career days) have been actually *hunting* for critical idiosyncratic incidents to interconnect utterances like Example 2.1 with the phenomena of politeness and impoliteness. While in many post-2010 studies this pursuit of extraordinary has somewhat lost its momentum (see an overview in Terkourafi & Kádár 2017), it is still not overreaching to argue that many politeness scholars continue to pursue interest in 'interesting' instances of language use. This is particularly valid for research on impoliteness where the nature of the data normally represents the realm of the extraordinary.

The study of interaction ritual offers a perspective which is different from that of linguistic politeness research in two major respects. First, the study of ritual requires the researcher to focus on the default and 'regular' aspect of language use, including instances where the participants simply follow 'boring' routines (Coulmas 1981), such as welcoming someone in a conventional way, as in Example 2.1. In other words, a ritual perspective involves a focus on the ordinary rather than the extraordinary. As Chapters 3 and 4 of this book will show, this perspective does not mean that ritual data itself is boring or even ordinary for some, or that the ritual pragmatician can afford ignoring cases when an idiosyncratic event disturbs the flow of a ritual and upsets the expectations of various participants. However, the ritual pragmatician is advised to interpret instances of extraordinary behaviour through the lens of ordinary: instead of seeing idiosyncrasies as some 'extras' to the conventionalised and often ritual aspect of interpersonal interaction in the manner of politeness scholars like Watts (2003), for the ritual pragmatician idiosyncrasies are meant to represent often predictable pragmatic *breaches* through which one can interpret the ritual phenomenon being breached.

Second, studying the default and 'regular' ritual realm of language use implies that the ritual pragmatician normally pursues a simultaneous interest in all three pillar-units of language use, i.e., expressions, speech acts and discourse (see House & Kádár 2021a). As stated above, politeness research prefers much background information to study utterances like Example 2.1. It also often struggles with bringing together expressions and speech acts with politeness and impoliteness (see e.g., Brown & Levinson 1987; Eelen 2001; Watts 2003 and many other classics of the field). More precisely, while cognitive politeness researchers such as Escandell-Vidal (1996) and Ruytenbeek (2019) used forms to examine politeness, the mainstream of linguistic politeness research has been dominated by the very reasonable argument – propagated by Eelen (2001), Watts (2003) and others – that it is difficult to pin down the relationship between form and politeness in a replicable way.[13] This is not the case with interaction ritual research: due to the ritualist's focus on the conventional ritual aspect of language use in ritual contexts, the study of interaction ritual does not background expressions and speech acts and foreground discourse because ritual always manifests itself in conventionalised and formalised ways. For the ritual pragmatician, it is also often important to consider what is evident from a minimal utterance itself, provided that an utterance provides relevant information as regards basic pragmatic variables, such as the role relationship between the interactants and the public or private nature of an interaction, such as in Example 2.1. This, of course, does not mean that the ritualist may not pursue a discourse-analytic interest: in the spirit of what was summarised in Figure 2.1, one should argue that certain instances of language use can only be understood as ritual if one first considers the ritual context that brings such instances of language use to life.

Since Goffman's concept of interaction ritual involves both ceremonial and contact rituals, the pragmatic study of 'ordinary' (conventionalised) interaction not only involves examining ceremonial utterances, but practically any utterance and interaction where the interactants simply follow pragmatic expectations. Compare the following example with Example 2.1:

Example 2.2   A: Nice day, isn't it?
                       B: Yes.
                       A: Hm, bus is a bit late this morning.
                       B: Hm.

(Quoted from Edmondson & House 1981: 170)

Example 2.2 features the speech act Remark (Edmondson & House 1981: 98). Here, the Remark realised by A occurs in a typically ritual Type of Talk, i.e., Small Talk, where the interactants are supposed to exchange words with social symbolic rather than referential meaning. While Example 2.2 does not take place in a public and ceremonial context, unlike Example 2.1, it equally follows a highly conventionalised ritual pragmatic pattern. This is why many language users in English-speaking linguacultures tend to be aware of the fact that 'Nice day, isn't it?' is a typically phatic Remark, rather than a 'meaningful' informative utterance.

A formal aspect of language use such as a speech act Remark can, of course, become more relevant for politeness than ritual. Compare Example 2.3 with Example 2.2:

Example 2.3   A: I saw your wife with John at that new Italian restaurant last night.
               B: Really, there's supposed to be a new Spanish restaurant opening up
                   soon, isn't there?

                              (Quoted from Edmondson & House 1981: 173)

The speech act Remark here is very different from what we could see in
Example 2.2: in this interaction B realises Remark as an attempt to switch an
unpleasant topic back into ritual Small Talk. By so doing, he also indicates that
A talks out of line. From a politeness point of view, this interaction is of definite
interest because the Remark here strategically resolves a face-threatening
situation.

While interactions like the one featured in Example 2.3 are no doubt
important, they are far less routinous that the other interactions featured in
this section. So, we can argue that a fundamental advantage of the ritual
perspective in pragmatics is that ritual encompasses something much more
regular than linguistic politeness or impoliteness: it includes any instance of
conventionalised communally oriented interaction where individual pragmatic solutions are somehow backgrounded. The communal orientation of
ritual language use may have broader pragmatic implications than what this
technical term suggests – consider the following example:

Example 2.4   JULIANE: Ach, Daniel, you are always late.
               DANIEL: Well, J, I didn't miss anything because you were sleeping in
                   your armchair anyway.
               JULIANE: Stupid idiot!!

This is a typically ritual interaction which took place between the author of
this book and a dear friend and colleague of his. The author and his colleague
work together online on a daily basis and they swear a lot, in order to decrease
the stress of academic research. If anyone else overheard this interaction, not
mentioning being subject to such an abuse, this third party might have felt
offended. However, this had not been the case with the participants for whom
swearing represented an in-group ritual with recurrent pragmatic features,
which made swearing in their relationship 'harmless', in a similar way to
many other instances of ritual swearing (see Labov's previously mentioned
1972 seminal study). Example 2.4 is of course not irrelevant for impoliteness
and politeness research, but it represents a case where forms of language use
associated with impoliteness do not fulfil any one-off interactional function.
Rather, rudeness is locally and constantly reinterpreted here by the micro
community of the interactants as a form of ritual endearment: both participants
would have *missed* such ritual swearing and abuse in many interactional
episodes during their daily work.[14] Thus, in Example 2.4, individualised
impolite language use is ultimately far less (if at all) important in comparison

to the communal rapport building and face enhancing (see Spencer-Oatey 2000) ritual function of abuse.

Example 2.4 also points to a key aspect of the ritual perspective, which in my view distinguishes it from the politeness perspective, namely, that in the pragmatic study of rituals one often encounters and studies the ostensible aspect of language use. Ostension is a concept coined by semioticians,[15] and in previous pragmatic research on ritual such as Koutlaki (2020: 94) ostensible behaviour described the apparent conformity to customs and 'the enactment of self's and others' status' through behaviour which is potentially about something else than what meets the eye, as the word 'ostensible' suggests. For example, in the encounter above, both participants conformed to in-group ritual conventions of cursing as a form of endearment rather than offence, i.e., here we have an archetype of ritual ostensible behaviour in hand. As Chapters 3 and 6 of this book will show, when a ritual becomes interactionally complex, the participants often use 'polite' and 'impolite' behaviour not so much to be nice or rude to the other, but primarily to ritually display their own (pragmatic) competence either to the recipient or a broader audience. In other words, polite and impolite phenomena in such ritual settings are both self- and communally oriented (see Chen 2001) and often ostensive.

2.3.3   The Ritual–Politeness Scale

Example 2.4 represents a specific case in that here ritual swearing is 'disarmed'. In Chapter 3, a case study of trash talk will illustrate that ritual abuse can also become very offensive and as such meaningful and potentially sensitive to both the participants and the observers of the ritual. What brings together Example 2.4 with such instances of conflict is that in any ritually relevant interaction (and, I would argue, most of our daily interactions belong to this category) individual pragmatic solutions are backgrounded to the communal conventionalised and ritual form and role of interaction. Being backgrounded does not imply the complete absence of individuality in ritual: following the scalar view of Leech (1983), it is reasonable to argue that fully-fledged interaction ritual represents the conventionalised end and fully-fledged politeness and impoliteness the individual end of language use. It is reasonable to argue that so-called 'polite rituals' (manifestations of etiquette) are closer to the ritual than the politeness end of the above-outlined scale. It is also reasonable to argue that rituals which somehow 'go amiss' (see Chapter 3) are closer to the impoliteness and politeness end of this scale.

When discussing the communal orientation of ritual, it is also worth revisiting the argument that interaction ritual (just like politeness and impoliteness) is far from being a homogeneous phenomenon. In Kádár (2013), I set up a pragmatic typology of interaction ritual, arguing that interactions like

Example 2.4 represent in-group rituals, while cases like mediatised ritual trash-talk studied in Chapter 3 are social rituals. There are also lower-level ritual types,[16] but putting these aside here, it is valid to argue that the more in-group a ritual is, the more elusive the border between ritual and politeness and impoliteness becomes. While in social ritual it is normally easy to discern if one or more of the participants start to use individual politeness and impoliteness solutions beyond the realm of conventionalised and communally oriented and endorsed language use, it can be difficult even for the participants of an in-group ritual to clearly discern exactly when someone ventures beyond the pragmatic boundaries of a ritual. Consider the following example:

Example 2.5   JULIANE: When I die you should collaborate with stupid Ute
              (pseudonym).
          DANIEL: [silence] Now, watch it Juliane, that was *really* offensive and
              stupidly morbid.
          JULIANE: Ach, Daniel.

The interaction in Example 2.5 took place between the same interactants as Example 2.4. In one of their working sessions, while exchanging their usual ritual insults, the author's friend made a morbid joke that the author of this book found genuinely offensive because (a) the mention of death and (b) the mention of Ute who is regarded by the participants as a hopeless academic, and he immediately gave voice to being offended. Here, perceived offense trespassed the invisible and rather indetermined boundaries of ritual teasing.

In summary, the ritual perspective provides insight into a vast array of pragmatic phenomena. This perspective also offers an *alternative* analytic attitude to pragmatic context and behaviour than the politeness perspective. In conventional politeness and impoliteness research it would be odd, to say the least, to talk about 'polite and impolite contexts' because the phenomena of politeness and impoliteness come into existence primarily through the hearer's evaluations across interpersonal contexts (see Eelen 2001). This correlates with the phenomenon that politeness and impoliteness in their fully-fledged sense (i.e., as an end of a ritual–politeness scale) are individualistic albeit often conventionalised phenomena. When it comes to interaction ritual, on the other hand, it is perfectly valid to talk about 'standard situations' (see House 1989 above) where rights and obligations and the related ritual order of the interaction are clear to all participants, i.e., these situations provide *ritual contexts* (see also Figure 2.1).

2.4   The Key Pragmatic Features of Interaction Ritual

In what follows, I define the key pragmatic features of interaction ritual. These features will be referred to throughout this book.

From what has been argued in this chapter thus far, the following may transpire:
- interaction rituals occur in standard situations, and
- they also indicate the presence of such situations and the related rights and obligations of the participants (see the above-mentioned alternative analytic attitude to pragmatic context).

Furthermore, from the examples presented in this chapter it is evident that rituals
- are pragmatically salient for the participants even if the participants themselves may not always be aware of this salience until an interactional breach occurs,
- operate with conventionalised (recurrent) pragmatic features, and
- are realised with ratified roles (e.g., a sense of ratification is due to welcome someone, as in Example 2.1).

These pragmatic characteristics become very visible whenever we look at utterance and speech act-level manifestations of interaction rituals, such as the ones studied in the previous Section 2.3. However, the same pragmatic features also recur in more complex and interactionally co-constructed rituals.

To prove this latter point, in the following I provide an excerpt from Kádár and Szalai (2020), where a colleague of mine and myself examined the ways in which members of a Roma community in Transylvania socialise young children within their community into the interactional practice of ritual cursing. In order to understand the importance of this socialisation process, it is important to consider that cursing in this community is often believed to have the power to cause real harm. Because of this, it is fundamental for young children to be able to distinguish between teasing – and the related 'harmless' use of cursing – and 'real' uses of cursing. In the following example, two older female members of the Roma community, Kati and Teri, engage in playful ritual cursing with a young girl Zsuzska:

Example 2.6   1. Kati Xal o beng adjeh, hi:::!
                        May the Devil eat today, huh!
               2. Teri Mula::h, mula:h, [ja:::j! ((pretends to be crying))
                        She has died, she has died, oy!
               3. Zsuzska ((laughs)) [@@@=
               4. Kati Mulah?
                        Has she died?
               5. Zsuzska ((partly crying, partly laughing))
                        =Na!
                        No.
               6. Teri Mulāh tji mami e Pitjōka:!
                        Your grandmother Pitjóka died!
               7. Kati . . .
                        Ne még mondjad úgy, mindjárt sír!
                        Do not tell it to her anymore, she is going to cry!

8. Zsuzska Na!
        No!
9. Kati ((to Zsuzska, consoling her))
        Na:, śej, či mulah!
        No, girl, she has not died!

(from Kádár & Szalai 2020: 21)

In lines 1 and 2, Kati and Teri playfully tease Zsuzska by ritually cursing her grandmother. In line 3, Zsuzska responds to the curses with laughter but also begins to cry, indicating that her laughter is more than a simple perception of humour. As the ritual exchange intensifies, Zsuzska appears to be confused as to whether the cursing is meant to be harmful or not. In line 4, Kati appears to notice this confusion: she asks Zsuzska whether Teri's claim – made in an intentionally overexaggerated tone – that Zsuzska's grandmother has died is true, to which Zsuzska answers 'no', in line 5. However, Teri's next curse in line 6 forces Zsuzska to the brink of tears again, and in line 7 Kati intervenes to decrease the 'pressure' of the interactional ritual on the child, by requesting Teri to reduce the intensity of the cursing. She also consoles the child in line 9.

The ritual features outlined above are clearly visible in the interactionally co-constructed ritual Example 2.6 representing the unit of discourse. The rights and obligations and the related standardness of the situation are straightforward: without these, the socialisation process could not properly work, and the cursing would become abusive. Also, considering that ritual here aims to help the child to acquire skill in cursing, the interaction clearly operates with a recurrent pragmatic inventory and very clear ratified roles, as witnessed by the intervention of the adult Kati in line 7. The interactional salience of the ritual is clear if one considers the emotively loaded responses of the child.

Along with the above-outlined basic pragmatic features, Example 2.6 also points to various more complex features of ritual:

• Most importantly, the presence of a *ritual frame* (see also Kádár & House 2020a) and a related moral order of things,

and the related operation and presence of

• mimesis,
• (self-)display,
• escalation (for rites of aggression) and
• liminality.

Part II of this book will introduce various of these pragmatic properties of ritual in greater detail, so here I only outline them briefly. Note that not all interaction rituals clearly necessarily operate with *all* four features listed with bullet points above. For example, it is difficult to use concepts such as ritual (self-)display for the utterance-level study of rituals (see Section 2.3). In other words, the more one focuses on the pragmatic unit of discourse in the study of interaction ritual, the more important these distinctive features become.

As the present section will show, the concept of ritual frame is by far the most important among the various features of ritual, and in the rest of this section I devote special attention to this notion.

2.4.1   Ritual Frame: An All-encompassing Concept

The concept of 'ritual frame' needs to be discussed separately from the other features of interaction ritual listed above because it is an all-encompassing characteristic which is responsible for the existence of practically *all* pragmatic features of ritual. Furthermore, ritual frame is a *precondition* for ritual to occur: it brings the ritual to life and it comes into operation whenever a particular interactional ritual unfolds. As the renowned anthropologist Victor Turner (1979: 468) argued in his ground-breaking study:

> To look at itself, a society must cut out a piece of itself for inspection. To do this it must set up a frame within which images and symbols of what has been sectioned off can be scrutinized, assessed, and, if need be, remodelled and rearranged.

Turner described ritual frame as a physical space: there is a separated area in many tribes for a ritual to take place, and once one enters this area, specific behavioural rules apply and rights and obligations are clearly defined. As Goffman (1974) pointed out, in modern urbanised societies we may have fewer such spaces, and the indication of ritual frames often takes place vis-à-vis ritual language use, indicating awareness of a virtual ritual frame in standard situations (House 1989). Ritual frame implies the presence of an interactional moral order (see Wuthnow 1987 and Douglas 1999), i.e., an expected order of things according to which the ritual interaction should unfold (see above; see also a detailed discussion of ritual and moral order in Kádár 2017).

Let us now discuss the phenomena of mimesis, (self-)display, escalation (for rites of aggression) and liminality outlined above. In a ritual frame, the participants' behaviour is not only meant to follow pragmatic conventions, but also they often *mimetically* re-enact the interaction ritual. As Chapter 5 will show, mimesis not only involves simple reciprocation (see Edmondson 1981) which is present in many daily rituals (such as mutual greeting), but rather talking in an 'alien' voice, by taking up assumed roles in the interaction, just like actors on the stage (rather than engaging in 'crossing', see above). Mimesis is particularly visible in Example 2.6 where the adult participants prompt the child to mimetically engage in cursing as part of the language socialisation process.

The interaction ritual featured in Example 2.6 also has a sense of 'lavish and ornate' *display* as Bax (2010: 58) puts it: the participants curse practically all the time during the interaction because the ritual frame allows and even prompts them to do this. In other words, they put cursing on display as part of the ritual, and they also engage in a self-display in the sense that they as adults showcase their own skill in realising this ritual phenomenon.

Along with this sense of 'overexaggeration', the ritual frame here also triggers a sense of *escalation* – a phenomenon which characterises rites of aggression only (see Chapter 3). That is, the longer the ritual lasts, the more intensive it becomes.

Finally, the interaction ritual brings the participants into an altered – i.e., *liminal* – state of mind and status, also in terms of language use. That is, they pass a certain sense of threshold, by leaving behind the boundaries of their ordinary pragmatic constraints and related rights and obligations.

As this brief analysis of Example 2.6 illustrates, the different features of interaction ritual are in an intrinsic relationship: once a ritual frame prompts them to emerge, they tend to emerge in combination. Accordingly, while in Part II of this book I will highlight each of them in different case studies, such an emphasis does not mean that any of these ritual features are somehow 'stand-alone'. Also, what always needs to be remembered is that all these features are 'products' of the ritual frame that underlies any interaction ritual, and which very often also imposes constraints on these pragmatic features. For instance, in Example 2.6 the ritual frame implies that mimetic liminal aggressive (self-)display in ritual needs to be kept within conventional pragmatic boundaries, even though the interaction leads to an escalation where the socialised person bursts out into tears.

2.4.2   Ritual Frame Underlying Methodological Approaches to Ritual

The concept of ritual frame is so important in the study of interaction ritual that it always influences methodological approaches through which the pragmatician can capture ritual (see a more detailed discussion in Part III). Let us here present Figure 2.1 again, in a revised form:

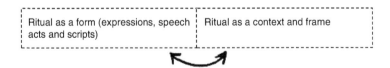

Figure 2.2 The role of ritual frame in research on interaction ritual.

As Figure 2.2 shows, there are two ways in which pragmatics-anchored ritual research may operate. Firstly, the researcher may focus on a pragmatic unit of analysis – expressions, speech acts and routinised or scripted parts of discourse – as a departure point of analysis, hence associating a form of language use with ritual. As Section 2.3 of this chapter has shown, forms of language use like expressions and speech acts tend to gain a ritual function in an actual interaction ritual frame: one can only study their ritual function in a rigorous and replicable way if one considers their conventional use(s) in the interaction ritual frame of specific contexts. The arrow in Figure 2.2 therefore shows that forms of language use which one associates with ritual can only be reliably studied if their use is considered through the concept of ritual frame. Even expressions and speech acts which are very closely associated with ritual in the popular sense, as well as scripts of ceremonies may be no exception to this. One may argue that archetypal formal manifestations of ritual, such as 'Amen', are ritual (see more in Chapter 8). However, even in the study of such expressions, and realisations of 'ritual' speech acts such as Greet, and scripts like prayers, one needs to consider their situated use in various data if one wants to tease out exactly how they are used in interaction, exactly when they gain a ritual function, and how they evolve over time. In other words, in the study of ritual as a form one may need to consider *exactly when and how* a particular form associated with ritual becomes ritual.

Secondly, if one approaches ritual as a pragmatically abstract phenomenon, one unavoidably needs to break it down to replicable pragmatic units. While 'rite of passage', for example, is certainly a ritual from the anthropologist point of view, for the ritual pragmatician it only represents an event and a context, which imposes certain preset rights and obligations on the participants and observers in the form of a conventionalised ritual frame. The pragmatician in turn examines exactly how the frame of such a ritual influences language use.

2.4.3   Ritual Frame Influencing the Pragmatic Typologisation of Ritual

The concept of ritual frame also helps us to consider how interaction rituals can be captured through a typology, which approaches ritual according to the types of behaviour the ritual frame prompts to emerge. While I will outline such typological considerations in more detail in the following Chapters 3 and 4, let us outline its basics at this point. While all interaction rituals help social structures to reinforce or reformulate themselves, this reinforcement or refor- mulation can take place in two entirely different ways: either through 'orderly' or seemingly 'disorderly' ritual events. Following Turner's (1979) seminal thought, I will refer to the former orderly event types as rites taking place in 'structure' – i.e., the normal society – and the latter disorderly event types as rites taking place in 'anti-structure', i.e., a social grouping (or '*communitas*') which is allowed to temporarily violate the ritual behavioural boundaries of ordinary social life. However, somewhat differently from Turner who pursued interest in societies and cultures rather than language use, I will distinguish conventionalised language use taking place in structure and anti-structure as 'rites *of* structure and anti-structure'. Importantly, both these ritual types operate with a well-defined ritual frame and an underlying moral order, i.e., structure and anti-structure represent a typology of ritual frames. An advantage of this simple typology is that it is finite and centres on the (dis)orderly nature of rituals, and as such it is more advantageous from the pragmatician's point of view than categorising rituals according to their context of occurrence.

2.5   Conclusion

The present chapter has provided a departure point for what is to be discussed in the rest of this book, by positioning interaction ritual and defining its key pragmatic features. The chapter first presented a brief review of previous pragmatic research on ritual, and also explained why Goffman's notion of interaction ritual is particularly useful for the pragmatician. As a next step, I discussed why a ritual perspective on language use is at least as (if not more) relevant for the study of ordinary language use than the politeness perspective. Following this, I provided an overview of the key pragmatic features of interaction ritual, including both those features which can be described through 'standard' pragmatic technical terms such as conventionalisation, and others which are not parts of the standard terminology of pragmatics and interaction studies, such as liminality. I argued that the concept of ritual frame is an all-encompassing notion, which always needs to be considered in the pragmatic study of ritual.

In the following Chapter 3, we will continue the journey started in this chapter, by taking a closer look at interactional rites of aggression and the question as to why the ritual perspective provides a fundamental tool to understand such rituals.

2.6   Recommended Reading

Edmondson, W., House, J. (1981) *Let's Talk and Talk about It: A Pedagogic Interactional Grammar of English*. München: Urban & Schwarzenberg.

The reader might have noted that I drew many illustrative examples in this chapter from the seminal work of Edmondson and House (1981), a classic of pragmatics and ritual. This is not only because Edmondson and House (1981) – like many early pragmaticians – foregrounded ritual over politeness, but also because their study provided ground-breaking insights into the relationship between certain expressions, speech acts and types of discourse and interaction ritual. This book has recently become available in a revised and extended form:

Edmondson, W., House, J., Kádár, D. (2023) *Expressions, Speech Acts and Discourse: A Pedagogic Interactional Grammar of English*. Cambridge: Cambridge University Press.

The following section represents a description of Small Talk, which Edmondson and House defined as a typically ritual Type of Talk and described its recurrent pragmatic features through their interactional typology of speech acts.

The central types of illocution which characterize Small Talk are informative in nature, i.e. Remarks, Tells, and Discloses (possibly Opines), and, necessarily, the matching Requests for Illocutionary Acts, which these informative illocutions may Satisfy. Requests for free goods belong more readily to Small Talk than to Business or Argumentative Talk, and thus some Requests for non-verbal goods will also be found in Small Talk if the non-verbal goods Requested counts as a free good. Phatic, ritual or hearer-supportive illocutions such as the Thanks, Minimise, and Congratulate may occur commonly also, without, of course, being specific to this Type of Talk.

We have already pointed out that the dividing line between Small Talk and Business or Argumentative Talk is not clear-cut, and further that in certain constellations (for example casual contacts, among familiars or non-familiars). Opening Talk naturally leads to Small Talk without any clearly discernible dividing line occurring. Small Talk therefore does not exclude other Type of Talk. Thus for example Small Talk may follow Business Talk before a Closing, often to ratify the social relationship after a business negotiation. If one member has obtained a commitment from the other, for example, he may go on to flatter or smooth his conversational partner via Small Talk, indirectly assuring him that the obtaining of the commitment was not the only point of the conversational contact. A concrete illustration is a case in which a tutor tells his student how bad his essay is in a tutorial, and then starts talking about the college football team of which the student is a keen member. The convention of serving drinks after a company board meeting formalises this procedure: it is remarkable, in fact, how members can switch their Type of Talk in such circumstances – two persons who have been attacking each other fiercely in a meeting may be observed "chatting" about their gardens or holiday plans a few minutes afterwards. (Edmondson & House 1981: 222)

3 Order in the Extraordinary: More on the Ritual Perspective

3.1 Introduction

In this chapter, I will explore the ritual perspective on language use in more detail. Chapter 2 has shown that the ritual perspective provides insight into language use in ordinary and mundane contexts where the interactants simply act according to what is expected, following social conventions of civility. Yet, the ritual perspective also provides a strong interpretive framework for seemingly *ad hoc* extraordinary scenes of aggression, like the ritual Roma interaction featuring cursing in Chapter 2 (Example 2.6). Such extraordinary ritual manifestations of aggression have their own social conventions just like rites of daily civility, but such conventions are usually different from what members of other societies or social groups find normative and acceptable. Ritual cursing, for instance, which is normative for one ethnic group, may sound menacing for members of other groups, often leading to racist stereotypes and prejudices. A clear advantage of the ritual perspective is that it allows the researcher to describe exactly what is going on in such rituals in a rigorous and replicable way, and on a par with rites of civility, by moving beyond sweeping stereotypes and prejudices. And the importance of the ritual perspective does not exhaust here: it also helps the linguist to systematically examine a cluster of other, less 'exotic' aggressive interaction rituals, which do not 'belong' to one particular group but rather 'the whole' of a society, or at least one of its major subgroups. This chapter focuses on such latter rituals, which represent the realm of extraordinary to some degree in our lives.

Typical examples of everyday rites of aggression include boxing and football matches, the roasting of celebrities on the TV, and scenes where a politician clashes with a heckler in a mediatised event. These rituals are not 'extraordinary' in the sense that – unlike Roma cursing – few may find such rituals 'alien', i.e., they represent a standard situation and a related well-known ritual frame. Further, unlike in the case of Roma cursing, many lay observers may not even use the word 'ritual' in its popular sense to describe such rituals. One may even argue that such rituals are ordinary in the respect that they tend to be expected to occur by both those who participate in them and others who observe them.

However, rites of aggression represent the realm of extraordinary in a pragmatic sense because they are liminal in nature, i.e., the rights and obligations holding for ordinary life are turned upside-down while such rituals are performed. This is why many may feel a sense of voyeuristic pleasure when watching televised aggression and other forms of mediated ritual aggression: the viewer knows that what is happening is meant to happen – i.e., aggression is under some sense of control or supervision – while the aggressive event helps the viewer to temporarily leave the boundaries of his ordinary life.

This chapter presents a case study involving an incident that happened during a high-profile Mixed Martial Arts (MMA) event. MMA events usually involve press conferences, public talks and social media exchanges, in the course of which the fighters exchange messages. These exchanges are followed by the actual match, which is an event that attracts both a physical audience and pay-per-view watchers. MMA events represent rites of aggression, in which the rights and obligations holding for ordinary life are turned upside-down. The build-up of MMA matches tends to become an interaction ritual where the antagonists exchange – and are often expected to exchange – increasingly aggressive, and very often ridiculing, insults. Such insults conventionally represent ritual insulting, that is, the participants are licensed and expected to insult each other within certain boundaries, in order to showcase their 'toughness' and align themselves with their supporters. Ritual aggression in such events may become escalated over the build-up of the event, often with the aid of (social) media. Ritual insults do not necessarily terminate at the end of the match: ridiculing between the antagonists (and their fan groups) often continues after the event, as part of the aggressive ritual.

I will argue that through the ritual perspective one can conduct a pragmatics-anchored study of the dynamics of such rites of aggression, by focusing on various layers of evaluations and reactive language that such events trigger. Methodologically, I will proceed in one particular way according to what was outlined in Figure 2.2 in the previous chapter. The figure is presented here in a modified form:

Analytic foci: Ritual as a form of interaction (breaches and evaluations/reactive language use as part of ritual Argumentative Talk)	Departure and arrival point: Ritual as a context and related frame

Figure 3.1 The procedure in this chapter.

As Figure 3.1 shows, the goal of the analysis here is to understand the pragmatic dynamics of an interaction ritual which may be too complex to be described as a 'ritual' from the pragmatician's point of view. In fact, different observers may not even unanimously agree on whether the phenomenon under investigation is ritual or not, i.e., whether the build-up, climax and post-event interactions of MMA matches represent a 'ritual' in the popular sense of the word. This is partly because language use during these phases is often aggressive and seemingly *ad hoc* in nature, and also because the ritual spans across phases which may manifest themselves in a longer stretch of time. Thus, following the procedure already mentioned in Chapter 2, the current case study attempts to capture this abstract ritual by trying to interconnect it with a pragmatic unit of analysis, and interactional evaluations and reflective behaviour triggered by this unit. More specifically, I examine a speech act through which the frame of the interaction ritual under investigation is perceived to be breached, and subsequent evaluations and metapragmatic language use through which the participants and observers of the event reacted to this perceived breach. Evaluations and reflective language use not only help the pragmatician to capture behavioural expectancies and mores – i.e., the broader ritual frame – of MMA events, but they also provide a pragmatic anchor for interaction analysis. More specifically, they represent a specific Type of Talk – Argumentative Talk (Edmondson & House 1981; Edmondson et al. 2023) – typically realised in a communally-oriented ritual way as a form of 'fan talk'. That is, as the analysis will show, evaluative utterances centering on a particular speech act which is perceived to have breached the ritual frame tend to be communally oriented and operate with clearly identifiable and recurrent interactional features. This community (more precisely, *communitas*, see more below) orientation and recurrent features are what turn Argumentative Talk here into ritual 'fan talk'.

The incident under investigation occurred between two very well-known MMA fighters. Before the match, one of the participants was perceived as going beyond the boundaries of 'acceptable' insulting, and his insults resulted in personal hostility against his antagonist. During the match, the participant who triggered the hostility was perceived as attempting to de-escalate the aggression by uttering what may be understood as a speech act Apologise. These breaches opened up significant ambiguity, which increased through the involvement of social media following the event. This ambiguity manifested itself in a complex cluster of evaluations by the participants and the observers of the mediatised event.

The case study in this chapter includes a wealth of rude expressions. However, in the spirit of the previous Chapter 2, such expressions will not be interpreted as 'impoliteness'-related ones. Individual impoliteness behaviour which participants and observers may find intolerable even when rudeness is the norm can easily emerge in a rite of aggression, in particular because such rituals are liminal and tend to result in escalation. However, for the ritual pragmatician, impoliteness in the individual sense is always only of a secondary importance for two reasons. Firstly, individual impoliteness through which a participant breaches the ritual frame is only a departure point to capture the pragmatic conventions and the moral order of the ritual itself. Secondly, as I argued elsewhere (Kádár 2014), overly individual pragmatic behaviour in any ritual – and in particular in rites of aggression – is ephemeral unless it becomes conventionalised. This is because ritual prefers mimetic behaviour to such a degree that many participants of social and ingroup rituals tend to disapprove and sanction saliently individual behaviour. The perhaps only exception to this is the case of those rituals where the *raison d'être* of the ritual is to engage in a creative or 'virtuoso' form of ritual self-display behaviour, i.e., where the participants are expected to 'overperform' each other in the realisation of a particular ritual (see Chapter 6).

The structure of Chapter 3 is the following: Section 3.2 provides a background for the case study analysis, by first presenting a set of interaction ritual concepts through which rites of aggression can be studied in a replicable way and in parallel with ordinary rites of civility. Here I will discuss the typological considerations touched on in Chapter 2 in more detail. Section 3.3 introduces the case study of this chapter, Section 3.4 presents the analysis and the results and Section 3.5 concludes the chapter.

3.2   Background

Before moving to the case study analysis, it is useful here to discuss two technical terms – 'rite of anti-structure' and 'escalation' – which are relevant not only for the analysis itself but also for presenting aggressive rituals in the same typological frame as ordinary rites of civility.

3.2.1   Rites of Anti-structure

Thus far, in this chapter I have used the expression 'rites of aggression' to refer to a group of rituals representing the realm of extraordinary. In his seminal work, the renowned ritualist Victor Turner (1982: 44) described such rituals in a more technical (and arguably more sound!) way, as rites taking place in 'anti-structure':

I have used the term "anti-structure," [. . . to describe] the liberation of human capacities of cognition, affect, volition, creativity, etc., from the normative constraints incumbent upon occupying a sequence of social statuses, enacting a multiplicity of social roles, and being acutely conscious of membership in some corporate group such as a family, lineage, clan, tribe, nation, etc., or of affiliation with some pervasive social category such as class, caste, sex or age-division.

As Turner argues, events which remove the individual from the expected flow of daily life are 'anti-structural' if they set into motion an alternative order that differs from the normally expected 'structural' order of 'civil' behaviour. Anti-structural events are often of an interaction ritual scope for various reasons, as previous pragmatic research by Koster (2003) pointed out, and also as I argued in my previous work (Kádár & Robinson-Davies 2015; Kádár 2017). As such, anti-structural events tend to have various common features:

(a) They are often public or at least unfold as if an audience was present, which accords with the communal orientation of interaction ritual in general;
(b) They are anchored in rights and obligations and related moral perceptions of 'acceptable' and 'unacceptable' in an aggressive context;
(c) They operate with conventionalised pragmatic features, even though these conventionalised features may be very different from what counts as 'conventional' in other domains of social interaction;
(d) Perhaps even more than other rituals, aggressive rites of anti-structure are also emotively invested (Collins 2004);
(e) They come into existence through an escalatory build-up, in the course of which the participants often insult each other as part of the drama of the ritual (see Turner 1979).

Turner used the term 'structure' to distinguish the ordinary life of the 'normal' society from 'anti-structure' which represents temporary events in which the participants are afforded to do things that they are not allowed to do in their ordinary lives. Structure and anti-structure are in a symbiosis: anti-structural events are designed to reinforce structural ones. To provide an example, in tribal societies – which Turner studied in depth – rites of passage typically represent the realm of anti-structure: during such rites the participants are removed from the rest of the tribe and they are allowed to do many seemingly unruly, adventurous and violent things that would be normally sanctioned. However, all such deeds ultimately help the participants to reintegrate into the society as its full members, and so they are as much endorsed (or, at least, tolerated) by the tribe as ordinary social rituals. Due to Turner's interest in tribal social life, he devoted less attention to 'structure' than to 'anti-structure': in his framework he distinguished 'rites of separation' through which the individual gets separated from 'structure' to become part of a temporary society labelled as '*communitas*' (see more below), and 'rites of re-incorporation' through which the individual returns to structure. Since in this book I am interested in the pragmatic features of both urban rituals and other orderly ritual events of historical and modern daily life as well as unruly rituals, and I aim to study them on a par by considering their joint pragmatic features, in the following I will use Turner's terminology in a somewhat altered way. More specifically, I distinguish 'rites *of* structure' and 'rites *of* anti-structure' as part of a ritual typology, in order to distinguish ritual frames that trigger civil behaviour from others triggering aggression. Figure 3.2 illustrates how this typological adaptation of Turner's work differs from Turner's original viewpoint:

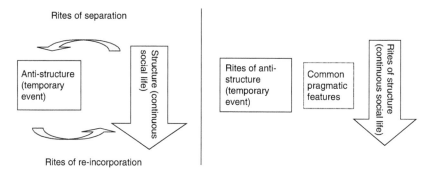

Figure 3.2 A pragmatic reinterpretation of the Turnerian ritual typology.

The left-hand side part of Figure 3.2 illustrates Turner's original typology, while the right-hand side illustrates the typology adopted in this book. An important rationale behind using Turner's typology in an altered way is that while in modern urban lives rites of separation and re-incorporation may continue to exist, they are less important than their tribal counterparts.[1] Further, many anti-structural interaction rituals – including the one studied in this chapter – are so much normative that no rite of separation is needed for them to unfold. The above-outlined typology implies that individual rituals ('rites of . . .') can be treated as part of a broader ritual system.

Along with the typological view afforded by the concept of rite of anti-structure, Turner's theory builds on two notions which characterise any aggressive ritual, and which provide insight into the communal role and evaluative effects of rites of anti-structure: *liminality* and *communitas*. *Liminality* – which is to be discussed in Chapter 7 – is not specific for anti-structural rituals, but it is particularly visible in them: it refers to the alteration of rights and obligations in ritual. As noted in Chapter 2, not all rituals are necessarily liminal: contact rituals in the Goffmanian sense rarely change the rights and obligations of participants. Here we should reiterate that the more interactionally complex a particular ritual becomes, the more likely discourse features such as liminality and ritual (self-)displaying behaviour occur. The reason why liminality tends to be very visible in rites of aggression is then not only because rights and obligations temporarily change in the anti-structure, but also because rites of anti-structure tend to be interactionally complex. Importantly, liminality has degrees: one may argue that a rite of anti-structure is fully liminal to those who take part in it, while for observers (and the same may apply for observers of a structural ritual) it is only *liminoid* in Turner's sense because they only observe the ritual.

Communitas is different from liminality: it is not a standard ritual concept in that in the Turnerian worldview it only comes into existence in the anti-structure: it refers to a temporal social formation which includes the participants of an anti-structural ritual. *Communitas* is not the same as 'in-group' – a ritual typological concept I proposed in a previous book (Kádár 2013) and in which anti-structural rituals often emerge. In-groups may have both structural and anti-structural rituals, whereas members of a *communitas* may often only have ephemeral relationship while the anti-structural ritual lasts. Communitas is also often fluid: for example, the antagonists of a mediatised rite of anti-structure may be technically in-group to a certain degree because they have a relatively constant relationship in the sporting world, while their online fans do not usually know them or each other in person, i.e., they may never have a fully-fledged in-group relationship with them or with each other.

Liminality and *communitas* provide insight into the fact that in liminal situations the altered rights and obligations are valid to all participants, and so any rite of anti-structure has a strong power to create temporary communities. In terms of aggression, these concepts imply that in a rite of anti-structure the participants are not only allowed but also encouraged to defy the norms holding for ordinary life situations within certain boundaries, and that such rites tend to create 'camps'. The concepts of liminality and *communitas* also help one understand why in many rites of anti-structure the interactional frame prompts those who perform the ritual to display their 'toughness', while certain manifestations of behaviour which count as 'ordinary' and desirable in daily interaction may be evaluated as inappropriate and even revolting.[2] Manifestations of 'toughness' have a fundamental role in creating *communitas*, and they may preclude forming 'civil' relationship between both the antagonists and their 'camps' before the climax of the ritual.

The existence of *communitas* implies that many types of aggressive rites of anti-structure tend to operate with a complex participation framework (Goffman 1974, 1981) due to their public nature: along with the participants directly involved in the performance of the ritual, they assume the presence of ratified hearers and – when they are mediatised – also that of synchronous and asynchronous audiences, including the audience that is physically present and other audiences who watch the event later (see also Knoblauch 2014; Dobs & Garcés-Conejos Blitvich 2013). Further, all rites of anti-structure revolve around the moral order. For example, many competitive sports events have an ethos of 'sportsmanship', influencing the moral order underlying such events.

3.2.2 Escalation

Any complex (above utterance level) interaction ritual prefers excessive display (see Chapter 2). However, rites of anti-structure tend to represent social dramas culminating in an escalation of offensive behaviour. For example, in MMA events studied in this chapter, escalation is often as it were 'coded' in the DNA of the events since ritual insults are expected to be exchanged during the build-up of a match. Such ritual insulting is popularly called 'trash talk', and its goal is to involve as many viewers as possible into the social drama.

The phenomenon of conflict escalation – i.e., the exchange of gradually intensified messages – has been studied widely in areas such as social psychology (see e.g., Felson 1982; Berkowitz 1994). In pragmatic research, both Jay (2000) and Culpeper (2011: 205–206) pointed out that being offended 'produces a state of emotional arousal' which increases 'the likelihood that they will retaliate in kind'. This arousal transforms into escalation if the participants have time and opportunity to respond to one another (see Bax 2010). As Vladimirou et al. (2021) argue, in order for escalation to occur, the participants do not necessarily have to be antagonists: one can observe instances of escalation also when the participants are united against a person or a cause, and exchange ever more hostile messages. Even in such a case there is of course antagonism, but the antagonists here are not present in the exchange of hostile messages. All types of escalation involve 'ritual chains' of insults (see Collins 2004), which make the words exchanged more and more offensive.

The pragmatic dynamics of escalation may be best captured if one considers when and how 'tolerable' aggression in a rite of aggression gets violated and interpreted as a 'slur'. For example, during trash talk in MMA events, the fighters usually ridicule the opponent's skill and utter threats. With the aid of (social) media, trash talk can go on for a long period of time before the fighters meet in the cage (the latter represents the climax in the tripartite ritual structure of build-up → fight → post-fight interaction). It perhaps goes without saying that insults can go very far in trash talk as part of escalation. But it is important to distinguish the notion of 'insult' – a pragmatic phenomenon expected and accepted in the aggressive ritual of trash talk – from the phenomenon of 'slurs' which are usually sanctioned in MMA events, and which, unlike insults, are unexpected. Dynel and Poppi (2019: 10) define the phenomenon of 'slur' as follows:

A taboo remark usually but not always used to deprecate, disparage or derogate a targeted member of a select category, such as ethnicity, race or sexual orientation.

When insulting becomes a slur, it tends to trigger morally loaded reflections that the moral order underlying the ritual frame of the interaction ritual has somehow been violated. Once such a scenario occurs, any perceived attempt of the antagonists to de-escalate the ritual, i.e., to remove personal hostility, opens up negative evaluations because such an attempt contradicts the expected flow of aggression.

3.3   Case Study

The case study presented in this chapter is an incident comprising a so-called 'grudge match'. A 'grudge match' refers to a sports event in which the participants go beyond the expected degree of antagonism and take the rivalry and antagonism onto a new personally offensive level.

In October 2018, a highly popularised match took place between the leading MMA athletes Conor McGregor (Ireland) and Khabib Nurmagomedov (Dagestan, Russia). Prior to the match, McGregor – who had been the most well-known MMA fighter in his weight class at the time – insulted Nurmagomedov through a chain of religious and racist slurs during the trash talk building up the event. At the time of the grudge match, Nurmagomedov was the champion and McGregor (the previous champion) wanted to reclaim his previous status after being inactive in the sport for a longer period. McGregor was (dis)reputed for his 'skill' in trash talk. However, on this occasion he went too far according to many commentators and fans: his slurs trespassed the generally rather liberal boundaries of the moral order of MMA events due to their explicitly religious and racist nature. While offenses have been frequent in the history of MMA, racist and religious slurs have been mostly avoided, and not surprisingly the grudge match under investigation escalated in a mass brawl: after defeating McGregor, Nurmagomedov jumped out of the cage and attacked the training partner of McGregor. Meanwhile, his training partners attacked McGregor in the cage and the latter fought back immediately. All the participants were, in turn, suspended by the organising Ultimate Fighting Championship. Nurmagomedov himself reflected on the chain of events by arguing that 'he lost his cool after defeating Conor McGregor because the Irishman disrespected his father, religion and country ahead of the fight',[3] i.e., he argued that due to McGregor's exceptionally offensive trash talk the event transformed into a kind of 'culture clash'.

The match lasted for four rounds, and in round three McGregor and Nurmagomedov exchanged words which were audible due to technology (the presence of a cage-side microphone). The following excerpt narrates what happened in the interaction:

Example 3.1   The UFC [Ultimate Fighters' Championship] have released audio of Khabib Nurmagomedov's and Conor McGregor's exchanges during their Lightweight title fight at UFC 229 in Las Vegas last weekend.

Nurmagomedov defended his 155 pound belt with a convincing performance against McGregor that saw him submit the Dubliner via a neck crank in the fourth round.

Both fighters entered the fight with tensions at a high after a strenuous build up that saw a bus attack at a UFC 223 media day used as the main driver in promoting the fight.

Nuramgomedov, as he has done in previous fights, began talking to McGregor during the fight and requested that they 'Talk now' as he rained down punches on top of the former two-weight world champion.

McGregor was also picked up saying, 'It's only business' at the end of the third round.

Nurmagomedov jumped out of the cage and attacked McGregor's teammates after this fight and the Russian said at his post-fight press conference that the Crumlin native had crossed lines during the promotion of the fight, a point which McGregor seems to reference during the fight by saying 'it's only business'.

(Retrieved from: www.sportsjoe.ie/mma/audio-emerges-conor-
mcgregor-khabib-nurmagomedov-said-fight-
180880 [last accessed 6 June 2023])

Of the two utterances, Nurmagomedov's 'Let's talk now', which can be interpreted as a speech act Invite (Edmondson & House 1981: 98; see also Edmondson et al. 2023), realised in a ridiculing manner, is a reference to McGregor's previous moral trespasses during the trash talk. Nurmagomedov uttered this speech act on various occasions as he locked McGregor on the mat and delivered vicious punches on his head. More interesting for us here is McGregor's utterance 'It's only business', which he uttered later as the referee separated him from Nurmagomedov at the end of the round. This utterance was understood by many as a speech act Apologise, while others understood it as a speech act Opine operating as a marketing promotion move by means of which McGregor wanted to reprimand his opponent for failing to behave professionally, i.e., according to the standards of MMA matches. The utterance was not clearly audible, and in various *communitas* wild speculations started about what McGregor actually said. All these speculations were centred on the notion that McGregor might have said something which was meant to de-escalate a ritual situation that could not be de-escalated at that point, and as such his utterance was at odds with the prevailing moral order and ritual frame of the aggressive interaction ritual on hand. Interestingly, post-event discussions of this utterance confirmed the validity of this interpretation: there was a huge media backlash about McGregor's (perceived) Apologise.

To analyse what happened here, a corpus was built, consisting of online reports and evaluative comments about McGregor's utterance 'It's only business'. The corpus also included post-event interviews with the fighters and social media postings of the fighters where they discussed this utterance, as well as online comments on these interviews and postings. Table 3.1 describes the corpus:

Table 3.1 *The McGregor corpus*

Type of data	*Reports on the match (including what McGregor said)*	*Comments on the report websites/MMA chatrooms featuring the event*	*Post-event news interviews with the fighters/ social media postings of the fighters*	*Comments about the post-event news interviews with the fighters/ social media postings of the fighters*
Overall number of cases	32	330	9	291

As Table 3.1 shows, the following four data types and related evaluative threads were involved in the present investigation:

1. What (seems to have) happened according to the observers of the event, i.e., reporters covering the match. Such observations themselves were relatively 'objective', or at least they were cloaked as objective, and so they only provide insight into the ritual event, the words of the participants during the build-up, and behavioural expectations about the moral order of the event, rather than being parts of the rite of anti-structure itself.
2. How fans of the fighters evaluated what was reported. Such evaluations represent a fundamental part of the rite of anti-structure beyond the actual clash.
3. The ways in which the antagonists engaged in the (re-)interpretation of the instance that causes ambiguity in the match ('It's only business'), in the course of interviews/postings. Similar to the above evaluative category, such reactive language use is part of the rite of anti-structure, aiming to trigger alignment between the participants and their *communitas*.
4. How fans of the fighters reacted to the fighters' (re-)interpretation (in particular that of McGregor).[4]

Evaluations manifesting themselves mostly as speech acts Opines and Tell tend to be ritual in the literal sense of the word: they typically represent ritual Argumentative Talk (Edmondson et al. 2023) in the form of 'fan talk', reflecting on (de-)escalation. Through such Argumentative Talk *communitas* is formed.

The case study analysis investigates the following two interrelated research questions, centring on the concepts of liminality and *communitas*:

1. Which factors were responsible for evaluations in ritual Argumentative Talk to emerge about McGregor's alleged 'apology' in the liminal event of the grudge match?

2. How did evaluations evolve over time and how was *communitas* responsible
for this 'evolution'?

The analysis presented in Section 3.4 follows these research questions:
Section 3.4.1 focuses on the first research question, while Section 3.4.2 centres
on the second research question. The aim of studying these questions is to show
that while rites of anti-structure can evolve very quickly and can be ambiguous
on the one hand, they follow a definite sense of moral order and they are
communally oriented in nature, i.e., they are not critically different from any
other interaction ritual.

3.4   Analysis

The present analysis centring on *liminality* and *communitas* started from
a simple empirical observation that the circumstances of the production of
McGregor's utterance 'It's only business' triggered significant ambiguity.
Following this observation, factors triggering ambiguity in the liminal rite of
the MMA event were categorised.

3.4.1   Factors Triggering Ambiguity

The Manner of Recording and Addressivity/Participant Structure

Many observers of the grudge match appeared to have wondered whether
what McGregor said was recorded accidentally or not. This is understand-
able if we consider that any perception of accidentalness puts this utterance in a very different interpretive frame than if it had been uttered
clearly with the public in mind, i.e., if it clearly occurred within a ritual
frame. In other words, we have here the case of ambiguous addressivity,
in particular concerning whether the utterance was addressed to
Nurmagomedov as an individual, or as an opponent in front of fans.
Along with addressivity, it is worth considering here participant structure
in Goffman's (1981) terms: ambiguity might have been triggered also by
the lack of clarity regarding whether the utterance was meant for the
audience or not.

Thirty out of thirty-two interviews in the corpus that report on the utterance
'It's only business' include the formulations 'New footage' and/or 'Cageside
microphone picked up', as the following examples illustrate:

Example 3.2   New Footage Features Audio During Khabib-McGregor
Even more footage has come out of the highly-talked [sic.] about
Khabib Nurmagomedov vs. Conor McGregor fight from UFC 229,
and in this case, Nurmagomedov is the one doing the talking.

Example 3.3   Cageside microphone picked up Conor McGregor comment after third
               round
               There was always going to be plenty of talk in the Octagon in the main
               event of UFC 229.

Both formulations in Examples 3.2 and 3.3 show that what McGregor said was
not part of the official recording, but rather it was caught accidentally – i.e., it
did not occur as part of the ritual frame – which coincides with the fact that in
rites of anti-structure things can happen extremely quickly, in particular as
liminal escalation kicks in. If the utterance was a clearly audible part of the
original media coverage, which viewers subscribed for during the pay-per-view
match, there would have been far fewer speculations as regards what exactly
occurred. However, as it happened, the footage became a hotbed of speculation.
As Hutchins and Rowe (2012) argue, such speculations often emerge when
footage of sports events featuring language use are circulated on the Internet.

What Was Said?

The next factor triggering ambiguity refers to what McGregor said exactly.
Given the ambiguity of the above-mentioned production circumstances, this is
an interesting issue to look into, all the more so because, immediately after the
grudge match, the fans, the media and even the fighters themselves engaged in
debates about McGregor's words.

Example 3.4   Conor McGregor APOLOGY: Did UFC star apologise to Khabib dur-
               ing fight? What did he say?
               CONOR MCGREGOR took aim at Khabib Nurmagomedov's religion
               and father in the build-up to their UFC 229 showdown but did
               McGregor apologise for his trash talking during the fight?

                              (Retrieved from: www.express.co.uk/sport/ufc/1028799/
                                       Conor-McGregor-apology-did-McGregor-apologise-
                                                    to-Khabib-UFC-229-what-did-he-say
                                                             [last accessed 6 June 2023])

As this extract shows, various media outlets raised queries about the actual
wording of McGregor's utterance. The liminal dynamics of rites of anti-
structure often triggers such a sense of ambiguity and, consequently, a degree
of deniability (Peet 2015). Due to this deniability, MMA fans also started to raise
questions with regards to what was said, as the following example illustrates:

Example 3.5   Did Conor Mcgregor [sic.] really say 'it's only business'?

                              (Retrieved from: www.youtube.com/watch?v=
                                      JssUM4BEXj0 [last accessed 6 June 2023])

Although many of McGregor's fans attempted to interpret the utterance as
a non-Apologise (see below), hence engaging in ritual argumentative 'fan talk',

McGregor himself did not try to do this but rather he soon denied that his words were 'It's only business' (and therefore he also implicitly denied that he had performed a speech act Apologise). On both Twitter and in media interviews, McGregor claimed that his actual words had been 'don't be bitching' – which was interpreted by some as 'it's only business' – hence claiming that he attempted to mock Nurmagomedov in accordance with the ritual expectations of 'toughness' in MMA matches:

Example 3.6   MMA superstar Connor McGregor has apparently denied his infamous 'it's only business' line muttered to champion Khabib Nurmagomedov in their UFC lightweight title bout, apparently suggesting he said 'don't be bitching'.

(Retrieved from: www.rt.com/sport/448665-conor-mcgregor-khabib-bitching-business/ [last accessed 6 June 2023])

McGregor's version of the utterance – representing a ritually realised speech act Disclose aimed at his *communitas* – is significant for how others may evaluate the event because by being 'tough' he could cast Nurmagomedov as a 'moaner' and position himself as a person reacting with mockery to such 'moaning' (see more below). As scholars such as Balteiro (2019) argued, 'bitching' is an expression often used about 'feminine' behaviour in sports events, and as such its use portrays Nurmagomedov as a 'weak' fighter. Not surprisingly, various fans in the *communitas* of McGregor accepted this interpretation, and despite his final loss, hailed McGregor as a star fighter who remained 'tough' all the time during the fight, i.e., they produce the speech act Remark to ritually reinforce the ethos of their *communitas*.

It is also relevant to note that various fans not only accepted what McGregor claimed, but also came up with their own interpretations of the utterance, as the following thread illustrates. The fact that interpretative discrepancies occurred not only between the fans themselves but also between McGregor and his fans illustrates the potentially extreme ambiguity and community orientation of liminal aggressive rites of anti-structure whenever it becomes unclear what an antagonist actually said:

Example 3.7   User A
Three months ago
He doesn't say 'It's only business'
He says 'Fun and Kisses'

User B
Three months ago
Conor said that he said dont be bitching which is impossible to hear for therefore the only other outcome would be khabib's [sic.] which is it's only business

User C
Two months ago
Khabib: He said 'It's only business'
Conor: I said 'Don't be bitching'
Conor fans: He said 'It's only kisses'
Audio: 'Iz songly bizzes'

User D
Two months ago
@User A lets be realistic bro. After being manhandled and utterly mauled the man was making a plea for mercy.
It is what it is. Conor was mentally broken and emasculated.

User E
Two months ago
That Irish fuck doesn't speak clearly, so he said, 'it's only business'.

(Retrieved from: www.youtube.com/watch?v=
eoCRweN6wFI [last accessed 6 June 2023])

Interestingly, these postings were made after McGregor's explanation. 'User C' in the thread is supposedly a fan of McGregor; however, instead of accepting McGregor's version, User C comes up with his alternative interpretation, realised in the form of the speech act Opine 'It's only kisses'. The above thread also illustrates that commenters tend to be divided into opposite camps of *communitas*, and that the ambiguity of an utterance may prompt various commenters to engage in complex evaluations and explanations. For instance, the commenter User C realised a virtual communally oriented 'enregisterment' (Agha 2005), by imitating what different parties claimed to have heard.

As regards the fans' metacomments, it is important to note that such comments were not only centred on accent, but also various fans provided surprisingly innovative pragmatic interpretations of McGregor's utterance, as the following thread illustrates:

Example 3.8   He said fine punches 'foine poonches'

Hmm, it does sound more like he's saying 'don't kiss us'

Why else would Khabib [Nurmagomedov] react the way he did if Conor said anything that was not antagonizing?

Sounds pretty obvious to me that he says 'It's only business' but that doesn't necessarily mean he was apologising. He could have easily have meant 'I don't give a shit if you're upset, it's only business to me.'

(Retrieved from: https://forums.sherdog.com/threads/
so-did-conor-really-say-its-only-business
.3846803/ [last accessed 6 June 2023])

These comments from the MMA website 'Sherdog' illustrate that accent is only one of the factors that influenced interpretations and subsequent evaluations of McGregor's utterance. The third comment in the thread refers to Nurmagomedov's reaction to McGregor's utterance by claiming that McGregor could not have said 'It's only business' because that would not have triggered an antagonistic evaluation. This also implies that McGregor must have ridiculed Nurmagomedov, hence attempting to further escalate rather than de-escalate the aggressive rite of anti-structure already mounting at the event. The fourth commenter, on the other hand, appears to have assumed that McGregor did in fact say 'It's only business', but rejects the one-sided interpretation that this is a speech act Apologise, suggesting instead that it might just as well have been a self-referenced utterance explaining McGregor's own intention.

The examples thus far have illustrated that all interpretations of the event – manifested as argumentative 'fan talk' – are centred on two entirely different scenarios, namely, McGregor saying (a) 'It's only business' or (b) 'Don't be bitching', 'It's only kisses', etc. Importantly, however, these two interpretations do not trigger binary evaluations: (a) 'It's only business' triggered both positive and negative online evaluations, as the extracts studied in this section have illustrated, whereas (b) variants of the other version lend themselves to being interpreted as manifestations of ridiculing Nurmagomedov.

What Was Meant?

The question what was said is relevant to another issue: what was meant? In the corpus of this case study (see Table 3.2), the number of comments that accept that McGregor uttered 'It's only business' is as follows:

Table 3.2 *Comments accepting McGregor said 'It's only business' in the corpus studied*

Type of data	Comments on the report websites/MMA chatrooms describing the event	Comments about the interviews with/ postings of the fighters (post-event)
Overall number of comments	330	291
Comments on the utterance 'It's only business'	171	203

The study of this group of comments has revealed that it was not only the media itself which speculated about whether McGregor realised the speech act Apologise or not (see Example 3.4), but also many commenters who accepted that McGregor did in fact say 'It's only business' started to think about his intended meaning. The following interpretive patterns emerged in this set of comments:

1. Justification
2. Disclose: A speech act operating as a ritual marketing promotion move within the ritual frame of the MMA event

Clearly, the former interpretation triggers negative evaluations because justification often operates as a pragmatic component by means of which the speech act Apologise is realised (see Vollmer & Olshtain 1989).[5] However, the other interpretation is suitable to trigger positive evaluations because promoting professionalism in the form of a speech act Disclose is morally endorsed in this particular ritual frame. The following thread illustrates the evaluations that these interpretations trigger:

Example 3.9   *When Conor said 'It's only business' during the Khabib fight, what did he mean? (Quora discussion)*

> *User A*
> *Answered 16 October, 2018*
> *I personally was extremely shocked when I heard it.*
> *[. . .]*
> *By saying, 'It's only Business', Conor was trying to justify his supposed 'trash talking'.*
> *Conor was trying to tell Khabib, 'Hey look, I insulted your father, spoke shit about your religion, your country, but that was only in the name of business'.*
> *Guess what? This doesn't work with a fellow Dagestani to whom legacy, honor and pride is everything.*
>
> *User B*
> *Answered 15 October, 2018*
> *Conor McGregor is an incredible fighter, but he's an even better promoter – of himself, of the sport, and of the UFC.*
> *The UFC brings some of the greatest competitive MMA fighters in the world to the centre stage, but make no mistake: the UFC is in the entertainment business, and businesses rely on marketing to survive. McGregor is one of their best tools, and he knows it.*
>
> *User C*
> *Answered 15 October, 2018*
> *This is the true colors of the real champion Mcgregor. It was all about promoting the fight, or in simpler terms business. He was always like this throughout his career.*
>
> (Retrieved from: www.quora.com/When-Conor-said-It-s-
> only-business-during-the-Khabib-fight-what-
> did-he-mean [last accessed 6 June 2023])

The first of the commenters refers to the previously discussed phenomenon of addressivity, by claiming that McGregor's addressee was Nurmagomedov. However, the second and third commenters in the thread position McGregor as a 'representative' of the interest of the organiser UFC and the fans as well, i.e., they implicitly argue that the utterance 'It's only business' was addressed to the audience. The implication of these evaluations in ritual argumentative 'fan talk' is that it was actually Nurmagomedov who behaved unprofessionally, which also shows that these evaluations represent the formation of *communitas*.

The Timing of What Was Said

The timing of the utterance – and a sense of time in general – is also important in the evaluations of the utterance as a manifestation of ritually rough and tough ridiculing *versus* cowardice. Due to the mediatised nature of the grudge match and the fact that McGregor's utterance was presented only in post-event footage, ambiguity emerged as regards exactly when this utterance was made. This ambiguity emerging in the liminal scene influenced evaluations. In the match, the utterance was made in round three, which was the only round in which McGregor scored better than Nurmagomedov. The media itself did not raise the matter of timing, but timing became a topic of discussion in online ritual argumentative 'fan talk', and interestingly McGregor himself retrospectively referred to timing on his Facebook page as evidence for the fact that his utterance was a manifestation of rough ridiculing:

Example 3.10   *'Don't be a bitch, bitching. The same thing I said to khabib [sic.] at the end of round 3. My round,' McGregor wrote. 'Don't be bitching! Every single round bitching to the referee. He was even bitching in the fourth round from mount position. It baffled me.'*

(Retrieved from: https://nl-nl.facebook.com/thenotoriousmma/videos/
let-the-record-show-i-like-paulie-malinaggi-here-is-a-confrontation-
between-us-r/387260908747662/ [last accessed 6 June 2023])

The media reacted to this explanation with some caution: while no official media outlet had explicitly challenged McGregor's explanation, various media forums voiced a sense of implicit doubt regarding its validity, on the grounds that it was provided much later after the event. That is, in these evaluations timing became important not in the sense of when the utterance was made, but rather in a reflective sense, i.e., in the context of when the explanation occurred. For instance, 'Bloodyelbow', one of the key MMA websites, mentioned the following:

Example 3.11   Is this lengthy and somewhat bizarre post all so McGregor could explain that he actually said 'don't be bitching' instead of 'it's only business'? With the way it's written, that does seem to be the case, but it's curious that he waited three months and needed a long back story and video 'proof' to make his case.

(Retrieved from: www.bloodyelbow.com/2019/1/12/18179590/
conor-mcgregor-deny-telling-khabib-its-only-business-malignaggi-
altercation-proof-ufc-mma [last accessed 6 June 2023])

Some of those online commenters who accepted McGregor's explanation pointed out that the match was circulated online in many edited forms, and it is due to such editing that McGregor's critics failed to realise that it was made at the end of round three. His critiques and members of the other *communitas*, on the other hand, argued that even in round three he was not dominating Nurmagomedov, and so any claim regarding the timing of the utterance is invalid. The following thread illustrates such debates:

Example 3.12   User F
One month ago
The 'it's only business' line has been taken out of context on every video I've seen. It came after round 3 – the round Conor won. It is edited in after round 2 on every video.

User G
One month ago
Connor didn't win a round. He was getting owned the whole time, stop being a fanboy.

(Retrieved from: www.youtube.com/watch?v=eoCRweN6wFI
[last accessed 6 June 2023])

The analysis thus far has shown that rites of anti-structure can trigger intensive (and excessive) ritual argumentative 'fan talk' when an individually formulated slur uttered during the escalatory event can either be evaluated as a violation of the moral order of the ritual, or as an utterance through which the moral order was reinforced. However, all such evaluations are centred on a common moral order underlying the ritual, i.e., they are not *ad hoc* and follow the communal nature of the ritual.

3.4.2   Diachronic Development of Evaluations

The Antagonists' Interpretations from a Diachronic Perspective
The fact that events unfold in a potentially very fast and ambiguous way in aggressive liminal rites of anti-structure raises another question – the second research question of this case study analysis – namely, whether the antagonists themselves can be affected by differing interpretations of what was said over time. In other words, can time increase the ambiguity surrounding a rite of anti-structure, and if yes, does *communitas* have any role in this? It is

necessary here to recall that MMA athletes like McGregor and Nurmagomedov are celebrities who use social media such as Facebook and Instagram to exchange messages and boost their images. The analysis of the corpus of this case study has revealed that Nurmagomedov did not challenge McGregor's (re)interpretation of the utterance, but rather integrated it into his own ridiculing of McGregor, hence gaining face in front of his fans constituting his *communitas*.

As Example 3.13 illustrates, right after the grudge match, Nurmagomedov interpreted McGregor's utterance as a 'plea for mercy', and as such he understood it as 'It's only business', i.e., a realisation of the speech act Apologise:

Example 3.13 [transcript] He tried to talk with me, with me, about erh, it's only business you know, this meant for me please calm down, don't smash me

(Retrieved from: www.youtube.com/watch?v=ssT2-Abh9cQ
[last accessed 6 June 2023])

However, this line of interpretation changed after McGregor released his own version of the event on Facebook:

Example 3.14 In an Instagram post directed at former sparring partner and ex-world boxing champ Paulie Malignaggi [an adversary of McGregor] on Saturday, McGregor seemed to hint that he told his Russian opponent 'don't be bitching' in an effort to stop him complaining to the referee for perceived fouls from McGregor, with footage of his using the same phrase to Malignaggi during their confrontation in 2017.

Khabib nevertheless responded with his own post on Instagram of the moment he submitted McGregor with the caption 'You will live with this shame all your life, bi ... ', stopping short of using the full expletive but leaving a heavy hint as to who he considered to be the real 'bitch' in the matter.

(Retrieved from: www.rt.com/sport/448665-conor-mcgregor-khabib-bitching-business/ [last accessed 6 June 2023])

In this posting, Nurmagomedov used the expletive 'bitch' in reaction to McGregor's 'bitching' remark. It would be speculative to argue that Nurmagomedov actually believed what McGregor claimed: it might well be that he assessed that engaging in a debate would belittle his own position, whereas successfully ridiculing the other is a strong resource in the context of the aggressive liminal rite of anti-structure.

In sum, both antagonists reinterpreted what was said retrospectively. Such reinterpretations of the ambiguous utterance make sense if we consider that they took place as a form of public discourse online.

The Temporal Development of Evaluating Evaluation (Meta-evaluation)

As part of the evaluative complexities that surround ritual argumentative 'fan talk' in aggressive rites of anti-structure of pragmatically ambiguous scope, such as the incident under investigation, it is also relevant to note that fans – many of whom are divided into camps – often evaluatively reflect on each other's evaluations. Considering that fans often aim to defend their own champion and their own (virtual) *communitas*, they often criticise evaluations made by members of the other camp as being 'subjective' (see Baumgarten et al. 2012), i.e., they engage in a war of words as part of the rite of anti-structure.

As far as the corpus of this case study is concerned, some MMA fans accuse each other with being 'subjective' by providing racial and/or ethnic rationalisations, as the following example representing a chain of speech acts Opine illustrates:

Example 3.15   *People forget conor [sic.] is irish [sic.] all he cares about is fighting and getting paid..thats why he always says all i wanna do is fight and have proper knock..even after the fight he tweet good knock now for the rematch..the guy dnt give a damn..i'll tap for another 50 mill anyday.. the guy dnt care about losing..conor [sic.]got paid..khabib [sic.] hasn't yet because of his stupidness*

(Retrieved from: www.dailymail.co.uk/sport/ufc/article-6253151/
Its-business-Fans-think-Conor-McGregor-APOLOGISED
-Khabib.html%23comments [last accessed 6 June 2023])

In this comment, a McGregor fan refers to members of the other camp as 'people' who 'forget' and as such misjudge McGregor's utterances, which are claimed to make sense if one considers McGregor's ethnic background. Only a few comments in the corpus feature such racial/ethnic arguments. As Table 3.3 illustrates, the majority of the accusations are about the 'fanship bias' of the other camp.

Table 3.3   *Evaluative accusations in the corpus*

Type of data	Comments on the report websites/MMA chatrooms describing the event	Comments about the interviews with/postings of the fighters (post-event)
Overall number of comments	330	291
Racially/ethnically motivated comments about the evaluations of the other camp	14	18
Accusing members of the other camp with 'fanship bias'	48	39

As the figures in Table 3.3 show, it is only a minor portion of the commenters who attack each other. It is important to bear in mind that it is difficult to rigorously quantify such tendencies of evaluation in argumentative 'fan talk' because some-times there is no evidence for the fact that in a particular corpus (like the present one) a commenter 'belongs to' a particular *communitas* of a fan camp or not. Yet, as the figures in Table 3.3 show, accusing others with 'fanship bias' is much more frequent in the corpus of this case study than the other 'racial/ethnic' evaluative category. Irrespective of whether fan comments are racist or not, what is clear is that in the rite of anti-structure, evaluations get themselves evaluated over time, i.e., it is clear that aggressive rites of anti-structure trigger intensive meta-evaluative engagement.

The following thread illustrates a typical accusation of 'fanship bias':

Example 3.16   *Conor fans are so desperate for it not to be 'its only business' that they couldn't come up with something less stupid then 'don't kiss us'*

   It's pathetic bro lol
   They would Lie for a false idol lol

   (Retrieved from: https://forums.sherdog.com/threads/its-only-business.3863741/page-2 [last accessed 6 June 2023])

As the present section has shown, evaluations of a controversial utterance can evolve over time, a fact which accords with the evolving nature of rites of anti-structure – argumentative 'fan talk' after the culmination of a clash is as much part of the ritual under investigation as the build-up of the event. The evolve-ment of such evaluations in Argumentative Talk is not arbitrary, i.e., they are centred on a general moral order underlying the ritual and also they are communally oriented (hence the potential clashes between evaluations grounded in the same moral order of an anti-structural sports event).

3.5   Conclusion

This chapter has continued the present journey into the realm of interaction ritual. The chapter introduced the concept of rite of anti-structure as a typological approach by means of which rituals are divided into structural and anti-structural ones. Anti-structural rites are intrinsically related to impol-iteness: as the data analysis has shown, the participants of such rituals make abundant use of rude utterances, offensive mocking and other forms of lan-guage use that traditionally 'belong' in one way or another to impoliteness. However, as we could see, impoliteness is only of a secondary interest to understand exactly what goes on in rites of anti-structure because ultimately these rituals – as any interaction ritual – are communally oriented. The only scenario where individual 'impoliteness proper' becomes salient in rites of anti-structure includes cases when an offence is interpreted as an individual slur, which is clearly at odds with what is normally tolerated in a rite of anti-structure, hence representing a violation of the moral order of events. The potential of this scenario is coded in the DNA of rites of anti-structure due to their escalatory nature: while rites of anti-structure tolerate aggression, certain things cannot be said and done in them, and yet such things may happen during escalation. However, at the end of the day even slurs tend to be re-evaluated and interactionally reconstructed in ritual Argumentative Talk in rites of anti-structure.

Following what was shown in Figure 3.1, the present analysis has studied a form of ritual engagement which is only ritual in the abstract sense of the word. That is, the ritual here may not be defined as 'ritual' in the popular sense because of its seeming *ad hoc* nature and also because it is not limited to 'trash talk' but also the fight itself, as well as all reflective interactions after the fight. The case study analysis examined the following research questions:

1. Which factors were responsible for evaluations to emerge about McGregor's alleged 'apology' in the liminal event of the grudge match?
2. How did evaluations evolve over time and how was *communitas* responsible for this 'evolution'?

The investigation has shown that aggressive rites of anti-structure trigger a complex cluster of evaluations, due to the high degree of ambiguity such liminal rituals often generate. Evaluations made by various participants and observers, which are also parts of the rite of anti-structure, contribute to the formation of *communitas*, and they often also further increase the ambiguity of what was said during the *liminal* event. However, evaluative utterances in argumentative 'fan talk' follow recurrent evaluative and argumentative patterns, akin to any communal ritual.

The present chapter has shown that a key advantage of the ritual perspective is that it allows us to observe seemingly very different manifestations of communally oriented language use – such as civil behaviour featured in Chapter 2 and aggression studied in the present chapter – as part of a broader phenomenon, either as a rite of anti-structure or a rite of structure. The following Chapter 4 will conclude the discussion of the ritual perspective, by taking the reader into yet another area of language use which can arguably be better explained from the perspective of ritual than politeness, by relying on the concept of 'rite of structure': instances of overly 'ordinary' political language use.

3.6   Recommended Reading

Turner, V. (1979) *The Ritual Process: Structure and Anti-Structure*. Ithaca, NY: Cornell University Press.
Victor Turner's classic is a must-read for the study of rite of anti-structure: Turner not only established a ground-breaking framework through which such

rituals can be studied, but also described his framework in a very reader-friendly way, making it accessible not only for anthropologists but also linguists and experts of other fields. In the following section, Turner discusses the concept of liminality:

The attributes of liminality or of liminal personae ("threshold people") are necessarily ambiguous, since this condition and these persons elude or slip through the network of classifications that normally locate states and positions in cultural space. Liminal entities are neither here nor there; they are betwixt and between the positions assigned and arrayed by law, custom, convention, and ceremonial. As such, their ambiguous and indeterminate attributes are expressed by a rich variety of symbols in the many societies that ritualize social and cultural transitions. Thus, liminality is frequently likened to death, to being in the womb, to invisibility, to darkness, to bisexuality, to the wilderness, and to an eclipse of the sun or moon.

Liminal entities, such as neophytes in initiation or puberty rites, may be represented as possessing nothing. They may be disguised as monsters, wear only a strip of clothing, or even go naked, to demonstrate that as liminal beings they have no status, property, insignia, secular clothing indicating rank or role, position in a kinship system – in short, nothing that may distinguish them from their fellow neophytes or initiands. Their behavior is normally passive or humble; they must obey their instructors implicitly, and accept arbitrary punishment without complaint. It is as though they are being reduced or ground down to a uniform condition to be fashioned anew and endowed with additional powers to enable them to cope with their new station in life. Among themselves, neophytes tend to develop an intense comradeship and egalitarianism. Secular distinctions of rank and status disappear or are homogenized. (Turner 1979: 95–96)

4 'Politeness' in the Realm of the Overly Ordinary: Concluding Notes on the Ritual Perspective

4.1 Introduction

The present final chapter of Part I of this book aims to bring the reader into yet another area where the ritual perspective may be more relevant than traditional politeness theory: the study of social protocols in public discourse, representing the realm of overly ordinary language use. By 'public discourse' I mean both monologues and instances of dialogues and polylogues that take place in public, mostly through mediatised events or written (online) pieces which are often available for members of the public. By 'social protocols' I mean forms of language use associated with 'politeness' – I call such forms 'social protocols' because in public discourse 'politeness' in the interpersonal sense is hardly needed, i.e., such forms at first sight may seem to be 'superfluous'. However, as this chapter will show, they gain an important ritual function in public discourse triggering all classic features of interaction ritual, including institutionalised rights and obligations holding for the participants, (awareness of) the presence of observers, strong perception of a ritual moral order underlying the flow of the interaction and so on.

Genres of public discourse can include rites of anti-structure – in the previous Chapter 3 we focused on such a case, featuring rudeness and incivility in a mediatised ritual. However, rites of anti-structure also encompass a wide variety of 'civil' events, including ones where aggression in hidden under a veneer of civility, such as debates in the British Parliament. The following example – drawn from Bull, Fetzer and Kádár (2020) – illustrates such an instance of language use which one may describe through the metaphor 'iron fist in a velvet glove':

Mr Speaker, for 10 years the PM [i.e. Prime Minister] plotted and schemed to have this job – and for what? No conviction, just calculation; no vision, just a vacuum. Last week he lost his political authority, and this week he is losing his moral authority. How long are we going to have to wait before the past makes way for the future?

Here the Speaker of the House is addressed in a clearly 'civil' way: the politician who utters the above barrage of speech acts Opines and Requests for information appears to 'elicit' the Speaker's view through rhetorical questions. However, it is not only that the Speaker of the House cannot and is not institutionally allowed to answer such questions, but also it is clear to all participants and observers of the event that what we have here is a fully-fledged attack on the Prime Minister as a third person. This attack is not significantly different from MMA trash talk from the ritual pragmatician's point of view: the event where it occurs triggers aggression which can escalate,[1] the participants are expected to attack each other within certain pragmatic boundaries (i.e., through exchanging attacks through the Speaker as a mediator), and attacks that violate the moral (and legal) order of parliamentary debates tend to be institutionally sanctioned. Also, similar to MMA trash talk, 'civil' face-threats here are only marginally relevant to traditional politeness theory: while through 'impolite' utterances attacks are made on the 'face' of the recipient, such attacks do not usually merely represent a clash between two individuals but rather one between two professional politicians representing political parties and electors.[2] One may rightly argue that successful ritual attacks, and the repelling of such attack, is not autotelic: they aim to improve the status and subsequent popularity of the participants of the rite of anti-structure in a competitive way. Thus, a body of the conceptual repertoire of traditional politeness research such as 'face-threat' (Brown & Levinson 1987), 'evaluation' (Eelen 2001) and so on are only marginally relevant in such settings for the study of phenomena normally associated with impoliteness (and politeness).

The same problem applies to what I define as 'social protocols' in this chapter, studied in public discourse representing rites of structure. Such protocols include expressions of deference, speech acts expected in public events (such as Welcome in a public ceremony, see Chapter 2), extended speech acts such as Congratulates in diplomatic correspondence and so on (see also Bendazzoli 2023). While many manifestations of social protocols have been studied under the politeness umbrella, I believe they can be far more reliably studied with the aid of interaction ritual, hence the reference to 'politeness' in inverted commas in the title of this chapter. This is because rites of structure where social protocols occur represent the realm of ordinary – or, one may argue, overly ordinary! – and as such they are normally scripted and provide little space for interactional salience (see Watts 2003). Thus, while social protocols seem to be very different from instances of ritual rudeness studied in Chapter 2, once we look at them with the cold eye of the pragmatician it becomes evident that they represent two sides of a coin: both of them represent ritual language use following rights and obligations. While one could argue that in terms of language use rites of anti-structure provide more creative 'freedom' than rites of structure, this is not always the case. For example, in a recent study (House et al. 2023) with a team of colleagues we examined diplomatic protocols which were very creatively used to threaten representatives of another country.

Since public rites of structure always take place in front of an audience, the target of social protocols in them can be complex, i.e., ambiguity may emerge as to whether an utterance or series of utterances are addressed to the community, the individual or both. Compare the following ritual welcoming speeches:

Welcome on board, Jason. I am sure you will make an excellent contribution to our company, which values outstanding IT skills like yours.

It's my pleasure to welcome Jason on board. I am sure Jason will make an excellent contribution to our company, which values outstanding IT skills like his.

The message of the two welcoming utterances – including the speech acts Welcome and Opine (Edmondson et al. 2023) – is essentially the same. However, the first utterance is addressed to the recipient, even though it animates the communal voice of the company, and as such the main function of the social protocol (or 'politeness', if one likes) here may be to build some form of 'rapport' (see Spencer-Oatey 2000) between the speaker and the recipient. However, in the second utterance the recipient is mentioned in the third person, and both the speech acts Welcome and Remark here may at least as much be oriented to the public as to the individual (i.e., this is a case of multiple addressivity). It would be naïve to argue that politeness does not operate *at all* in an individual way in public rites of structure like the one represented by these examples. For example, even the second welcoming above, which is less personal than the first one, could be uttered by a manager in the context of a company pub outing where the relatively impersonal and institutionalised welcoming words would be followed by sharing drinks and engaging in informal conversation.

However, there are instances of public discourse which clearly lack *any* individual and personal feature, representing the ultimate end of 'public' on a scale of interpersonal versus public communication. This chapter will focus on such discourse, by examining official Chinese written monologues – more precisely, news releases of official Chinese public announcements (*gong'gao* 公告, lit. 'public announcement', in Chinese). The analysis of this data will show that while Chinese public announcements are heavily loaded with honorifics and other manifestations of 'polite' language use, such instances of language use represent social protocols which can be far more reliably studied through the ritual perspective than through the lens of politeness.

The structure of this chapter is the following. Section 4.2 introduces a Goffmanian concept – 'alignment' – which helps one interpret the function of so-called 'politeness' (and 'impoliteness') in public discourse. I will argue that like many of Goffman's concepts, 'alignment' provides an excellent tool for the ritualist to describe what is going on in rites of structure when social protocols are used. Section 4.3. introduces the case study of this chapter, and Section 4.4 conducts the case study analysis. Finally, Section 4.5 provides a conclusion – here I also summarise what Part I of this book has covered.

4.2   Alignment

One may rightly ask why an 'author' (in Goffman's sense) would bother with engaging at social protocoling in public discourse, such as a piece of public political monologue with no apparent recipient. After all, the expression 'protocol' normally refers to conventions (and related rights and obligations) of pragmatic behaviour in events and genres where two or more actors interact with each other. While protocol may play an important role in monologues such as political notes exchanged between diplomats, why would one want to follow a particular 'polite' protocol in a written public monologue with no direct recipient present? Goffman (1981) provides a perfect answer to this question, by proposing the concept of alignment.

Alignment originates in Goffman's discussion of the participation framework. Goffman (1981: 128) argued that 'footing' is 'the alignment we take up to ourselves and the others present as expressed in the way we manage the production or reception of an utterance'. According to Goffman, the participants of an interaction may shift footings as they change their alignments with each other and third parties, and they indicate such changes with contextual and linguistic cues. Since the current chapter focuses on public monologic discourse, I interpret alignment here in a narrow sense, i.e., as the attitude of accepting an authoritative line of discourse. An author can both prompt others to align themselves with himself or a third party, and as part of this he may also align himself with someone who is above him in authority. If the author of a public discourse engages in any form of seemingly direct communication with a third party, e.g., by expressing deference to a political actor, the power triggered by the public medium through which his words reach the public provides a strong opportunity to create an authoritative line of discourse. Following social protocols with a third more authoritative party in such an authoritative line of discourse tends to have a strong capacity to trigger the responsive alignment of the receivers with the addressed political actor or organisation.

Considering that public political monologic discourse operates with strongly conventionalised features and also has a fixed ritual frame with clear ritual rights (and obligations), such discourse is apt to trigger alignment through social protocols. This phenomenon of alignment-triggering through 'polite' social protocols can be particularly visible in Chinese public announcements examined in this chapter as a case study. In the decidedly power-driven Chinese political culture where there is little direct communication between political decision makers and the public (e.g., in the form of electoral meetings), 'polite' social protocols are seemingly even more redundant than in 'Western' political language use. Thus, in such a context it is arguably even more obvious that social protocols may simply have no relationship to interpersonal politeness but are parts of a public ritual. The goal of alignment-triggering here may always correlate with the actual goal of an instance of public discourse. For example, the case study below examines 'polite' social protocols in public discourse in the wake of a national social crisis where the public's trust and cooperation with policies needs to be reinforced.

Relying on the concept of alignment in the study of social protocols implies that the analyst needs to try to look beyond the apparent function of the words uttered, i.e., rely on the ritual concept of ostensible behaviour mentioned previously in this book. This is a line of thought that various experts of research on language and politics have advocated, drawing attention to the fact that 'politeness' in political language correlates with implicit communication (see, in particular, Harris et al.'s 2006 seminal study of the role of implicitness in political messages). Implicitness is particularly relevant if one aims to study a genre – such as Chinese public governmental announcements featured in the case study below – where implicitness is always lurking because political decision makers are simply *not meant* to directly and explicitly communicate with the public (see also Dou & Zhang 2007; Jiang 2006). The ritual view helps one interpret implicit pragmatic behaviour beyond individual language use: if implicit patterns of language use in political discourse recurrently follow pragmatic patterns and underlying rights and obligations, one can rightly assume that such patterns tend to be used and interpreted as part of a major social ritual. Yet, I use the expression 'ostensible behaviour' instead of 'implicit behaviour' because the former is a ritual term, which describes the fact that the goal of ritual is often different from what meets the eye.

4.3   Case Study

The current case study features Chinese public announcements (*gong'gao* 公告) made in the wake of major crises. Such announcements tend to be made as news is released at various governmental levels, including national, provincial and local (city) ones. The level at which a particular announcement is made bears relevance for its style and the use of social protocols in it, considering that in Chinese politics different governmental levels have strictly defined and clearly different power and related rights and obligations (Ma 2005), unlike in many 'Western' countries.[3] Chinese public announcements typically represent a public rite of structure where the author's goal is to reassure the public that political decision makers can resolve a situation in an orderly and hierarchical fashion (see Yang 1997; Kádár & Zhang 2019), hence aiming to trigger the public's alignment with the decision makers. The authors of such texts also often make promises of action to the public. The right of 'reporting' the details of an action plan is unevenly allocated across the news releases produced by the various administrative levels.

The data of the present case study consists of official Chinese releases of *gong'gao* during the vaccine scandal that erupted in China in the summer of 2018. This incident began when national media cautiously released information about a 'potential' problem with 'a limited number of vaccines'. It quickly became evident that the situation was significantly more serious than this euphemistic wording had suggested: a vast number of patients had been improperly vaccinated against life-threatening illnesses such as rabies. This was not the first vaccine scandal in recent Chinese history: there had been a chain of similar events, including an incident in 2007–2008 (Shanxi Province), one in 2009 (Jiangsu and Hebei Provinces) and one in 2016 (Shandong Province). The gravity of such cases was exacerbated by the fact that many felt that the companies involved had not been sufficiently sanctioned. For instance, Changchun Changsheng, the company responsible for the 2018 incident, only received a penalty of several million Renminbi, an extremely modest sum compared to the size of the company and its annual profit. From the outset of the 2018 incident, authorities and decision makers at various levels of the state administration were prompt to react: immediately after the release of the first report on the incident, they repeatedly promised a thorough investigation of the case and strict punishment for those responsible for the production of substandard medicine. The reactions of these leaders and other Chinese political figures were portrayed to the public primarily through *gong'gao* announcements featured in official news releases.

This case study was conducted on the basis of a corpus consisting of thirty national-level public announcements, five provincial-level announcements and five local-level announcements that were made in the media following the outbreak of the incident. The overall size of the corpus is 32,891 Chinese characters. The above-mentioned thirty public announcements were released during a period of fifteen days between 16 and 30 July 2018, following the earliest report of the incident on 12 July. This limited timeline stems from the nature of *gong'gao*, which is a ritual genre that conventionally operates in contexts where formal legal action has *yet to take place* and appears mainly in the official media which has been permitted to act as the voice of the authorities. As the incident developed, actors at various administrative levels – spanning the highest-level decision makers such as Xi Jinping (General Secretary) and Li Keqiang (Premier), to the leaders of the cities affected by the incident – announced their reactions to the incident. Their announcements were disseminated by the main official media outlets: Chinese official national-level news agencies, such as Xinhua, released details of the *gong'gao* made by Xi Jinping, Li Keqiang and the national governing body while, for example, provincial news, such as the official news site of Jilin Province, released reports that included both information on the *gong'gao* and the local government reaction to the incident. By 30 July 2018, the case was passed on to criminal investigators, and so formally ceased to be a part of the *gong'gao* agenda.

4.4   Analysis

The study of the present *gong'gao* corpus has shown that Chinese public announcements always follow a bipartite ritual structure:

1. The first section of *gong'gao* reports tends to provide a deferential discussion of the actions that Chinese authorities have taken at the time of the report. Without exception, this narrative is centred on the political leaders of China by emphasising their individual agency. In the corpus studied, the authors discuss the immediate measures that Xi Jinping and Li Keqiang had taken by the time the event was reported in the official media. This focus on the agency of those who hold leadership positions is a key form of facework that has its roots in the hierarchical structure of Chinese politics. Importantly, such descriptions of the leaders' actions are heavily loaded with forms of 'polite' social protocols – most typically, formal expressions that gain a conventional honorific function. Further, as the analysis below will show, the use of such protocols closely relates to the level of the news release, i.e., the lower a news outlet is in the governmental hierarchy (national > provincial > local), the more ubiquitous and intricate the social protocols it provides. As this brief description at the outset of the present case study analysis may already illustrate, while social protocols in the structural ritual under investigation could be described through the lens of politeness, they have very little to do with politeness in the interpersonal sense.

2. The second section of *gong'gao* announcements focuses on the collective action that decision makers and investigators intend to take in the future. As the analysis will illustrate, this second section of the reports is not simply an 'objective' announcement of action plans, but rather it features a further implicit attempt – along with the first part – to trigger the public's alignment with the leadership, without addressing members of the public directly. The manner of reporting correlates with the position of the given news outlet in the administrative hierarchy. This part of Chinese public announcements also tends to be heavily loaded with social protocols.

   The following data analysis will be divided into two sections: here I will contrastively examine national- and provincial-level texts to illustrate how the use of 'polite' social protocols vary between them, hence illustrating that in this rite of structur social protocols follow strict ritual patterns, and as such have little to do with 'politeness' in the conventional sense.

4.4.1   Social Protocols in Public Announcements Featured in National-level Chinese News

Let us commence the analysis by introducing the original Chinese and gloss of a *gong'gao* news text which was released at the national level. The text includes both the first and second parts of this news item for illustrative purposes, but the analysis will only focus on the first section.[4]

Example 4.1   新华社北京 7 月25日电为 贯彻落实 习近平总书记、李克强总理关于长春长生生物科技有限责任公司违法违规生产狂犬病疫苗案件的 重要指示批示精神, 7 月 23 日 国务院调查组赶赴吉林, 开展长春长生违法违规生产狂犬病疫苗案件调查工作。

7月 24 日, 国务院调查组组长、 市场监管总局党组书记、 副局长毕井泉主持召开调查组第一次全体会议, 传达学习 习近平总书记、李克强总理等中央 领导同志 重要指示批示精神, 要求调查组 深入学习领会 习近平总书记 重要指示精神, 坚决贯彻落实 李克强总理 重要批示要求 [...]

会议要求, 要重点围绕七个方面开展工作。一是彻查涉案企业违法违规行为, 全面查清违法违规事实和涉案疫苗流向, 做好调查取证工作;二是依法严惩违法犯罪行为, 严肃查处涉案企业, 对直接责任人等涉案人员要依法严惩; 三是对公职人员履职尽责进行调查, 发现失职渎职行为的要严肃问责;四是科学开展风险评估, 研究提出分类处理救济措施;五是要妥善处理涉案企业后续工作;六是要回应社会关切, 及时公布案件调查进展情况, 普及疫苗安全科学知识;七是要研究改革完善疫苗管理体制的工作举措, 建立健全保障疫苗质量安全的长效机制。根据工作需要, 调查组下设案件调查组、监管责任组、综合组和专家组等工作组。

Xinhua News reports on 25 July: The State Council Investigation Unit [*immediately*] implements the instructions of General Secretary Xi Jinping and Premier Li Keqiang about the illegal activities of Changchun Changsheng Biotech Ltd. Based on the higher instructions of the General Secretary and the Premier, on 23 July the Investigation Unit proceeded to Jilin Province to investigate the matter of substandard rabies vaccines produced by the named company.

On 24 July, Bi Jingquan – the Principal Investigator of the State Council Investigation Unit and Party Secretary and Deputy Director of the State Administration for Market Regulation Bureau – held the first comprehensive meeting to study the instructions of General Secretary Xi Jinping, Premier Li Keqiang and other important Cadres. Based on their higher instructions, the Principal Investigator demanded that the Investigation Unit was to intensively learn from General Secretary Xi Jinping and to determinedly implement the instructions and requirements in the key comments of Premier Li Keqiang. [...]

As an outcome of the conference, the delegates confirmed that they will deliver work on the following seven areas: First, they will thoroughly investigate the illegal actions of the corporation involved and will comprehensively investigate criminal activities in the corporation and the market flow of vaccines produced by the named company. Second, an action will be initiated to severely punish any behaviour that turns out to be illegal, in compliance with law. They will seriously examine the corporation involved in the incident and impose severe sanctions on persons directly responsible for the incident. Third, they will investigate the public officials' fulfilment of their duties. Acts of dereliction should be seriously investigated. Fourth, they will conduct a risk assessment, propose classified measures for disposal and remedies based on research. Fifth, they will address the social crisis caused by the incident. Sixth, they will respond to public concerns with the timely disclosure of information on the investigation and disseminate scientific knowledge about vaccine safety. Seventh, they will carry out research on operational measures to improve and reform the current vaccine management system and establish and strengthen/develop long-term mechanisms for the maintenance of vaccine quality (and) safety. The Investigation Unit constitutes subordinate working units including a case investigation unit, a regulatory responsibility unit, an integrated unit and an expert unit.

(Retrieved from: www.gov.cn/xinwen/201807/25/content_
5309213.html [last accessed 6 June 2023])

The announcement in Example 4.1 features an active form of deferential ritual rhetoric which may be somewhat alien to readers with no background in Chinese. Xinhua News, being the voice of the national-level authorities, ritually endorses here the individual actions of the leaders by emphasising their agency in resolving the crisis. Due to its national status, the news release remains silent about the actions of individuals below the leadership level: the only other person mentioned alongside Xi Jinping and Li Keqiang is the Principal Investigator. However, his action is also framed as being of a subordinate status: the text only states that he 'demanded the Investigation Unit' to implement the higher-order actions of the leaders.

One can distinguish two types of social protocols in announcements like Example 4.1. Firstly, such reports tend to be heavily loaded with formulae that express a deferential meaning in the ritual context in which they occur. Table 4.1 provides an overview of such expressions which occur in the examples featured in this case study:

Table 4.1 *Expressions in the case study which gain deferential meaning in the ritual context*

1.	贯彻落实 落实 坚决贯彻落实	*guanche-luoshi* *luoshi* *jianjue-guanche-luoshi*	'to implement higher orders'

2.	重要指示批示精神
	
	重要批示要求
	重要指示精神
		zhongyao-zhishi pishi-
		    jingshen
		zhongyao-pishi-yaoqiu
		zhongyao-zhishi-
		    jingshen
			'very important comments and instructions' (in reference to the actions of a higher-ranking person)

3.	传达贯彻 传达学习	*chuanda-guanche* *chuanda-xuexi*	'to transfer the words of a higher-ranking person to others for study' and implement (their important instructions and comments)
4.	深入学习领会	*shenru-xuexi-linghui*	'to deeply learn and comprehend' (from a higher-ranking person)
5.	领导同志	*lingdao-tongzhi*	'leading comrade'
6.	要求 讲话要求	*yaoqiu* *jianghua-yaoqiu*	'demand', a verbal form which indexes power and expresses respect
7.	高度重视	*gaodu-zhongshi*	'to attach a great importance to'
8.	全力配合	*quanli-peihe*	'to cooperate fully'

While these expressions may be used in written – and some in spoken – interaction, they are different from what can be regarded as the 'standard' formulaic inventory of Chinese politeness. Further, the repetitive way in which the authors of Chinese public announcements such as Example 4.1 use such expressions shows that these expressions are part of a social ritual: for instance, in the two relatively short texts that are featured in the current case study analysis, there is a total of fourteen such formulae. The use of these expressions shows that they are not 'polite' in the proper sense of the word: the direct recipient of these expressions is not a leader or any individual because the expressions occur in ritual narratives which tell the readers about the ways in which a community of decision makers (e.g., the 'State Council Investigation Unit' in Example 4.1) position their prospective actions with regard to the individual instructions of the leaders. In the context of a crisis scenario, this sense of indirect (self-)displaying deference is likely to trigger the acceptance of the leaders' authority in the management of the crisis. In turn, this acceptance communicated in a ritual frame by the media gains the capacity of implicitly triggering the public's alignment with the leaders and their actions.[5]

Secondly, social protocols are also present in national level *gong'gao* announcements beyond actual expressions, i.e., in the way in which actions are temporally positioned. When discussing the reactions of the national leaders, *gong'gao* reports indicate the promptness of their responses.

Notably, the authors do not use such words as 'quick' in this context to refer to the actions of Xi Jinping or Li Keqiang, i.e., it remains the reader's task to draw this implication. However, when one considers that the text states that the agenda which has been established for the meeting of the State Council Investigation Unit follows the then-already-available reflections of the national leaders, it is evident that these leaders are being positioned as acting promptly. Once again, since *gong'gao* does not represent a form of interpersonal communication, it is very likely that these manifestations of 'politeness' are being aimed at the public, i.e., they form part of alignment triggering.

4.4.2   Social Protocols in Public Announcements Features in Provincial-level Chinese News

Public *gong'gao* announcements made at lower administrative levels operate with more complex 'polite' social protocols than their national-level counterparts, as illustrated by the following example:

Example 4.2   长春长生生物科技有限责任公司违法违规生产疫苗案件发生以来，省委副书记、省长景俊海高度重视，先后16次作出具体批示指示，并于7月22日、23日主持召开专题会议，全面调度处置工作。7月23日晚上，景俊海连夜主持召开案件处置工作指导组第一次会议，传达贯彻习近平总书记重要批示指示精神，落实李克强总理批示指示精神，按照巴音朝鲁书记在省委常委会议上的讲话要求，研究具体举措。他强调，要全力配合国家调查组，[...]

Since the incident of illegal vaccine production of Changchun Changsheng Biotech Ltd., the Vice Secretary of the Provincial Committee of the Chinese Communist Party and the Governor of the Province Jing Junhai attached great importance to the incident; [so far, he has released as many as sixteen specific instructions and comments relating to the incident. In addition, he also held two subsequent special meetings on 22 and 23 July respectively, to thoroughly take care (of the incident). On the very night of 23 July, Mr Jing hosted the first meeting of the Guidance Group for the dissemination of the Changsheng vaccine incident, in order to study and implement the important instructions and comments made respectively by General Secretary Xi Jinping and Premier Li Keqiang. Furthermore, he emphasised that actions need to be made in accordance with the demand made by Provincial Party Secretary Bayinchaolu in his speech to the Standing Committee of the Provincial Party Committee. He stressed that we must cooperate fully with the State (Council) Investigation Unit to thoroughly investigate the facts [...]

(Retrieved from: www.jl.gov.cn/zw/yw/jlyw/201807/
t20180724_4945608.html)

One can observe at least three different types of social protocols in this brief text:

1. The text expresses deference towards Jing Junhai, the Governor of Jilin Province. While in national-level news reports, such as Example 4.1, only national leaders are featured with individual agency, in this case Jing occurs both as an 'author' and an 'animator' in Goffman's (1981) terms. On the one hand, he is positioned as a *loyal* animator: the news article emphasises that he 'attaches great importance' to and works the 'whole night' on the implementation of the policies of the higher authorities. On the other hand, he is also positioned as an 'author' at the local level: the news report emphasises his agency in resolving the crisis, for example, by stating that he has released as many as sixteen public comments and has held subsequent meetings immediately after the onset of the incident.

2. The text mediates deference towards the higher authorities, by directly quoting Jing Junhai's words such as 'must cooperate fully' (*quanli-peihe* 全力配合). Such narrations represent a form of deference that is recurrent in provincial- and local-level reports.

3. Finally, the text also mediates camaraderie between actors at the local level: it features camaraderie between Governor Jing and the Provincial Party Secretary Bayinchaolu, who are peers at the provincial adminis- trative level. The expression of such camaraderie reinforces the mes- sage that political decision makers are actively collaborating to resolve the crisis.

The relative abundance of 'polite' social protocols in public *gong'gao* announcements released at lower administrative levels shows that the fre- quency and pragmatic characteristics of such protocols negatively correlate with administrative power. This does not imply that organisations with less power are supposed to communicate in a more 'polite' way than their more powerful counterparts in crises. The situation is rather that such announce- ments at various levels are released as part of a major social ritual where authors of texts dispatched on the lower level tend to be more actively engaged in social protocoling in order to showcase their solidarity with, and loyalty to, higher-level organisations, hence attempting to trigger the public's similar alignment with those who make decisions.

In summary, the case study analysis here shows that, despite their monologic nature, Chinese *gong'gao* engage in intricate 'polite' social protocoling. That is, such texts not only deploy a rich vocabulary of deference indicating expres- sions, but also make use of strategies of social protocoling such as the temporal representation of events, reporting on the collaboration between political deci- sion makers to resolve a crisis, the eagerness of lower-level decision makers to comply with the orders of higher-level authorities and so on. The analysis has also shown that the intensity of social protocoling in *gong'gao* correlates intricately with the administrative level and related power where a given pronouncement is released.

4.5   Conclusion and Summary of Part I

In this chapter I have studied rites of structure. The analysis has shown that the ritual perspective can more promptly capture what is pragmatically happening in certain rites of structure – such as public political monologues – than the politeness perspective. The communal function of public rites of structure prompts one to look beyond interpersonal phenomena (or phenomena often interpreted in an individual sense) such as 'face'[6] and consider issues such as triggering alignment in Goffman's sense. Many temporally longer rites of structure are more 'monotonous' than rites of anti-structure: while they tend to have mimetic and (self-)displaying features like any ritual, there is no escalation in them and – simply put – *nothing interesting seems to happen in them*. Yet, as the case study in this chapter has shown, in fact such rituals transpire to have intriguing pragmatic features if we consider them through the ritual perspective.

Figure 4.1 summarises the key features of interaction ritual discussed in Part I of this book:

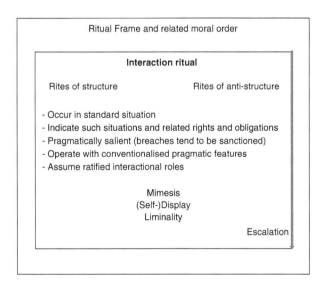

Figure 4.1 The key pragmatic features of interaction ritual.

As Figure 4.1 shows, all interaction rituals share a number of core pragmatic features – for example, any interaction ritual occurs in a context which counts as standard for some or all the participants. Also, any ritual can be categorised according to Turner's concept of rite of structure and rite of anti-structure. Arguably, ordinary day-to-day urban rituals in Goffman's sense represent unseen rites of structure. However, as Chapters 3 and 4 have shown, there are also many important and more complex rituals in our daily lives, which represent rites of anti-structure (Chapter 3) and rites of structure (Chapter 4). Turner's concept is of course only one typological way through which inter-action rituals can be categorised – for example, I previously proposed a typology where I distinguished social versus in-group rituals, as well as lower-level ritual types (Kádár 2013). I believe that the important analytic power of the typology of structure and anti-structure resides in that it captures different manifestations of ritual on a par, i.e., it focuses on what brings together rather than separates all types and forms of ritual.

Figure 4.1 shows that the ritual frame and a related moral order underlies all characteristics of ritual. The down-pointing arrow in Figure 4.1 represents inter-actional complexity. As Chapter 2 has shown, interaction rituals can manifest themselves in relatively simple forms such as individual speech acts and short routine interactions. Such interactions often only operate with the key basic features of ritual outlined in the upper side of the central box in the figure. However, interaction ritual also has a number of features – mimesis, (self-)display, liminality and escalation – which tend to occur in interactionally more complex rituals, such as the ones studied in Chapters 3 and 4. Mimesis, (self-)displaying behaviour and liminality tend to be present in any interaction ritual, whereas escalation is primarily relevant to rites of anti-structure.

Since thus far this book has only studied the phenomenon of escalation, in the following Part II we will continue the present journey into the pragmatics of ritual by providing a more detailed analysis of mimesis, (self-)displaying behaviour and liminality, which are interactional features triggered by the ritual frame in interactionally complex rituals.

4.6   Recommended Reading

Goffman, E. (1979) Footing. *Semiotica* 25(1/2): 1–29.

Goffman's work has heavily influenced the ritual framework of this book, including the case-study analysis presented in this chapter. The present recommended reading features a longer example from Goffman's seminal 1979 study where he discussed the concept of alignment as part of footing and participation. While Goffman's interpretation of alignment is more complex than how I (rather liberally) used it in this chapter, the following example features alignment in the exact way in which it has been interpreted in this chapter, i.e., as a way of accepting an authoritative line of discourse.

Consider a journalistically reported strip of interaction, a news bureau release of 1973 on presidential doings. The scene is the Oval Office, the participants an assemblage of government officers and newspaper reporters gathered in their professional capacities for a political ritual, the witnessing of the signing of a bill:

WASHINGTON – (UPI) – President Nixon, a gentleman of the old school, teased a newspaper woman yesterday about wearing slacks to the White House and made it clear that he prefers dresses on women.

After a bill-signing ceremony in the Oval Office, the President stood up from his desk and in a teasing voice said to UPPs Helen Thomas: "Helen, are you still wearing slacks? Do you prefer them actually? Every time I see girls in slacks it reminds me of China."

Miss Thomas, somewhat abashed, told the President that Chinese women were moving toward Western dress.

"This is not said in an uncomplimentary way, but slacks can do something for some people and some it can't." He hastened to add, "but I think you do very well. Turn around."

As Nixon, Attorney General Elliott L. Richardson, FBI Director Clarence Kelley and other high-ranking law enforcement officials were smiling, Miss Thomas did a pirouette for the President. She was wearing white pants, a navy blue jersey shirt, long white beads and navy blue patent leather shoes with red trim.

Nixon asked Miss Thomas how her husband, Douglas Cornell, liked her wearing pants outfits.

"He doesn't mind," she replied.

"Do they cost less than gowns?"

"No," said Miss Thomas.

*"Then change," commanded the President with a wide grin as other reporters and cameramen roared with laughter. (*The Evening Bulletin *[Philadelphia], 1973)*

This incident points to the power of the President to force an individual who is female from her occupational capacity into a sexual, domestic one during an occasion in which she (and the many women who could accord her the role of symbolic representative) might well be very concerned that she be given her full professional due, and that due only. And, of course, the incident points to a moment in gender politics when a President might unthinkingly exert such power. Behind this fact is something much more significant: the contemporary social definition that women must always be ready to receive comments on their 'appearance', the chief constraints being that the remarks should be favorable, delivered by someone with whom they are acquainted, and not interpretable as sarcasm. Implied, structurally, is that a woman must ever be ready to change ground, or, rather, have the ground changed for her, by virtue of being subject to becoming momentarily an object of approving attention, not – or not merely – a participant in it.
(Goffman 1979: 1–2)

Part II

Ritual Frame in Interaction: The Complex
Interactional Features of Ritual

Synopsis

Part II of this book includes three chapters, which introduce the reader to phenomena that one can usually witness only in complex rituals: mimesis, (self-)display and liminality. Chapter 5 focuses on the phenomenon of mimesis, devoting specific attention to an understudied, albeit important type of mimesis, namely 'performative mimesis'. Performative mimesis differs from its more broadly studied 'interpersonal' counterpart (reciprocating what the other says) and which typically occurs in complex and longer stretches of interaction ritual. The concept of 'performative mimesis' refers to contrived interactional performance whereby the performer sustains mimicking a pre-dated interactional schema, just like an actor in a theatre manages a performance on stage by enacting a role. The chapter includes a case study which describes performative mimesis in Chinese university military training courses, representing an understudied ritual drawn from the realm of higher education in China.

Chapter 6 investigates the phenomenon of (self-)displaying behaviour, by considering how various degrees of ritual self-display behaviour can be distinguished from one another. The chapter shows that display should be viewed as a phenomenon which by default is a concomitant of ritual, but which can intensify and become self-oriented if a ritual becomes complex in general and competitive in particular. As a case study, the chapter investigates a corpus of historical Chinese letters written by an epistolary expert to various recipients, including both 'ordinary' recipients such as patrons, family members, lovers and so on, and fellow epistolary expert friends representing 'professional' recipients. With this latter audience he engaged in a playful competition as to who can be 'more' (intricately) deferential to the other.

Finally, Chapter 7 discusses liminality. Liminal rituals have a sense of irreversibility and they come together with strong metapragmatic awareness: if the moral order and the related frame of the ritual are violated, both the participants and the observers tend to become alerted and engage in intensive metapragmatic reflections. The chapter will present a case study focusing on the liminal rite of workplace dismissal.

5   Mimesis

5.1   Introduction

This chapter explores the phenomenon of mimesis from a pragmatic point of view. All interaction rituals are mimetic. The chapter will devote specific attention to an understudied, albeit important type of mimesis, namely 'performative mimesis', which differs from its more broadly studied 'interpersonal' counterpart and which typically occurs in complex and longer stretches of interaction ritual. The concept of 'performative mimesis' refers to contrived interactional performance whereby the performer sustains mimicking a predated interactional schema, just like an actor in a theatre manages a performance on stage by enacting a role. This notion of performative mimesis originates in the following Goffmanian (1959: 17) idea:

> When an individual plays a part, he implicitly requests his observers to take seriously the impression that is fostered before them. They are asked to believe that the character they see actually possesses the attributes he appears to possess, that the task he performs will have the consequences that are implicitly claimed for it, and that, in general, matters are what they appear to be.

The difference between performative mimesis and interpersonal mimesis can be described as follows. Interpersonal mimesis always occurs in ordinary conversation where it implies ritual 'reciprocation' (Edmondson & House 1981: 204). Interpersonal mimesis is particularly likely to occur in the ritual phases of Opening and Closing Talk (see House & Kádár 2021a; see also Chapter 11), and also in conventionalised ritual exchanges (see Ide 1998), including religious ceremonies where reciprocation may not necessarily imply that the participants say exactly the same things. The following is a typical interactional example of reciprocation:

A: Hello John
B: Gosh, hello, Mary. Haven't seen you in ages – how are you?
A: Oh, I am fine, thanks. How's life been treating you then?
B: Oh, not too bad, you know.

(Cited from Edmondson & House 1981: 204)

Interpersonal mimesis not only covers mimicking each other in such conversational routines. Rather, a sense of participant 'convergence' also occurs in daily conversations when a specific subject or practice recurs between the participants, as in a recurring complaint or an ongoing joke. For instance, Donald (2013: 189) referred to reciprocal mimetic games in the following terms: 'Someone invents a move; the next one imitates it, and perhaps adds something new, and so on.'[1] In summary, interpersonal mimesis represents an important but relatively simple type of mimesis, encompassing both 'meaningful' and 'meaningless' ritual behaviour in the literal sense.

As opposed to interpersonal mimesis, performative mimesis implies re-enactment but not reciprocation, in that the recipient of this form of mimesis is not supposed to reciprocate in kind. Furthermore, this type of mimesis is not limited to certain phases of an interaction but rather tends to be present over entire interaction ritual events, which are ritual in the more abstract sense. Performative mimesis is different from 'crossing', which was discussed previously in this book. Crossing 'involves a distinct sense of movement across social or ethnic boundaries and it raises issues of legitimacy which, in one way or another, participants need to negotiate in the course of their encounter' (Rampton 1995: 485). The operation of performative mimesis does not necessarily entail social or ethnic differences, and also this form of mimesis, unlike crossing, can become normative in certain institutional ritual settings, and as such it is not an ephemeral part of an interaction.

Figure 5.1 – which is an adaptation of Figure 2.1 in Chapter 2 – illustrates the relationship between interpersonal and performative mimesis:

| Interpersonal mimesis – particularly frequented in ritual as a form, e.g., in 'ritual' forms of language use like exchanges of speech acts | Performative mimesis – particularly frequented in ritual as a context, i.e., in a variety of contexts in which rights and obligations are preset and where the interaction is communally oriented |

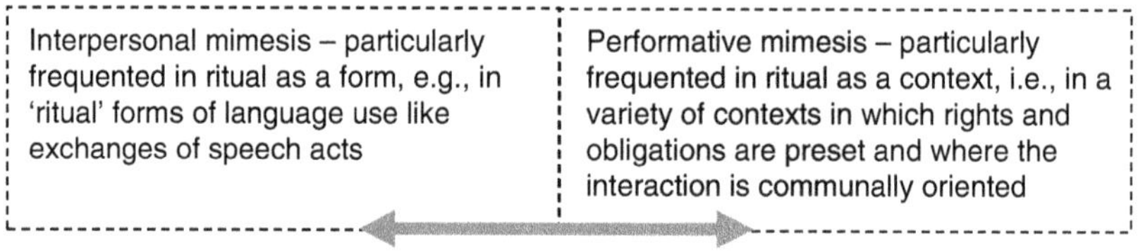

Figure 5.1 Interpersonal versus performative mimesis.

The double-headed arrow which was featured in previous versions of this figure occurs in an altered form in Figure 5.1, in order to illustrate that interpersonal and performative mimesis differ from each other in a tendential way. That is, interpersonal mimesis is arguably frequented in ritual behaviour which one normally interprets through forms, e.g., exchanges of speech acts (see e.g., a How-are-You → How-are-You exchange). Performative mimesis, on the other hand, can be observed in complex rituals where ritual can be approached as a context or a cluster of contexts, such as the MMA event studied in Chapter 3.[2]

As its name suggests, performative mimesis represents a ritual 'performance'. More specifically, in Goffman's terminology, performative mimesis involves a 'contrived [ritual] performance' (Goffman 1959: 70), consistently mimicking a perceived or 'scripted' form of pre-existing behaviour, which counts as conventionalised and normative in a particular context. Liminal ritual events (see Chapter 3) and liminoid theatre performances (Turner 1979) are the most representative scenarios in which performative mimesis occurs. In such scenarios, the participants' normal status and related behaviour are changed, and this change triggers performative mimesis.

In order to investigate performative mimesis in interaction, as a case study the current chapter examines aggressive mimetic behaviour in Chinese university 'military trainings' (*junxun* 军训), by focusing on the recurrent expressions and speech acts that recur in such events. 'Military training' refers to a university course, during which first-year students in Chinese institutions of higher education receive physical training from 'officers' (*jiaoguan* 教官) who are usually second- or third-year students. While in both real army trainings and university trainings the participants receive hard physical training, in university military classes the participants do not receive any proper martial education, and also usually none of the participants is a real army person. Due to the fact that army language is conventionally aggressive, i.e., aggression in such language is conventionalised and normative, in the case study of this chapter I devote particular attention to how aggression plays out in ritual performative mimesis.

The goal of examining this case study is to identify langue-based evidence for the social operation of the important and understudied performatory type of the cognitive process involved in mimesis. As was mentioned in Chapter 2, various key ritual notions such as mimesis are relatively rarely used in mainstream pragmatic research, and so it is important to attempt to pin them down through strictly language-anchored inquiries. From the pragmatician's point of view, the cognitive process of performative mimesis can be most reliably captured if we examine recurrent ritual pragmatic behaviour in naturally occurring interactions, where the interactants deliberately re-enact (see Bax 2010) language use that does not naturally 'belong' to them. In this respect, it is particularly helpful to explore settings such as Chinese university military trainings, in which the participants make attempts to re-enact a ritual which, by default, is part of another institutional setting – in the present case, a scenario orchestrated by a real army officer. This ritual re-enactment process comes to life in university military training when student 'officers' attempt to talk as army personnel as part of the anti-structural rite of passage of the training, although of course after the training sessions they and the trainees both need to relapse into their ordinary lives (i.e., the 'structure') as students.

The structure of this chapter is the following. Section 5.2 introduces the case study in more detail, also including the methodology and data of the case-study analysis. Section 5.3 presents the case-study analysis. Finally, Section 5.4 provides a conclusion.

5.2   Case Study: Chinese University Military Training Courses

When I first observed university military training as an academic working in China, I felt stricken by the ritual nature of such events. These quasi-military trainings operate in a ritual frame with strictly defined temporary rights and obligations and exhibit recurrent pragmatic features. They also have a complex participatory structure: they take place in the sports field (*caochang* 操场) of universities, and the participants include trainers, students and official delegates of the university occasionally observing the events, as well as many eavesdroppers passing by and/or using the sports field simultaneously. Further – importantly for this chapter – such university military trainings trigger performative mimesis because the student 'officers' need – and are expected – to ratify (Goffman 1967) their role as quasi-representatives of the army by mimicking military language, hence leaving the boundaries of their 'normal' lives.

Clearly, Chinese university military trainings are archetypical anti-structural rites of passage: they are liminal events that transform the status of the participants. By going through a military training, first-year new arrivals at a university are transformed into 'proper' members of the community of a Chinese university. The trainings are centred on a military ethos: the students not only need to go through the physical exercises, but they are also required to participate in emotionally loaded communal activities such as singing and chanting. An important incentive for the students to cope with this compulsory rite of passage is that military trainings are conventionally regarded as sources of long-term friendships between the participating students.

University military trainings were originally more 'authentic' than they are at present, in that while this ritual always mimicked real army training sessions, it used to be held by actual army officers until 1999. In that year, Chinese universities significantly increased their student intake and the number of Chinese army specialist trainers proved to be insufficient to cope with this sudden expansion. Subsequently, Chinese universities gradually replaced army people with student-trainers and decreased the length and intensity of military training courses. Currently, military training is a compulsory course, usually without credit. Thus, Chinese university military trainings have increasingly evolved into a performative mimetic ritual process over the years.

5.2.1   Methodology

In this case-study analysis, I pursue a strictly language-anchored approach, in order to attempt integrating mimesis in the mainstream of pragmatic research. Engaging in performative mimesis implies that the trainers realise expressions and speech acts in ways which would be sanctioned in ordinary circumstances. These expressions and speech acts indicate, and raise awareness of, the mimicked army setting in which the trainers have specific rights and obligations as quasi-army 'representatives'. This quasi-character needs to be emphasised consistently, considering that the student trainers' rights only last as long as they are on the training grounds. The question of course emerges how student trainers can manage this mimesis, considering that those who act as trainers at universities are likely to have never been inside an army because there is no general conscription in China. An answer to this question resides in the historicity (see Kádár & Culpeper 2010) of university military trainings in Chinese universities: as the course used to be held by army people, student trainers are likely to have 'inherited' the conventionalised pragmatic inventory of these ritual events as part of an 'institutionalised tradition' (Volkov 1991). The institutionalised ritual frame of the aggression implies that the participants are provided with rights and obligations not normally holding for their lives, and this is why the pragmatic behaviour of trainers makes sense only in the particular inherited institutional setting of trainings: a fellow student who is cast in the role of the trainer has the right to be 'aggressive' only on the training ground. While ritual aggression in general has a sense of 'temporariness' in that it can only unfold unsanctioned while the ritual itself is ongoing, university military trainings are different from other forms of aggressive institutional ritual such as forms of political and courtroom aggression in that the role of the trainer who is endowed with the right to be aggressive is not permanent – unlike, for example, that of a judge.

The methodology of this case study is based on the assumption that certain expressions and speech acts are constitutive of a situation that is standard and normative for the participants. The notion of 'standard situation' was mentioned on several occasions in this book, and it was originally proposed by House (1989: 115) who argues, in the context where a Request is realised by means of an expression, as follows:

The notion of a standard situation involves participants' rather fixed expectations and perceptions of social role. Role relations are transparent and predetermined, the requester has a right, the requestee an obligation, the degree of imposition involved in the request is low, as is the perceived degree of difficulty in realizing it. In a nutshell, the participants know where and who they are. Clearly, the distinction between a standard and a nonstandard situation is not clear-cut.

It is clear that university military trainings are highly standardised for the participants. In 1985, the revised version of the *Military Service Law of the People's Republic of China* stipulated that high school students are also required to take part in such courses, and that middle and primary schools should also organise so-called 'defense education' courses (see He & Sheng 2014). Thus, practically all Chinese students have already experienced military trainings before entering the university system, and so they are likely to have both pragmatic experience and expectations regarding the dynamics of this university course.

To a certain degree 'standardness' is a relative value, in that it represents a scalar value in Leech's (1983) sense. However, what interconnects all standard situations is that the rights and obligations holding for the participants is immediately clear to those who are familiar with such standard situations, without detailed contextual information. Due to the prevalence of rights and obligations in standard situations such as military trainings, such situations may be best interpreted as ritual in the abstract contextual sense (see Figure 5.1). Expressions used in such situations indicate the participants' awareness of the standard situation and broader ritual frame in a particular context – in other words, these expressions can be described as Ritual Frame Indicating Expressions (RFIEs).

I will discuss the concept of RFIEs, which I developed with Juliane House, in more detail in Part III of the present book. What is important to mention at this point is that RFIEs have an intrinsic relationship with speech acts. In some linguacultures such as Chinese, RFIEs are particularly 'speech-act anchored', i.e., they often indicate the realisation of a certain speech act. As part of the methodology of this case-study analysis, I will therefore not only examine various RFIEs by means of which the trainers mimic real-life army trainings, but I will also analyse speech acts – indicated by these RFIEs – that characterise these training sessions. It is important to note that, as we argued in House and Kádár (2021a), an RFIE can become the Head Act of a speech act such as Request.

As the case-study analysis will show, as part of performative mimesis student trainers recurrently realise very direct Requests ('Request (to-do-x/not-to-do-x); see Edmondson & House (1981: 97), displaying the requestive strategy 'mood derivable' (see Blum-Kulka et al. (1989: 278). Directness refers to the degree to which the speaker's illocutionary intent is apparent from the locution. The category 'mood derivable' refers to the employment of phenomena such as raw imperatives (e.g., 'Go away'). It is clear that the very direct mood derivable Request is constitutive of real-life military trainings, and the fact that it is typical of the university course under investigation is evidence of the importance of performative mimesis in this setting.

The methodology of the case study is qualitative in nature, i.e., a team of colleagues and myself examined recurrent RFIEs and speech acts in the data without quantifying them. While it would have been highly productive to combine this approach with a quantitative examination, the circumstances of the data collection prevented doing this.

Similarly to what has been argued elsewhere in this book, the concept of ritual frame that underlies communal behaviour beyond the dyadic level prompts one to look at aggression in the data beyond the politeness (and impoliteness) paradigm. In this setting, aggression may manifest itself in expressions and speech acts that appear to be 'impolite' or 'rude' in an interpersonal sense; however, in our case their primary function is *not* to cause offence (see e.g., Culpeper 2011) but rather to reinforce rights and obligations and the related ritual frame of the interaction, beyond the scope of strict-sense interpersonal impoliteness. While the trainers may sometimes overstep their roles and speak particularly harshly, by default it is not only their right but also their institutional normative obligation to appear to be aggressive. This obligation is particularly important in contexts like the one studied in this chapter in which mimetic behaviour is prevalent: simply put, the trainers need to be (and are expected to be) aggressive to resolve the potential ambiguity caused by the fact that they are 'step ins' for real army personnel. In the analysis of aggression in the data studied in this chapter, the team of researchers with whom I worked on the data collection devoted particular attention to the prosodic features of how trainers talk, considering that army language tends to be associated with specific prosodic features such as vowel lengthening.

5.2.2   Data

This case study is based on a corpus of university military trainings, which was collected at a university in the northeast of China in September 2019, during the annual army training session of the university. Before starting the data collection, the students who helped me collect this corpus first asked the university's permission to audio-record the training sessions. As part of this procedure, they only requested the consent of the trainers because our team did not transcribe or use anything that the trainees uttered during the events, nor did we reveal the personal details of any participant. This was mainly due to technical reasons: the students' utterances were barely audible during the extremely loud training sessions. In addition, asking the consent of all the trainees would have been disruptive for the training course.

The participants in the recorded data included four volunteer instructors: two female and two male students. These instructors trained two groups, with each group consisting of 120 first-year students, being led by both a male and a female trainer. The whole-day training sessions lasted for a period of two weeks, which is standard for university military trainings in China. I requested each of the trainers to attach MP4 audio-recorders onto their uniform and keep the recording running during all the sessions. Overall, the audio-recorded corpus consists of nearly ten hours of interaction. The relatively low amount of recording can be explained by the fact that during the training sessions verbal interaction only represents a minor proportion of the entire training, and also that a large proportion of the recorded speech turned out to be inaudible. Following the training course, my students transcribed the utterances of the trainers, by using conversation-analytic conventions. In accordance with these conventions, the examples below feature both Chinese characters and the Pinyin Romanisation of these characters.

5.3   Analysis

In this analysis, I first investigate the use of RFIEs in the corpus and following this I analyse recurrent speech acts mimicking real-life army trainings. In a sense, this is an 'artificial' division because RFIEs often indicate speech acts, i.e., RFIEs and speech acts are only distinguished in the present analysis as different units of analysis rather than different phenomena.

5.3.1   Ritual Frame Indicating Expressions

Ritual frame indicating expressions used by student trainers in the present corpus can be divided into two major groups: (1) expressions which are directly 'borrowed' from army language, and (2) other expressions which gain an army-like function in the particular standard situation of university military trainings.

The first group of RFIEs, directly borrowed from army language, are compulsory in particular moves of the army trainers. Some others do not represent army language *per se* but sound aggressively 'army-like' in the standard situation of university military trainings. Example 5.1 represents the use of RFIEs belonging to the former category:

Example 5.1   齐步走 ! 立定 !
               Qi: bu::: (…) ↑*z::ou* ! *Li:: ding* !
               ↑ March::: (…) ! Sto::p !

Here the trainer uses the RFIEs *qibuzou* 齐步走 ('march') and *liding* 立定 ('stop'). These RFIEs are typical elements of real army language, and it is not surprising that they prevail in the corpus of the present case study. As the transcript of Example 5.1 indicates, the aggressive prosody of these RFIEs mimics that of proper army trainings,[3] in particular the rising intonation, primary stress and lengthened syllables are conventional prosodic features that army trainers frequent in many linguacultures as they bark their orders.

A similar 'borrowed' RFIE in our corpus is *douyou* 都有 ('attention'), the use of which illustrated by Example 5.2:

Example 5.2   全体都有, 向右转。
Quan t:i *dou y::ou* , xiang y:::ou zhuan.
Everybody, ate::ntion ! Tur:::n left.

Similar to the RFIEs *qibuzou* and *liding* in Example 5.1, the RFIE *douyou* in Example 5.2 – uttered with lengthened syllables – represents conventional army language.

The second category of RFIEs in the present corpus consists of various expressions which do not represent military language as such, but rather indicate the standard situation of university military training, in which they mimetically re-enact the aggressive language use associated with the army. The most typical RFIE by means of which this mimetic re-enactment is performed is the second-person T pronoun *ni* 你. The Chinese language distinguishes between this T form and its V counterpart *nin* 您 (see a detailed pragmatic analysis in House & Kádár 2020). The T form *ni* is practically always used between Chinese university students in ordinary interactions. However, in the corpus of this case study this T form typically occurs in a sentence-final position and it is uttered in a saliently lengthened way, as the following examples show:

Example 5.3   你们两个特别低, 你 !
Ni men liang ge te bie di, n::i !
You both kick your legs too low. Y::ou !

Example 5.4   腿抬高!立定!怎么回事你?累了吗你?
Tui ↑ *tai g:::ao! L:::i ding! Zen me hui shi* n::i *? Lei le ma* n::i *?*
Legs ↑ u:::p! Sto:::p! What's the matter with y::ou ? Are you tired, y::ou ?

In Example 5.3, *ni* transforms into an RFIE, indicating a very direct speech act Request and the related right of the trainer to intimidate his trainees 'for their own good', as well as the obligation of the trainees to comply with the direct Request. In Example 5.4, *ni* occurs twice, following the above-discussed military RFIE *liding* 立定 ('stop'). Here *ni* is again produced in a sentence-final position, and it is uttered with a significantly lengthened syllable. In this utterance, this RFIE operates as an interactional resource for the trainer to intimidate the recipient – an underperforming first-year student – by boosting the sarcastic overtone of the utterance.

Another typical expression in the present corpus representing the second category of RFIEs is *da-baogao* 打报告 ('to report to someone'). This expression can occur in many other institutional settings, such as ordinary classrooms. What makes it salient in the context of university military training sessions is its semantic and pragmatic meaning: asking for a report represents the right of a lecturer, and so in normal circumstances this form can be uttered as a Request by a higher-ranking person towards a lower-ranking recipient. Thus, in the standard situation of military training, this expression positions the trainer student as a superordinate who can give an 'order', i.e., realise a direct Request, and the recipient as a subordinate who must follow this 'order'. The following example illustrates the use of this RFIE:

Example 5.5 刚才动了的人 打报告 。刚才谁动了? 有多少人 打报告 ?
Gang cai *dong le de ren* (..) ↓ *da bao g::ao* . *Gang cai shui d::ong* ↑ *le?*
You duo shao ren ↓ *da bao gao* ?
The person who moved just now makes a ↓ repo::rt to me . Who ↑ mo::ved? How many people have ↓ reported to me ? (Shouting).

In Example 5.5, the RFIE *da-baogao* is uttered twice, which can be interpreted as an aggressive escalation of the Request, triggered by the repetition.[4] Furthermore, the RFIE is recurrently uttered in a lower pitch, which increases its aggressive tone (see e.g., Frick 1986).

The RFIEs studied thus far are clearly anchored in the speech act Request. In the following, let us examine interactional patterns through which subcategories of this speech act are mimetically realised in the present corpus.

5.3.2   Speech Acts

The standard situation of university military training triggers a specific type of Request, namely, Requests realised in their most direct form, i.e., 'raw imperatives' which are often referred to as 'mood derivable' (see Blum-Kulka et al. 1989). In the present study of the student trainers' Requestive behaviour, my colleagues and myself also considered how mood derivables are modified through the use of 'upgraders' and 'downgraders' (see Edmondson & House 1981).

Mood Derivable

As we could see in Section 5.3.1, RFIEs borrowed from army language (see Examples 5.1 and 5.2) tend to occur when a particular Request is realised as mood derivable. Along with such RFIEs, there are also other lexical forms indicating raw imperatives in very direct Requests; in the present corpus, such forms typically include verbs of prohibition. The most typical of such words in Chinese university military trainings include *bie* 别 ('don't') and *buyao* 不要 ('you shouldn't'). The following examples illustrate the use of these expressions:

Example 5.6 别 讲话!
BIE ↓ JIANG ↓ HU:::A!
DON'T ↓ TAL:::K! (shouting)

Example 5.7   不要把步子加快。
               Bu yao ba (..) bu zi (.) jia kuai.
               Don't (..) quicken (.) your pace.

Along with verbs of prohibition, there are also other conventionalised forms embedded in raw imperatives, as the following example illustrates:

Example 5.8   后边快一点, 快一点。
               Hou bian (..) < *kuai yi dian*>, < *kuai yi dian*> .
               People in the back (..) < hurry up>, <hurry up> .

In Example 5.8, the student trainer recurrently deploys *kuai-yidian* 快一点 ('hurry up'), which is a conventionalised very direct Request in Chinese. *Kuai-yidian* is conventionally associated with parental language, and so it expresses here a patronising tone (see more below).

Lexical Upgrading
A typical form of lexical upgrader deployed by student trainers is *buxiang* 不想 ('I don't want'), a modal verb which occurs in Requests (not-to-to-do-x). If this verb occurs in strong prohibitive Requests, it nearly always expresses a sense of patronising impatience, as the following example shows:

Example 5.9   这里所有人, 向后转, 转体, 我不想再强调了。向后转, 一、二, 向
               后转, 不错。 向左看齐, 看齐的时候别撩头发, 我最后再提醒你们
               一遍。
               Zhe li suo you re::n, xiang ho::u zhuan, zhuan t:::i, wo bu xiang *zai (..)*
               <qiang diao l:e>. Xiang ho::u zhuan, yi, er, xiang ho::u zhuan, bu cu:::
               o. Xiang zuo kan ↓ qi, kan qi de shi hou (. . .) bie liao tou fa, wo zui hou
               zai ti xing ni men yi bian.
               Everybo:::dy here, turn ba::ck, turn your bo:::dy, I don't want to (..)
               <emphasise it again:> ((impatient)). Turn ba::ck, one, two, turn ba::ck,
               go:::od. Look ↓ left, don't touch your hair (. . .) when you look left. I am
               telling you for the last time.

Another type of lexical upgrader that recurs in our corpus includes negative adjectives indicating criticism. Such adjectives typically boost the Request, by negatively positioning the requestee. The following examples illustrate the use of such adjectives:

Example 5.10   太乱了, 听我口令吧。
               Tai luan le, ting wo kou ling ba.
               Too disordered . Follow my order.

Example 5.11   都踢得软绵绵的, 用点力。
               Dou ti de ruan mianmian de , yong dian l::i.
               You all kick softly . Use more str::ength.

Example 5.12   这样动作很丑。
   Zhe yang dong zuo hen chou.
   This movement is ugly.

My definition of 'negative' is not semantically defined but is rather based on the contextual meaning of the adjectives. For instance, in Example 5.11 the trainer scolds the students by claiming that their marching kicks are made too 'softly' (*ruan mianmian-de* 软绵绵的), which is apparently a negative evaluation in the particular context. As Examples 5.10, 5.11 and 5.12 all illustrate, prosody plays an important role in exacerbating the power of the adjectives: trainers who were recorded in the present corpus tend to put heavy primary stress on either the adjectives (Example 5.10) or their modifiers (Examples 5.11 and 5.12). In terms of mimesis, such adjectives position the student trainer as an 'expert': considering that the trainers only have slightly more experience than the trainees, strong evaluation provides them with a certain sense of expertise and authority (see also Blackwell 2010 on the relationship between evaluation and authority).

Yet another form of lexical upgrading includes the use of the gambit or discourse marker 'starter' (see Edmondson & House 1981; see also House & Kádár 2021a). Starters are used whenever the speaker starts his turn of talk, by alerting the hearer of the fact that the speaker is now about to say something. This gambit again positions the student trainer as an 'expert', considering that it is very often used in educational settings by the powerful party, i.e., typically a teacher. In terms of mimesis, in university military trainings this starter is particularly powerful, due to the fact that the trainings take place in universities where all the participants are familiar with the communicative style of teachers. In university military trainings, the most typical starter that the trainers use to introduce what they want to say is *lai* 来 ('right'):

Example 5.13   来，所有人，停！
   L:ai *(..) suo you ren, t::ing*!
   Ri:ght (..) everybody, sto::p.

Example 5.14   来，就第一列男生练！
   <Lai *(..) jiu di yi lie nan sheng*> ↓ *lian*!
   <Right (..) only the boys in the first row> ↓ practice! (heated)

Syntactic Upgrading
In the corpus of the present case study, syntactic upgraders most typically manifest themselves in the form of aggressive interrogative sentences boosting the Request. There are two types of such interrogatives: those that operate in the form of Request (to-do-x), and those expressing Request (not-to-do-x). The following examples illustrate the operation of the Request (to-do-x) category:

Example 5.15   七班在最后面, 八班在最中间, 九班在八班后面, 记住了吗?

Qi ban zai zui hou mian, ba ban zai zui zhong jian, jiu ban zai ba ban hou mian, ji zhu le m::a ?

Class Seven is at the back, Class Eight is in the middle, Class Nine is at the back of Class eight, remember, ye::s ?

Example 5.16   听懂没?

Ting dong ↓ mei ?

Understand ↓ don't ?

Example 5.17   明白没?

Ming bai ↓ mei ?

Get ↓ don't you ?

Examples 5.15, 5.16 and 5.17 are similar in that the interrogative particle or tag question[5] that expresses the question is uttered either with extended syllables (Example 5.15), or in a lower-stressed pitch (Examples 5.16 and 5.17). Such prosodic features make the Request appear angry and aggressive, and as such they upgrade the Request. This upgrading function seemingly contradicts the default pragmatic function of questions, which consists of rendering an utterance more indirect (see Blum-Kulka et al. 1989: 281). Notably, the instructors in the corpus regularly use tag questions in an abbreviated form: for instance, in both Examples 5.16 and 5.17 the tag question structure *youmeiyou* 有没有 ('x, don't you') is abbreviated to the substandard form *mei* 没. In many other university settings, students often use such abbreviated forms when they interact with each other, and also in various Chinese dialects the use of this form is acceptable. However, in our case, the above-discussed prosodic features do not afford the recipient to interpret such expressions as 'casual', 'friendly', 'dialectal' and so on, but rather they reinforce the aggressive nature of the ritual frame triggered by the standard situation of university military training.

Examples 5.18, 5.19 and 5.20 illustrate the operation of aggressive interrogatives expressing Request (not-to-do-x). In the corpus of this case study, Requests (not-to-do-x) are manifested as 'tirades', during which the trainer attacks the undesirable behaviour of the trainees:

Example 5.18   你们现在干嘛 呐?整个草坪上就你们一列, 还嬉嬉闹闹!主席台上的教官看不见吗?

Ni men xian zai gan ma ↓ n::a ? Zheng ge cao ping jiu ni men yi l::ie, hai xi xi ↓ nao nao! Zhu xi tai shang de jiao guan kan bu jian ↑ m::a ? ((fennu))

What are you doing ↓ e::h ? You are the only te::am who is ↓ sloppy and frolic on the whole lawn. Can't the instructors on the rostrum see you ↑ e::h ? (heated)

Example 5.19   你是在这儿吗?那后边人咋跑啊?
Ni shi zai zhe er ↑ma? Na hou mian ren zha pao ↑a::?
Are you here ↑eh? How can the people behind you run ↑e::h?

Example 5.20   还需要我喊一二一吗?还有三天, 就汇报表演了!
Hai xu yao wo han yi er yi ↑m:::a? Hai you san tian, jiu hui bao biao
yan (.) l:::e. (fennu)
Do you need me to say one, two, one ↑ha:::h? There are only three days
left before the formal perform:::ance! (heated)

In terms of prosodic features, these aggressive interrogatives operate exactly
like their Request (to-do-x) counterparts. Examples 5.18 and 5.19 illustrate
a recurrent phenomenon in the corpus: student trainers tend to deploy interrogatives to 'bombard' the trainees with unpleasant questions (see Ainsworth
1993). The only significant prosodic difference between such interrogatives
and their Request (to-do-x) counterparts is that the former are often uttered in
a high pitch, as Examples 5.18, 5.19 and 5.20 all illustrate. This high pitch adds
a sense of 'talking down' to these questions and the speech act Request in
a broader sense (see Bryant & Fox Tree 2005 on high pitch as a manifestation of
'talking down').

Along with aggressive interrogative sentences, conditional clauses are also
deployed in the corpus as syntactic upgraders, as the following example illustrates:

Example 5.21   不行, 排头就换人。
Bu x:::ing, pai t::ou (. . .) jiu huan ren.
[If] you ca:::n't do well, I will let others (. . .) stand at the hea::d of the queue.

A noteworthy characteristic of such conditional clauses is that student
trainers tend to omit the conjunction. In university military training sessions,
conditional clauses regularly introduce a threat realised through the Request, as
in Example 5.21.

Lexical Downgrading

Downgraders are relatively rare in the corpus, which is not surprising considering that aggression in such settings is meant to be escalated rather than
downgraded. However, when these downgraders do occur, their use is paradoxical in that they do not have any mitigatory function, that is, 'downgrading'
here does not operate in the conventional sense of the word. Rather, just as the
abbreviated (not-to-do-x) interrogatives examined in the previous section,
instances of downgrading in the corpus convey a sense of 'talking down' to
the addressees. The following preposition *geiwo* 给我 (roughly '[do it] for me')
is the main lexical downgrading form in our corpus:

Example 5.22   来，所有给我听口令。
Lai (..) suo you ren gei wo <ting wo kou li::ng>.
Right (..) everybody <listen to my passw::ord> for me.

Example 5.23   坚持住了，后腿也给我绷直，别后仰，脚尖给我下压。
Jian chi zh:u l::e, hou tui ye gei wo beng zh::i, bie hou y:ang, jiao jian gei wo xia ↓ya.
Hold o::n, keep your back legs stra::ight for me , don't le:an backwards, ↓ press your toes down for me .

'Talking down' in the case of such utterances derives from the fact that the use of the preposition *geiwo* adds a quasi-familial tone to the utterance. Yet, this quasi-familial tone is clearly insincere and as such decidedly patronising, considering that the ritual frame of the interaction precludes any sense of social or emotional closeness between the trainer and the trainees. In a sense, *geiwo* positions the trainer as a parent figure, talking down to immature children. Such forms of language use could indeed occur in parental contexts, like when a parent is trying to make a child eat (e.g., 'eat x for me'). In terms of mimesis, it is a noteworthy fact that some trainers – like the one featured in Example 5.23 – repeat the patronising *geiwo*, which thus represents an attempt to talk like a senior army figure.

5.4   Conclusion

This chapter presented mimesis, by dividing it up to the two categories of performative and interpersonal mimesis. Performative mimesis, unlike interpersonal mimesis, only occurs in relatively complex interaction rituals. This is why in Figure 4.1 in Chapter 4 mimesis was featured on a par with (self-)displaying behaviour and other features of complex rituals. Yet, mimesis in some form is arguably present in any type of ritual behaviour if, for nothing else, due to the conventionalised nature of rituals.

The present chapter has examined performative mimesis in a ritual context where the performer of the ritual mimics pragmatic patterns over the course of an entire event. Such behavioural patterns may have various origins, spanning scripted texts in theatres to inherited interactional traditions (as in the present case study). Certain ritual scenarios such as university military trainings trigger performative mimesis, which fit into the Goffmanian (1959: 70) notion of contrived performances mimicking a form of behaviour that somehow pre-dates, and is re-enacted in, the actual interaction. The pragmatic category of performative mimesis is essentially different from its interpersonal counterpart, with the latter involving reciprocation, in particular in the ritual phases of opening and closing a conversation.

When people mimic a perceived ritual frame through a contrived perform-ance, they use certain expressions (RFIEs) as well as specific conventionalised realisations of speech acts, in order to indicate their own and other participants' situated rights and obligations. Such RFIEs and speech acts typically indicate awareness of the standard situation and the related conventions holding for the participants, and as such they operate as reminders of the fact that little face-work is necessary for all the participants. This, in turn, makes aggression normative in anti-structural ritual contexts. In the present case study of Chinese university military trainings, student trainers typically deploy RFIEs either borrowed from army language or used in a way to evoke aggression associated with army language. The trainers frequented the speech Request in particular. Requests in the trainings tend to be realised as mood derivables and in upgraded or downgraded forms. Further, while the speech act Request can be downgraded by the student trainers, paradoxically such downgrading does not imply mitigation of the Request in this particular context.

Performative mimesis implies a suspension of disbelief while the partici-pants interact within the ritual frame. A representative pragmatic evidence for the effect of this ritual frame in which suspension of disbelief unfolds is prosody studied in this chapter, which differs in the ritual frame of university military trainings from how prosody often operates in everyday contexts. Student trainers often employ a distinctively army-like prosody, i.e. unlike in scenarios of everyday interaction they engage in performative mimesis to create an illusion, which the trainees are expected to accept due to the rights and obligations triggered by the inherited institutional tradition of university military trainings.

After describing the phenomenon of mimesis, in the next Chapter 6 we cover another phenomenon which can be observed in interactionally complex rituals: (self-)display.

5.5   Recommended Reading

Donald, M. (2013) Mimesis theory re-examined, twenty years after the fact. In Hatfield, G., Pittman, H. (eds.), *Evolution of Mind, Brain, and Culture.* Philadelphia, PA: University of Pennsylvania Press, 169–192.

Merlin Donald is a Canadian psychologist and neuroscientist who has done ground-breaking work on mimesis and, as part of this, he has also provided invaluable insight into the relationship between mimesis and ritual. The excerpt below is from Donald's state-of-the-art overview of mimesis (Donald 2013: 167–170, 186–187):

Mimesis was conceived as an archaic (more than 2 million years old) neuro-cognitive adaptation that formed the initial foundation of a distinctively human mind sharing culture. This innovation ultimately enabled hominins to create the rudiments of a community of mind (or more properly, a community of brains). Although it was primarily an adaptation for refining skill, it was also the first step toward the formation of shared cognitive-cultural networks, so characteristic of human beings, which would serve as a means of accumulating culturally stored knowledge and skill. This had consequences for the future evolutionary trajectory of the hominin brain and the eventual shape of human culture. It also established the social conditions in which the later evolution of language became possible.

The mimetic dimension of culture endures, and in fact flourishes, in modern society. Human social life still begins with role-playing, which begins with simple mimetic action and gradually expands to include more elaborate social scenarios, such as becoming a mother, a soldier, a doctor, a victim. All these are modeled by role-playing children. Humans are unique in their tendency to experiment with the potential forms a given action might take in the future. This is especially evident in children, who routinely play with creating variations on their routine action patterns. An example might be to practice standing on one foot, making faces, crying, laughing attractively, or generating aggressive or intimidating sounds. Many games, even adult games, capitalize on this spontaneous motor generativity, and one of the consequences is the existence of mimetic "wit" as seen in games such as peek-a-boo, or in generating funny ways of falling down when struck. The facial exaggerations of silent film are perfect examples of mimetic wit. Such scenarios are common among children, and even adults, in human society.

The capacity for this kind of expressive play, and for refining skills, implies a major change in the executive management of action. This change created a channel, or mechanism, for the generation of a different kind of hominin culture, one where there was an incipient mechanism for capturing intentions and emotions in action, and thus "escaping" the solipsism of the central nervous system, through public action–modeling. This provided a means of achieving some degree of coordination and ritualization of group behavior. It also created the potential for rudimentary iconic and metaphoric gestures, including vocal gestures, which, in groups, can create elementary rituals, as in demonstrations of grief or triumph.

6   (Self-)Display

6.1   Introduction

This chapter focuses on the ritual phenomenon of (self-)displaying behaviour. Whenever our daily interaction gains a ritual character, we tend to display some social values or traits of personal characteristics, or both. In daily urban ritual encounters, (self-)display may not trigger any attention. However, as soon as it becomes 'lavish', it may become the subject of humour, as the following online description shows:

If you find yourself being polite to the point of painful (for you as much as everyone else), here's why it's time to stop.

It means you never have to have THIS conversation again . . .
– What do you want to do?
– I don't mind. What do you want to do?
– Ah I don't mind, it's up to you.
– No, no, it's up to you.

The reason why many find such an exchange irritating and/or humorous is that interaction rituals in daily contacts are not meant to make interaction unduly 'complicated'. Also, one may feel that the participants of the above interaction are overly obsessed with displaying how 'considerate' they are, i.e., self-display is 'overdone' here. Yet, in many highly ritualised settings, including both anti-structural and structural ones, it may turn out to be difficult to 'overdo' (self-)display because the ritual frame actually triggers such a form of behaviour. This is particularly the case if a ritual becomes competitive. The term 'competitiveness' here not only includes serious competition between the participants of a ritual, as in the case study featured in Chapter 3, but also playful exchanges, often manifesting itself in what Collins (2004) defined as ritual 'chains'.

To the best of my knowledge, in the pragmatic study of ritual it was Bax (2003a, 2010) who proposed first the concept of 'display'. Bax borrowed this notion from Goffman (1976) who used 'display' to describe ritualised communicational traits through which a value like femininity is conveyed and reinforced in social groups. Bax applied 'display' in a narrower pragmatic way, to capture ways in which '"excess", of veritable politeness' is manifested in historical language use. In this book, I use 'display' somewhat differently from Bax, even though the research presented here profited enormously from his ground-breaking work. That is, I use the term '(self-)display' in a bracketed form and distinguish 'ritual display' and 'ritual self-display' as two ends of a scale in Leech's (1983) scalar sense. I argue that in practically any ritual there is a sense of display: ritual itself displays a sense of awareness of the standard situation (House 1989) and a more abstract awareness of civility, politeness, etc. Because of this, the participants of a ritual often put a particular phenomenon on display. For example, by greeting a stranger through hiking one unavoidably showcases that one is aware of the norm of civility holding for hiking situations where one is expected to greet others even if one does not know them. When a ritual becomes pragmatically complex, the participants may be encouraged to make use of the displaying capacity of the ritual to reveal as much about their own knowledge of a certain topic or value, or their own skill in communicating in a civil, rude, humorous or other way, as possible. And once a ritual becomes competitive, display may be as much (if not more) centred on the self as on the other. To stick to the example of hiking, let us imagine the following scenario: one meets a group of fellow hikers on a mountain path, and when they clearly ignore our hiker by happily chatting and not looking at him, he shouts an angry 'Hallo' at them. What would happen in this case is that the ritual greeting would have the ostensive 'polite' message that the speaker is more aware of the norms of civility than the others, i.e., the ritual greeting would gain a competitive and self-displaying character. Also, such a greeting may easily become 'excessive' from a pragmatic point of view as it will be uttered more loudly than what is the norm.

Of course, the above is a simple and hypothetical example, and in this chapter I will consider how it is possible to distinguish between various degrees of (self-)display from a pragmatic point of view with the aid of a more complex case study. More specifically, the chapter will investigate a corpus of historical Chinese letters. In historical China, letter writing was a highly ritualised genre (see Kádár 2011; Kádár et al. 2023), with many 'excessive' pragmatic features, such as literary strategies to express deference to the other in overly intricate ways. The chapter will study a corpus of nineteenth-century Chinese letters written by an epistolary expert to various recipients, including both 'ordinary' recipients such as patrons, family members, lovers and so on, and fellow epistolary expert friends representing 'professional' recipients. With this latter audience, the author of the corpus under investigation engaged in a playful self-displaying competition as to who can be 'more' (intricately) deferential to the other. The presence of these twofold recipient groups therefore provides an interesting case to consider the question whether and how it is possible to distinguish different degrees of ritual self-display: while even letters written to 'lay' recipients represent self-display rather than simple display, they are much closer to the 'display' end of a 'display–self-display' scale than those written for 'professional' recipients and where the *raison d'être* of ostensive civility is to showcase the skill of the author.

As with other chapters, politeness behaviour is relevant for interaction ritual also in the case study of the present chapter. However, once again I will not consider politeness for its own sake because politeness in the present case is once again ostensive, i.e., it often serves a different goal than what meets the eye, in a similar way to protocols studied in Chapter 4

The structure of this chapter is the following. Section 6.2 provides a brief introduction into the ritual genre of historical Chinese letter writing and also introduces the data and methodology. Section 6.3 presents the case study, and Section 6.4 provides a conclusion.

6.2   Background, Data and Methodology

6.2.1   Background

Letter writing was perceived in historical China as a refined 'epistolary art' (*chidu wenxue* 尺牘文學) with distinctive (ritual) conventions. Although a sense of variation existed between historical Chinese epistolary subgenres because some letters were more practical and less 'ritual' in the popular sense of the word than others (see also Edwards 1948), in general Chinese letter writers tended to follow highly conventionalised themes and tropes and use language in an ostensive way. That is, they often followed a conventionally exaggerated emotive style, used refined vocabulary in markedly artistic ways (see Richter 2013), and indulged in extensive deference and (self-mocking) humour (see Kádár 2010).

The perception of letter writing as a form of art implied that experts of letter writing often used letters to put their skill on display for the reader. In historical China, the writing of epistles was an 'elite activity' (see Richter 2013: 50). However, many letters were not written by members of the elite, but rather clerks from the lower social strata who were paid to write letters for others. Some of these experts – the ones who were fortunate – worked in offices as subordinates of officials, while others earned their bread by servicing members of the largely illiterate public (interestingly, such expert letter writers still existed, e.g., among Chinese immigrants in Singapore in the twentieth century). Thus, many Chinese expert letter writers were often lower ranking literati who, however, were engaged in the writing of an elite genre, and epistolary engagement for them was often more than merely a 'job' – it was rather an opportunity to demonstrate their skill. Also, traditionally there was a sense of competition between expert Chinese letter writers because they often collected and published their own letters in collections, and the best of such collections became epistolary models. This competitive engagement, which can be observed in many rituals (see Bax 2010), became a hotbed for ritual self-display in many historical Chinese epistles which were written by clerks rather than members of the elite (see Kádár 2010). As I previously argued (see Kádár 2010), historical Chinese epistolary experts had their own communities and they often corresponded with each other partly as a pastime and partly as a friendly competition. While they tended to put their epistolary skill on display even when their recipients were 'lay' people such as clients to promote their epistolary services, once they addressed their letters to other experts, they intensified competitive ritual self-display.

6.2.2   Data

As a case study, this chapter examines a source that represents informal letter writing in late imperial China. 'Late imperial' denotes here the period between the fourteenth and twentieth centuries. The present research is based on sixty letters,[1] selected from the epistolary collection *Xuehong-xuan chidu* 雪鴻軒尺牘 (*Letters from Snow Swan Retreat*), which were written between ca. 1758 and 1811[2] by the office clerk Gong Weizhai 龔未齋 (1738–1811; Weizhai was Gong's 'study-name' and his birth name was E 萼). This edited collection, containing 186 informal letters of varying length written to various addressees by Gong, is considered by many as one of the most representative collections of late imperial Chinese letter writing (see Zhao 1999). Furthermore, it is one of the most 'popular' historical Chinese letter collections (see Kádár 2009), which was used as an 'epistolary textbook' during the nineteenth and early twentieth centuries and hence is often referred to as an epistolary 'model work' (*chidu mofan* 尺牘模範) by scholars of Chinese.

This source was chosen for the present case study primarily because of its representative feature, and also because artistic engagement and subsequent ritual self-display prevails in it. On this latter point, *Letters from Snow Swan Retreat* includes both letters written to ordinary recipients and others written to Gong's friends representing a small circle of intellectuals reputed for their literally skill. Gong Weizhai and most of his correspondents belonged to what was called the Shaoxing Masters' (*Shaoxing shiye* 紹興師爺) literary group.[3] The members of this circle – natives of the city of Shaoxing 紹興 in South Eastern Zhejiang Province who mostly worked in Beijing as office clerks and officials – became renowned for their skill in letter writing (as well as other literary activities).

6.2.3   Methodology

The case study of this chapter follows a contrastive pragmatic take (see an overview in House & Kádár 2021a): it comparatively examines ritual self-displaying behaviour in letters written to the above-outlined two groups of 'ordinary' recipients and fellow epistolary experts. In order to obtain comparable corpora, I chose twenty-eight letters from the *Xuehong-xuan* corpus, dividing them into two sub-corpora of equal size:

1. Fourteen letters written to recipients who were, to the best of my knowledge, not regarded as leading epistolary experts in the Shaoxing circle, i.e., were 'lay' recipients, and
2. Fourteen epistles written to other reputed experts in the same circle of literati, in particular Xu Jiacun 許葭村 (see more below).

In the first sub-corpus I only included letters where the recipient had more power than Gong, while the second sub-corpus included letters whose recipients were peers of Gong. Using the sociolinguistic parameters [+P] and [–P] in the selection of the sub-corpora helped me to investigate the following contrastive pragmatic question: is it possible that in [–P] settings Gong used what one would normally interpret as 'politeness' in a more intricate way than in [+P] ones? If yes, we may have a seeming paradox on hand because in the politeness paradigm [+P] is normally associated with a larger degree of politeness (see Brown & Levinson 1987).

In the following analysis I include two representative letters from these sub-corpora. I will approach ritual (self-)displaying behaviour in the two sub-corpora by devoting special attention to deference, humour and emotive discourse.

6.3   Analysis

6.3.1   Letters Written for 'Ordinary and Lay' Recipients

Example 6.1 represents a typical letter written to an ordinary recipient:

Example 6.1   答周介巖
會垣把晤, 快慰闊悰。坐我春風, 醉我旨酒, 感戚誼之彌殷, 比情交而更洽。
拙詩奉教, 獎譽過情, 豈范大夫初入苧羅, 以東施為西子耶?
荊 襄之間, 蓮花幕中, 誦美公者不絕口, 足下真軼倫超群哉!僕壯本無能, 老之將至, 猶復向東郭墦間, 唱蓮花落而屬酒肉, 其情已可想見。足下愛我深, 其何以策之?

Answer to Zhou Jieyan

I rejoiced at having the opportunity of seeing you again in the provincial capital and conversing after our long separation. You instructed me with noble words[4] and you made me drunk on fine wine – I am imbued with the greatest gratitude[5] for your kindness[6] and feel that our friendship has become even more harmonious.

Previously I sent you my worthless[7] poem in order to beg your esteemed opinion[8] of it. You commended the work despite its unworthiness and I wonder whether you did not appraise the work mistakenly,[9] just as if the High Official Fan[10] of old had mistaken the ugly Eastern Shi for the beautiful Western Shi when he went to the Zhulou Mountain for the first time.[11]

From Jingzhou to Xiangzhou[12] everyone who works in your esteemed office praises your name constantly. You, sir, indeed tower over your contemporaries in talent. But my humble self has been incompetent from an early age, and as the declining years approach, I can envisage naught but that I will continue my excruciating tasks in office. This work is like begging for my living; I am like the man of old who begged morsels from people who were sacrificing among the tombs beyond the eastern city wall – in his manner I will chant the beggars' song[13] and consume wine and flesh.[14] You, sir, love me deeply, and I wonder whether you could instruct me in how I should carve out my future?

(Kádár 2009: 36–37)

This is a letter to express gratitude to Zhou Jieyan who had a [+P] relationship with Gong.[15] Epistles representing the first group of fourteen letters studied, like Example 6.1, are heavily loaded with conventional honorific expressions. Perhaps the most important type of such expressions includes words that express self-denigration and the elevation of the recipient (see also Chapter 10). In historical colloquial Chinese (*jindai Hanyu* 近代漢語) texts such as novels that feature dialogues, such expressions usually consist of polysyllabic nouns (usually forms of address/reference) and verbs (in reference to the actions of the author/recipient). For example, the term *xiaoren* 小人 (lit. 'small person', i.e., 'this worthless person') denigrates the speaker and *gaojun* 高君 ('high lord') elevates the speech partner. *Xiaonü* 小女 (lit. 'small woman', i.e., 'worthless daughter') denigrates the speaker's daughter and *qianjin* 千金 (lit. 'thousand gold', i.e., 'venerable daughter') elevates the addressee's daughter. Interestingly, indirect honorific terms of address also exist in reference to objects such as the house of the speaker/writer (e.g., *hanshe* 寒舍, lit. 'cold lodging') and that of the addressee (e.g., *guifu* 貴府, lit. 'precious court'). Along with terms of address, another important historical lexical tool for elevation and denigration is the group of honorific verb forms, i.e., forms that deferentially describe the actions of the speaker and the addressee, such as *kouxie* 叩謝 (lit. 'thanking with prostration') and *fengshi* 奉事 (lit. 'offering service [respectfully with] both hands', i.e., 'respectfully take care').

The way in which the denigration and elevation forms operate in historical Chinese letters is more complex than what can be observed in dialogic texts. As I argued elsewhere (see Kádár 2010), in historical Chinese letters self-denigration and other-elevation tend to manifest themselves in what can only be described as *innovative* ways, due to the fact that the written medium affords significant leeway for the author to use expressions that would be difficult to use and interpret in the spoken medium:[16]

- Various deferential expressions convey their meaning as complex literary references (see also Richter 2013). For instance, in Example 6.1, the author uses *guoqing* 過情 (lit. 'beyond its condition', translated as 'despite its unworthiness') to deferentially denigrate his own work by downgrading the recipient's appraisal. This expression is a reference to the work of Mencius (*Lilou xia* 離婁下 [*Lilou, Part Two*] Chapter, Section 46), which contains the following statement: 故聲聞過情, 君子恥之 'Thus, a superior man is ashamed of a reputation beyond his merits.' Note that this is a 'simple' polysyllabic expression rather than a structurally and morphologically more complex form (see below); it is not a self-denigrating term that would be normally used in colloquial Chinese sources.[17] In a similar fashion, the author refers to the recipient's gift by using the expression *zhijiu* 旨酒 'luxurious wine' – this is a literary reference to the *Book of Odes* (II. 1. 161), which contains the following line: 我有旨酒 'I have good wine'. Similar to the expression *guoqing*, this is not a colloquial expression. The presence of such expressions does not preclude the use of more regular ones. For instance, in this letter the author also uses the standard elevating verbal form *fengjiao* 奉教 (lit. 'to accept with both hands [the recipient's] teaching', translated as 'beg your esteemed opinion').

- The author also uses literary analogies in a playful fashion, to express elevating and denigrating meanings. For instance, in Example 6.1 he recurrently refers to an anecdote from Mencius in order to denigrate himself. More specifically, he quotes the classic of Mencius (*Lilou xia* [*Lilou, Part Two*] Chapter, Section 61), which contains the following anecdote: a man of the ancient Kingdom of Qi boasted in front of his wife and concubine that he had feasted with honourable people while out during the day, but in fact he shamelessly begged for food around the city. The section *Dongguo fan jian* 東郭墦間 (lit. 'among the tombs of the eastern city wall') is cited from the following part of the story: 卒之東郭墦間, 之祭者, 乞其餘 'At last, he came to those who were sacrificing among the tombs beyond the outer wall on the east and begged what they had left over'. The author uses this anecdote to draw similarity between the man who shamelessly begged for food and drink and himself who works as an office assistant to earn his living, despite the fact that he knows this to be a worthless position. In a similar fashion, in the first section of the letter, the author refers to the well-known anecdote of the ugly woman Eastern Shi (*Dongshi* 東施) from the Taoist classic Zhuangzi as a humorous self-reference, by comparing his own works with the ugliness of Eastern Shi.

The above-outlined forms of deferential behaviour represent ritual self-display in two respects:

1. As Example 6.1 illustrates, elevation and denigration in historical Chinese letters is not simply a polite 'ritual': the creative and playful way in which such forms are used in epistles represent a ritual 'game' (see Goffman 1955). As part of this game, politeness in the conventional sense of the word is implicit rather than explicit. For instance, in Example 6.1 it remains for the recipient to interpret the author's reference to Mencius for himself. That is, there is a playful challenge involved in the ostensive 'polite' practice of historical Chinese letters of this sort – even though, as the analysis of Example 6.2 will demonstrate, the challenge in the case of the present letter is relatively small.

2. Along with this deferential game, practices of elevation and denigration also represent self-display due to its complexity. The sociologist Randall Collins (2004) described ritual (self-)display as a form of 'energy investment', and indeed if one examines the text it is evident that Gong invests a significant portion of the letter to creating complex elevating and denigrating messages, mainly through Informative speech acts Tell and Opine (see Edmondson & House 1981). While Chapters 10 and 11 will discuss speech acts in more detail, it is worth briefly defining these speech acts at this point: both Tell and Opine are Informative speech acts, but while Tell presents information as a matter of fact, Opine presents it in a 'subjective' way, i.e., as the speaker's opinion. If one considers the ubiquity of such complex realisations of elevation and denigration in the letter, one can certainly argue that Gong laboriously displayed his awareness of the conventions of letter writing. However, given the fact that he was a reputed epistolary expert, it is very likely that 'laboriousness' here involves ritual self-display rather than the simple display of his awareness of epistolary conventions.

Along with deference, the letter also includes ritual forms of gently self-mocking humour, as Gong Weizhai humorously assumes that the recipient made an error by positively evaluating his work. This humorous narrative is recurrent and is part of the practice of ritual epistolary self-display. Various sinologists like Mair (1978, 1984) also noted this humorous and playful characteristic of Chinese letter writing practices, i.e., this pragmatic characteristic of the *Xuehongxuan* corpus fits into a broader pragmatic pattern.

Along with deference and humour, the emotive features of Example 6.1 are also worth noting. Upon examining letters in the corpus, it transpires that the recipient is bombarded with emotions. Such emotive discourse is not *ad hoc*: the study of the corpus shows that it follows conventionalised tropes, i.e., emotive discourse in the letters studied is also clearly part of ritual ostensive behaviour. In Example 6.1 one can witness the following elements of emotive discourse:

- In the first section of the letter, Gong discusses his friendship with the recipient, by describing their relationship as *bi qing jiao er geng jia* 比情交 而更洽, which can be literally translated as 'being on better terms than friends'. In the corpus studied, there are as many as 124 such references to friendship, that is, it is clearly a conventionalised and ritual trope.
- In the second section, the author engages in an ostensive self-denigrating description of his feelings of being humble.
- In the third section, the author realises complaining through a speech act chain of Tells and Opines: he complains about the decline of his career, which is a theme that recurs in some form in ninety-seven out of the 186 letters in the corpus. As Sinologists like Shields (2015) demonstrated, such lamentations were frequented by Chinese literati, and so once again this is a typical manifestation of ostensive ritual behaviour.

6.3.2   Letters Written for 'Expert' Recipients

The following letter was written to Xu Jiacun who was a close friend of Gong Weizhai, and who was the other most renowned 'star letter writer' in the Shaoxing circle:

Example 6.2   與許葭村
病後不能搁管, 而一息尚存, 又未敢與草木同腐。平時偶作詩詞, 祇堪覆瓿。惟三十餘年, 客窗酬應之札, 自攄胸膈, 暢所欲言。雖 於尺牘之道, 去之千里, 而性情所寄, 似有不忍棄者, 遂於病後錄而 集之。內中惟僕與足下酬答為獨多。惜足下鴻篇短製, 為愛者攜 去, 僅存四六一函, 錄之於集。借美玉之光, 以輝燕石, 並欲使後之 覽者, 知僕與足下乃文字之交, 非勢利交也。
因足下素有嗜痂之癖, 故書以奉告。容錄出一番, 另請教削, 知許子 之不憚煩也。

To Xu Jiacun
During my convalescence I was unable to take up my brush and write.[18] Yet, as long as I still have breath left within me I shall not neglect our correspondence[19] and do not dare to die slowly in the manner of plants scythed down.

The poetic and lyrical works that I have casually written during my life are worthless. Nevertheless, for more than thirty years, in service far from home, I have written extensive correspondence in which I narrated my feelings with artless words.[20] Although these writings are a thousand miles distant from what one would call the art of letter writing, they record my various dispositions and I feel somewhat reluctant to throw them away. Therefore, after recovering from my illness I have copied and collected my correspondence. Amongst my letters, those which this humble servant wrote to you, sir, are by far the most numerous. It is regretful to me however, that most of your outstanding letters of various length[21] have been taken away by others who also admire your work,[22] and I have only one letter written in parallel prose in Classical Chinese left,[23] which I have copied into my collection. Thus, I would like to ask you, sir, to lend me your refined works[24] and let them illuminate my worthless collection,[25] like shiny jades lending glow to worthless stones. In this way the readers of my work will know that the relationship between you, sir, and my humble self was a true friendship between men of letters[26] and not the snobbish and greedy connection of some of the literati.[27]

As I know, sir, that you have an eccentric taste and find some pleasure in my badly written work[28] I write the present letter in order to humbly inform you about this matter.[29] If you allow me[30] to send a copy of the work to you, and fulfil my humble request by correcting it,[31] I will know that you, sir, like Master Xu of old, do not try to spare yourself effort.

(Kádár 2009: 158–161)

Deference, humour and emotive discourse are all present in this letter, just as in Example 6.1. However, if one compares these two letters, it becomes clear that Example 6.2 – and other letters in the second sub-corpus – includes increasingly complex ways in which deference is expressed to the recipient, compared to letters written to non-epistolary experts, such as the recipient of the letter featured in Example 6.1. If one considers that the recipients of letters like Example 6.2 had a [–P] relationship with the author, it becomes clear that the use of such saliently complex realisations of deference was less related to politeness in the conventional sense of the word than ritual self-display and related competition. Such ritual challenges in the present letter include the following:

1. *References to history.* For example, in this letter Gong refers to his own work by using the form *yanshi* 燕石 (lit. 'stone of Yan', i.e., 'a stone which looks like Jade', translated as 'worthless collection, like shiny jades enlightening worthless stones'). This is a rarely used honorific self-denigrating form of address, which describes the author's own work in contrast with *meiyu* 美玉 ('refined jades') – the latter serves as an honorific reference to the recipient's works. By using these terms, the author makes a reference to the anecdote *Song zhi yuren* 宋之愚人 (*The Crazy Man of Song State*). According to the fifty-first chapter (*Kanzi* 闞子, *Master Kan*) of the source *Taiping Yulan* 太平御覽 (Readings of the Taiping Era), once an insane man found a worthless stone that looked like jade (this jade-like stone is called Yanshi 燕石 in the source) and so he valued it very much. When he was warned by a guest that in fact the stone was not worth more than ordinary tiles and bricks, he became furious and assiduously guarded the stone ever after.

2. *Pieces of popular literature.* The section *yu caomu tong fu* 與草木同腐 (lit. 'rotting together with [cut] grass and trees', translated as 'die slowly in the manner of plants scythed down'), in which the author ritually narrates his lament, is a literary reference to the forty-ninth chapter of the popular historical novel *Sanguo yanyi* 三國演義 (*Romance of the Three Kingdoms*). In this novel the hero Kan Ze 闞 澤 (170–243), based on a real historical figure, utters the following words: 大丈夫處世, 不能立功建業, 不幾與草木同腐乎! 'A man of fortitude and courage cannot make progress in his social conduct if he grubs for money, and he should certainly not [idly] rot with [cut] grass and trees!'.

3. *Sources that need significant literary expertise.* For instance, in this letter Gong uses the rare honorific expression *fubu* 覆瓿 (lit. 'covering vessel', translated as 'worthless') in reference to his own work. This expression is a reference to the eighty-seventh chapter (*Yang Xiong zhuan* 楊雄傳, *The Biography of Yang Xiong*) of the *History of the Han Dynasty* (*Hanshu* 漢書). According to this source, Liu Xin 劉歆 (53 BC–23 AD) when reading Yang Xiong's works expressed his concern that Yang's books were too well-written to be understood by ordinary people; he used the following words: 吾恐後人用覆醬瓿也 'I am afraid that the men of later ages will only use [these works] to cover the jars in which they store sauces.'

While not all such deferential elevating and denigrating references are necessarily more 'difficult' to interpret than their counterparts in the previous example, in general they must have been complex forms to interpret, and a key is their diversity here. That is, by referring to sources of diverse origin and by using less standard forms, the author here clearly engages in a more playful ritual game than in Example 6.1.

In letters written to epistolary experts like Example 6.2, the use of such increasingly complex textual features as a form of ritual self-display also manifests itself in other forms, such as humorous self-references and complex wordplays. For instance, in the closing section of the letter featured here the author refers to the recipient by using the form 知許子之不憚煩也 lit. 'knowing that Xuzi spares no effort', translated as 'I will know that you, sir, like Master Xu of old, do not try to spare yourself effort'. Here Gong Weizhai makes a literary reference to *Mencius* (*Teng Wen-gong shang* 滕文公上 [*Duke Wen of Teng, First Part*] Chapter, Section 4). This source contains the following section: 何為紛紛 然與百工交易?何許子之不憚煩? '[Mencius said:] "Why does he [Xuzi 許子, i.e., Master Xu] have a confusing exchange with the craftsmen? Why does he not spare himself so much trouble?"'. This reference implicitly draws a parallel between Master Xu of old and the recipient Xu Jiacun, both having the family name Xu 許. As such, it also has a playful other-elevating meaning, since it compares the recipient to an ancient Confucian Master.

6.3.3   Contrastive Analysis

The case study has shown that while deference, humour and emotive discourse are used in a self-displaying way in both sub-corpora studied, the second sub-corpus includes increasingly complex ways in which deference is expressed to the recipient. Thus, referring again to Leech's (1983) scalar view, there is a comparatively higher degree of self-displaying behaviour in the second sub-corpus than in the first one.

As was noted, in the first sub-corpus I only included letters where the recipient of the letter had more power than Gong, while the second sub-corpus includes letters whose recipients were peers of Gong. Using the sociolinguistic parameters [+P] and [−P] in the selection of the sub-corpora helped me to investigate the following contrastive pragmatic question: is it possible that in [−P] settings Gong used what one would normally interpret as 'politeness' in a more intricate way than in [+P] ones? If yes, we may have a seeming paradox on hand because in the politeness paradigm [+P] is normally associated with a larger degree of politeness. The analysis of the two representative examples above has shown that this seeming paradox indeed exists. However, it gets resolved once we consider that it was the expertise of the recipients in the [−P] settings which triggered more competitive self-display, i.e., manifestations of 'politeness' are increasingly ostensive in such settings.

Figure 6.1 summarises the paradox which has been resolved in the case study analysis:

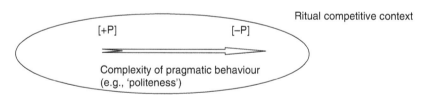

Figure 6.1   The paradox resolved in the case study.

The circle in Figure 6.1 shows that the ritual situation studied here represents a specific competitive context. Many interaction rituals, including the ones studied in Chapters 3 and 4, include such contexts, but one should bear in mind that (self-)displaying behaviour can also occur in non-clearly competitive contexts, such as ritual etiquette (see Paternoster's 2022 authoritative study). While historical etiquette also triggered (self-displaying) behaviour, the participants were normally required to follow conventions rather than 'compete' in the strict sense of the word.[32]

6.4   Conclusion

This chapter has investigated (self-)displaying behaviour. The case study has shown that one can distinguish various degrees of ritual self-display from one another. Thus, ritual self-display should not be seen as a homogeneous phenomenon: while any complex ritual tends to trigger (self-)displaying behaviour, competitive contexts are more apt to trigger such behaviour than other contexts. The chapter has shown that 'competitiveness' in ritual does not necessarily involve real competition like in Chapter 3, but also playful ritual exchanges.

In the following chapter, we will continue discussing the pragmatic features of complex rituals, by examining liminality.

6.5   Recommended Reading

Bax, M. (2010) Epistolary presentation rituals: Face-work, politeness, and ritual display in early-modern Dutch letter writing. In Culpeper, J., Kádár, D. (eds.), *Historical (Im)Politeness*. Bern: Peter Lang, 37–86.

The ritual expert Marcel Bax made ground-breaking research on ritual, including the notion of 'ritual display' studied in this chapter. Bax presented the concept of ritual display and the problem that it is difficult to capture such a display from the conventional point of view of politeness. Bax's research was way ahead of its time: he started to problematise politeness from a ritual perspective from the 1990s, even though he did not attempt to consider the role of ritual outside of the politeness paradigm. The following excerpt is from one of Bax's studies relating to the phenomenon of ritual display:

Apropos of the profuse display of politeness, the "humiliative" (Brown/Levinson 1987) or "hyperbolic" ... mode of negative politeness is only found in Hooft's [reference to the Dutch author studied by Bax; my insertion] letters to superiors and in letters to and from intimate friends. In the former category, 'excess' in address terms, benedictions, complimentary closes, and the writer's self-depreciation is a standard feature ... As such, it does not qualify as politeness in the Wattsian [i.e. Richard Watts'; my insertion] sense, because it is no more than expected – predictable, even. The prevailing 'ritual order' required such a formal, laborious, and refined approach from those lower on the social ladder, as can be concluded from what the manuals prescribe for letters to (wo)men of high station. In point of fact, doing less than what the interaction order required of lower-ranked individuals would have been highly marked at the time, and 'underachieving' would have amounted to a severe breach of epistolary etiquette, with all that that entails. Nevertheless, what we encounter in letters such as Hooft's letter of thanks to Frederick Henry ... are very resourceful, and very stylish, variations on ipso facto *deviations from the conventional way of putting things. To be sure, nothing in the manuals or in more standard 17th century correspondence comes even close to Hooft's suave way with the customary courtesies, so that his verbal display cannot but have produced a distinct communicative effect. It is not very likely, however, that this effect can be apprehended in terms of upholding or enhancing the reader's face.* (Bax 2010: 62–63)

7   Liminality

7.1   Introduction

A final distinctive feature of complex interaction rituals to be discussed in Part II of this book is liminality. Liminality is a term of anthropological origin, which has been used perhaps even more rarely in pragmatics than mimesis and self-displaying behaviour – it only occurred in the work of a very small circle of ritualists, such as Bax (2001, 2010).

Liminality comes from the Latin word *līmen* meaning 'threshold', and it gained momentum in anthropological research under the influence of Arnold van Gennep and Victor Turner who were already mentioned in this book. Similar to the notion of anti-structure discussed in Chapter 3, liminality in its original anthropological sense typically occurs in the narrower contexts of rites of passage, which bring the participants through a particular lifecycle 'threshold'. Furthermore, following Turner (1974), ritualists often distinguish tribal liminal events from modern and industrialised liminoid ones – the latter include theatre plays and performances where both the performers and members of the audience leave their ordinary lives behind for a short while, i.e., pass a threshold temporarily. As previously noted, in the current book the term 'liminoid' is not used because none of the case studies includes theatrical data – readers with interest in this area can find further information relating to this area in my joint work with the performing artist Siân Robinson Davies (Kádár & Robinson-Davies 2015). While certain datatypes studied in this book such as the MMA event in Chapter 3 have liminoid elements because they include an audience, they are not liminoid in the fully-fledged sense of the word. It is also important to clarify here exactly what the expression 'liminality' itself covers in this book as I use it in a specific pragmatics-anchored way, similar to 'anti-structure' (see Chapter 3). Since the concept interaction ritual covers a broad cluster of rituals, liminality in my view should not be restricted to the ritual triad of separation → liminality (*communitas*) → incorporation process as in a rite of passage (see Figure 3.2 in Chapter 3, although I did not include liminality in that figure). Rather, for the pragmatician, liminality is present in every complex ritual – including, for example, the epistolary rituals studied in the previous Chapter 5 – which remove one or more participants from the pragmatic conventions holding for 'ordinary' life. Yet, while certain conventions like epistolary (self-)display are only temporarily liminal, some others bring one or more participants into an interactional process which has long-lasting or even permanent effect on the participants. In other words, such rituals – which are the focus of this chapter – operate with a sense of 'irreversibility'. This sense of irreversibility not only includes rites of anti-structure but also rites of structure: for example, ritual public apologies (see Kádár et al. 2018; House & Kádár 2021b), which in my view are structural rather than anti-structural rituals, are typically liminal in nature because the person who realises such apologies passes a threshold with no return.[1] This implies that the public apologiser puts his face at the mercy of the public, i.e., even if the apology is accepted – although public apologies may never be unanimously accepted! – it represents a point of no return.

As Chapter 3 has already shown, liminality strongly correlates with an underlying sense of moral order. Since liminal rituals tend to have a significant impact on the participants, they are supposed to be realised according to often uncoded rights and obligations and pragmatic conventions. In rites of anti-structure, it usually comes from the nature of the ritual that the participants have to discern themselves what is afforded or tolerated by the moral order of the ritual. Yet, even in structural liminal rites – representing the realm of 'orderly' pragmatic behaviour – pragmatic conventions and the related moral order tend to be uncoded: unless a ritual is scripted, the participants need to formulate the ritual by following what they believe is acceptable in the frame of the ritual. Such pragmatic competence in ritual performance becomes particularly relevant in those liminal rituals which are public and where the person who realises the ritual has the role of the animator in Goffman's sense. In summary, the sense of irreversibility implied by liminality can be said to 'enhance' the moral order: while the moral order is clearly important in the operation of any ritual because violations of the ritual frame have impact on the participants rights and obligations (see Chapter 2), the participants may be more sensitive to perceived violations of the moral order in irreversible liminal rituals than in other simpler rituals.

Figure 7.1 visualises liminality as it is interpreted in this chapter:

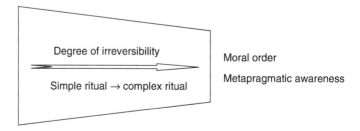

Figure 7.1 Visualising liminality.

As Figure 7.1 shows, irreversibility correlates with the pragmatic complexity of a ritual: simple interaction rituals such as urban context rituals may rarely have such a sense of irreversibility. This, in turn, also prompts one to reflect again on exactly what 'complexity' involves for the pragmatician when it comes to ritual. In my view, it can involve both interactional complexity (i.e., the way in which this notion has been interpreted in this book thus far) and relational complexity. Interactional complexity does not need an explanation. As regards the latter notion of relational complexity, it is relevant here to use again Example 2.1 from Chapter 2 (replicated here as Example 7.1), representing a public realisation of the speech act Welcome:

Example 7.1   It gives me a great pleasure to welcome here as our guest this evening Professor Quatsch from the University of Minnesota Junior.

(Quoted from Edmondson & House 1981: 193)

This Welcome is realised on the utterance level, and as such it is not complex in an interactional sense by default. However, it is complex in a relational sense because it has significant influence on the recipient. Therefore, if the person (author and/or animator) who realises this utterance 'tampers' with its default and expected style, the utterance becomes subject to complex evaluations and follow-up metaprag-matic comments and interactions, i.e., it also becomes interactionally complex – this is why interactional and relational complexity often come hand-in-hand. The trapezoid shape of Figure 7.1 indicates that the number of complex rituals is necessarily fewer than that of simple 'contact' rituals to use Goffman's previously mentioned term. Also, Figure 7.1 displays the previously mentioned argument that the moral order becomes salient when it comes to complex rituals with a liminal character, even though it is important in any ritual. This salience manifests itself in a strong sense of metapragmatic awareness of the realisation of the ritual.

In order to examine the pragmatics of liminal rituals in its whole complexity, in this chapter I present a case study featuring descriptions of 'inappropriate' workplace dismissals and subsequent metapragmatic behaviour reflecting evaluations. Such dismissals represent typical liminal rituals in the very sense of the word: they change the life of the recipient and as such they are very meaningful and irreversible. Workplace dismissal is a rite of structure: the person who realises such a ritual unavoidably acts as an animator on an institution's behalf, and so he is expected to follow strict pragmatic conventions and an underlying sense of moral order. However, as the case study will show, such conventions are rarely defined and coded, and so rites of dismissal can become controversial and subject to intensive metapragmatic reflections if they are perceived by some as 'inappropriate'. At the same time, quantitative evidence shows that most participants and observers tend to be aware of the moral order and contextually expected order of the liminal ritual.

Along with serving as an example *par excellence* for liminal rituals, workplace dismissal can also be said to be a piece of cake for the pragmatician because it is a 'secretive' urban ritual. While many – including myself when I started to study workplace dismissals – may think they know what such a ritual looks like, one (ideally) never, or at least rarely, encounters this liminal ritual in one's daily lives either as a participant or an observer. Also, as a pilot study outlined below will show, there is intriguingly little information about how such rituals should be realised on the official websites of larger companies. At the same time, perceived trespasses of the moral order of this confidential ritual tend to trigger public uproar and subsequent metapragmatic reflections on the ritual.

The structure of this chapter is as follows. Section 7.2 introduces the methodology and data of the case study, Section 7.3 provides the case study, while Section 7.4 concludes this chapter and Part II of the present book.

7.2   Methodology and Data

The present case study focuses on various types of evaluative metapragmatic reflections to perceived breaches of the moral order in the liminal rite of workplace dismissal. This metapragmatic lens[2] allows one to examine and even quantify how language users talk the moral order of the rite of dismissal into being when breaches occur. The metapragmatic focus also helps one to keep the scope of one's inquiry pragmatics-anchored, hence avoiding interpreting dismissals through 'abuse' and other psychological notions.

In a metapragmatic investigation of the present scope, it is worth considering the following phenomena:

- the metapragmatic stance (for an overview, see Jaffe 2009) of the narrative which reports on the liminal ritual event;
- follow-up metapragmatic comments.

As mentioned above, when the moral order is perceived to have been breached in a liminal ritual, metapragmatic awareness prompts both the participants and the observers to realise morally loaded metapragmatic comments. Such comments are often centred on norms – in the case of dismissal, such a typical norm is the breach of dignity, which triggers a strong sense of face threat (see Ho 1976;

Ting-Toomey & Kurogi 1998; Bargiela-Chiappini 2003). In the present book, I do not focus on norm(s), but rather on tendencies (or, one may say, conventions) of evaluations that breach the moral order underlying the rite of workplace dismissal trigger. Because of this, while I used 'dignity' as a search word together with 'dismissal' to identify relevant data, I did not attempt to speculate about exactly how 'dignity' should be interpreted from a pragmatic viewpoint.[3]

The present investigation has a tri-partite structure. First, I conducted a pilot study to examine whether rites of workplace dismissal are scripted or not. This was a key question to consider because if language use is prescribed by law or workplace regulations in such rituals, moral order may only be of a secondary importance to legal order when they are realised. When I started the present investigation, my hypothesis was that such rituals must be scripted to some degree, considering their impact on all parties included. Second, in the main analysis I examined breaches of the moral order through the lens of metapragmatics. This main part of the investigation was bipartite, i.e., I first investigated evaluative stances in reports of such breaches and then comments on such reports from both qualitative and quantitative points of view.

The corpora consist of the following:

- In the pilot study, I examined whether there is any legal criterion in Anglophone linguacultures as regards the interactional style of workplace dismissal. I also examined fifteen online workplace 'Dignity at Work' descriptions, in order to see whether they mention anything about dismissal. I collected these descriptions in an *ad hoc* fashion, by conducting a Google search.
- The first sub-corpus of the main body of this research consisted of 120 online narratives of Anglophone workplace dismissals in Britain, Australia and the United States, collected via Google searches (conducted in February 2017). This Google search was based on the two phrases 'unfair dismissal' and 'dignity at work' used together. The size of this corpus was established at 120 on a purely practical basis: as I read through cases that were triggered by the Internet search – which were then entered into a single file to facilitate the analysis – I wanted to ensure that the size of the corpus was manageable for both qualitative and quantitative purposes. I only included longer (above 300 words) narratives in the corpus.
- The second sub-corpus of the main study includes 341 online comments on the above-outlined 120 news accounts, collected from news websites such as the *Guardian* and the *Daily Mail* which allow those who have registered with the websites to comment on news items. Among the 120 incidents studied, only eighty-one are featured on websites that allow (evaluative) comments to be posted, and the online comments that I collected relate to these eighty-one narratives.

Table 7.1 summarises these three types of corpora:

Table 7.1 *The corpora of the case study*

Pilot study	First sub-corpus	Second sub-corpus
Fifteen 'Dignity at Work' descriptions	120	341, based on eighty-one websites

An advantage of studying these corpora is that they represent the different evaluative and related metapragmatic layers.

First sub-corpus: Online Reports on Incidents
• The majority of online narratives represent the views of the participants regarding both the dismissed person and the employer, in the form of quoting ('reporting') comments, hence reflecting the participants' evaluations of the appropriateness of the ritual. Only eleven texts exist in the corpus that report a dismissal without quoting the participants. In twenty-three texts the employer is reported as either declining to comment on the dismissal, or they are not featured. From the pragmatician's point of view, the lack of reporting on the employer's view of the incident is of equal interest to the comments made by the employer, since it represents a particular evaluation made by the author of the news.
• Importantly, narratives, like news reports, are not 'objective': an important goal of engaging in reflecting on the language of a rite of dismissal is to trigger reactions from a lay observer. Such reactions may be simply a passive interest (which implies that the given news is widely read), but also intensive metapragmatic participation (i.e., the readers will comment on those items of online news that permit this). As the present case study will show, narratives tend to represent evaluative stances, which implicitly influence subsequent evaluations and metapragmatic reactions (see also Houston et al. 2011).

Second sub-corpus: Comments on the Reports
• Online comments 'below' news reports are worthy of study from both qualitative and quantitative points of view because they reflect observer evaluations.

In sum, the two corpora provide insight into the following evaluation types:
• Employee/employer reported in the first sub-corpus: i.e., participant evaluations;
• The evaluative stance of the report in the first sub-corpus: i.e., quasi-professional evaluations;
• Commenter reactions in the second sub-corpus: i.e., lay evaluations.

7.3   Case Study

The present analysis consists of the following parts. In Section 7.3.1, I report on the pilot study where I considered whether liminal rites of workplace dismissal tend to be scripted, or not. Section 7.3.2 presents the study of the first sub-corpus and Section 7.3.3 presents the study of the second sub-corpus through the lens of the above-outlined three types of evaluations of perceived 'inappropriate' workplace dismissals.

7.3.1   Pilot Study

As mentioned above, in investigating the liminal rite of workplace dismissal I set out from the hypothesis that the language of such rituals must be scripted or legally prescribed to some degree. However, this hypothesis turned out to be false because only certain very specific realisations of dismissal are legally problematic in Anglophone linguacultures.

Legal frameworks acknowledge the fact that any dismissal may, inevitably, cause distress and pain; however, such frameworks only penalise those realisations of dismissal which are explicitly and demonstrably abusive (Perritt 2006: 6–96). As the pilot study has shown, workplaces themselves rarely define what they regard to be 'appropriate' and 'inappropriate' forms of dismissal, as far as interactional style is concerned. If one explores workplace descriptions of 'dignity at work' – which tend to be provided by many larger organisations – it becomes evident that these descriptions generally discuss broader 'principles' for the employer as to how to treat employees, rather than specific pragmatic conventions such as how a dismissal is meant to be announced. The following 'Dignity at Work Statement', taken from a university website, illustrates this point:

Example 7.2   All employees are entitled to:

- *a workplace free from bullying, intimidation, harassment or victimization*
- *experience no form of unlawful discrimination*
- *be valued for their skills and abilities*

> (Retrieved from: www.ucl.ac.uk/ion/equality-diversity-inclusion/challenging-bullying-harassment-victimisation-and-intimidation)

The vagueness of such descriptions correlates with the problem that, from a legal perspective, there is a fundamental difference between 'unfair dismissal' triggering legal consequences and 'unethical dismissal'. 'Unusual' pragmatic realisations of dismissal, which lack explicit rudeness, typically represent the realm of unethical and pragmatically ambiguous rather than unfair and unambiguous.[4]

On the basis of this observation in the pilot study, I set up a simple typology of *ambiguous* and *unambiguous dismissals*. One can argue that in unambiguously inappropriate dismissal normally the legal order gets violated, while in pragmatically ambiguous ones only the moral order is trespassed. The following examples represent these two types of the rite of dismissal:

Example 7.3   After reading about Angel Clark, the talk-radio host who was fired via Facebook recently, I got to think about what would be the worst way to get the bad news about losing your job ... Amazingly, however, nothing I imagined could top your stories ...

The Poster As Pink Slip
When I was in college I was fired from a job via a poster. My boss put up a neon pink sign in the break room that read 'Alyson, find a new job.'
– Alyson, former pizza delivery girl

(Retrieved from: https://energycentral.com/c/hr/10-firing-horror-stories-will-give-you-nightmares)

Example 7.4   Sacking by text was 'brutal and gutless'
9 May 2013
The sacking of a retail worker, after nineteen years of service, via a twenty-one-word text message, was 'brutal and gutless', the FW Commission has ruled.

(Retrieved from: https://workplaceinfo.com.au/termination/unfair-dismissal/cases/sacking-by-text-was-worst-brutal-and-gutless)

In Example 7.3 the employer explicitly and unambiguously violated the employee's dignity at work: the public display of humour in such a sensitive liminal ritual tends to be interpreted as being highly 'destructive' (see Billig 2005: 28). The narrator of the example also takes such an evaluative stance as he introduces the event in a moralising sarcastic way, by stating that 'nothing I imagined could top your [i.e., the featured] stories' (see Dadlez 2011 on 'moralising sarcasm'). Example 7.4 represents a pragmatically ambiguous dismissal: while the brevity and the medium of the dismissal are both negatively evaluated, the dismissal is not demon-strably intended to cause offence and, as such, it does not trespass the legal order. Pragmatically ambiguous dismissals often feature tension between legal and moral orders. For instance, while the dismissal featured in Example 7.3 caused a moral uproar, the employee was unable to sue the employer.

7.3.2   Study of the First Sub-corpus

The simple typology outlined above allowed me to categorise the first sub-corpus of 120 news accounts as follows:

Table 7.2 *Categorisation of the first sub-corpus*

Pragmatically (and legally) ambiguous dismissals	Pragmatically (and legally) unambiguous dismissals
112 online narratives	Eight online narratives (vulnerable employees who do not normally take a legal action)

As Table 7.2 illustrates, a statistically significant majority of the online narratives represent pragmatically ambiguous dismissals, which accords with the fact that unambiguous dismissals may have legal and financial consequences for the employer. It may also not be a coincidence that all of the eight unambiguous dismissals in the sub-corpus involve employees in low-skilled jobs like in Example 7.3. In the following, I devote more attention to pragmatically ambiguous cases, not only due to their statistical salience but also because they are clearly interesting for the ritualist to investigate as they lead to the following question:

Considering that such realisations of the liminal rite of dismissal are not demonstrably wrong, at least from a legal point of view, do participants and observers reveal metapragmatic awareness of a breach of a specific moral order?

In the study of the first sub-corpus, I investigated this question by examining both participant evaluations and the evaluative stance of the reports.

Participant Evaluations

Since the rite of dismissal is rarely scripted and pragmatically ambiguous dismissals are therefore not 'demonstrably' wrong, such cases allow the employer to have significant freedom when interpreting 'appropriate' behaviour in a particular situation. In the present sub-corpus of narratives, some employers defend their decision to dismiss employees in contradictory ways, while others opt to remain silent. Table 7.3 illustrates employers' evaluative reactions and the lack of such reactions in the corpus:

Table 7.3 *Employer reactions in the first sub-corpus*

11/120 narratives	24/120 narratives	85/120 narratives
Reporting the dismissal without quoting the employer/employee	The employer is reported as declining to comment on the dismissal	The employer expresses some form of regret; in four cases the employer formally apologises

This low frequency rate of apologising can be explained by considering the potential legal and marketing consequences of a corporate apology (see Fuchs-Burnett 2002). At the same time, these figures also show that the liminal ritual of workplace dismissal triggers a strong sense of metapragmatic awareness, and employers who authored and realised the ritual in a perceived inappropriate fashion also tend to acknowledge the breach of the moral order. Having argued thus, this acknowledgement often comes in a careful way: as Table 7.3 shows, only four out of eighty-five employers who expressed some form of regret realised a public apology, while the others only mentioned regret. While expressing regret can be a strategy to realise the speech act Apologise (see Blum-Kulka et al. 1989), in the corpus it tends to correlate with the speech act Justify (see Excuse/Justify in Edmondson & House 1981), as the following example shows:

Example 7.5   Licensee Stephen Howard has admitted 'sacking' staff members but says he had to act to bring in new people after what he claims were a number of issues with the existing workers.

(Retrieved from: www.mirror.co.uk/news/uk-news/
boss-justifies-sacking-shocked-staff-11833113
[last accessed 7 June 2023])

In this case, the employer admits that he has dismissed employees but justifies the claimed abruptness of the dismissal by referring to 'a number of issues with the existing workers'. By so doing, he makes an implicit appeal to a *competing* moral order of the liminal ritual, namely, that if an employee is 'problematic', the employer is entitled (and may even be expected) to dismiss him in writing and even in an abrupt manner. Such justifications can be reinforced by the fact that textual dismissal is not illegal. In many contexts, the written medium (and the pragmatic implications of this medium) can even be considered to be a preferred form of workplace dismissal, as the following legal excerpt illustrates:

Example 7.6   Communicating a dismissal decision by text should be a last resort but may be acceptable in limited circumstances. For example, where there is a concern that face-to-face contact may involve some genuine prospect of aggression or violence, or the employee had engaged in gross and willful misconduct and no possible explanation could alter the decision. It can also be necessary if an employee is unable to be contacted by other means.

(Retrieved from: www.hcamag.com/hr-news/is-it-illegal-
to-dismiss-someone-via-text-message-242567.aspx
[last accessed 7 June 2023])

Compared to employers, employees evaluate such instances of dismissal in an unanimously negative way, which is not surprising. In summary, the study of participant evaluations shows that even those perceived 'inappropriate' ritual dismissals which are not demonstrably wrong tend to be negatively viewed. This metapragmatic tendency correlates with the liminal irreversibility of the ritual.

Evaluative Stances of the Narratives

The study of the 112 narratives in the corpus shows these narratives share various evaluative features.

Title

Discourse analysts like Hartley (2013: 165) argued that title represents a prime opportunity for texts like news items to take an evaluative stance. This phenomenon can also be observed in the first sub-corpus where the titles of the reports represent negative views on perceived 'inappropriate' dismissals, as the following examples show:

Example 7.7   STAFF 'FUMING' AFTER NEW PUB LANDLORD SACKS THEM BY TEXT AND FACEBOOK MESSAGES

> (Retrieved from: www.mirror.co.uk/news/uk-news/boss-justifies-sacking-shocked-staff-11833113 [last accessed 7 June 2023])

Example 7.8   STAFF AT DUNDEE FURNITURE STORE 'SACKED BY TEXT TWO DAYS BEFORE CHRISTMAS'

> (Retrieved from: www.thecourier.co.uk/fp/news/dundee/579613/staff-told-by-text-two-days-before-christmas-they-had-lost-their-jobs/)

Both these titles include evaluations which were made by the dismissed staff members and, as such, they not only adopt stances themselves, but also influence the prospective evaluation of the reader. The expression 'fuming' in Example 7.7 reflects the anger that has been triggered by an allegedly 'unfair' dismissal, while reference to the media of the dismissal (both text and Facebook) justifies this evaluation. Similarly, in Example 7.8, the statement 'sacked by text two days before Christmas' is a reflection on the lack of care (see Haidt and Joseph's 2007 interesting discussion of 'harm and care' in the context of morality). In this latter case, the reported timing of the dismissal, and its medium, position it as inappropriate. While not all titles feature original quotes, there tends to be some implicit form of appeal to the expected moral order of things in a workplace dismissal in the majority of the titles in the corpus. The following example illustrates this point:

Example 7.9   CLAIMS WORKERS SACKED BY TEXT-MESSAGE

> (Retrieved from: www.dailymail.co.uk/news/article-182944/Claims-workers-sacked-text-message.html#ixzz55ZaBIS3B [last accessed 7 June 2023])

While this title does not feature an explicit evaluation, the fact that 'by text-message' is included in the title indicates that the narrator construes the irreversible rite of dismissal as controversial. Practically all the 112 narratives studied feature an evaluation in the title.

Foregrounding Information

The concept of foregrounding has been widely studied (see e.g., Leech 2008); essentially, it refers to the ways in which a text structures information. A recurrent feature of the narratives in the corpus is that, following the title, the author first presents the alleged inappropriate behaviour, and he only introduces the circumstances that have led to the perceived inappropriacy after that; this is usually followed by reporting on the reactions of the employees, and then the reactions of the employer.

Example 7.10

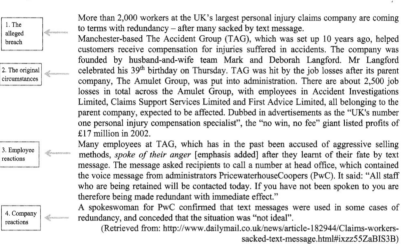

1. The alleged breach

More than 2,000 workers at the UK's largest personal injury claims company are coming to terms with redundancy – after many sacked by text message.

2. The original circumstances

Manchester-based The Accident Group (TAG), which was set up 10 years ago, helped customers receive compensation for injuries suffered in accidents. The company was founded by husband-and-wife team Mark and Deborah Langford. Mr Langford celebrated his 39th birthday on Thursday. TAG was hit by the job losses after its parent company, The Amulet Group, was put into administration. There are about 2,500 job losses in total across the Amulet Group, with employees in Accident Investigations Limited, Claims Support Services Limited and First Advice Limited, all belonging to the parent company, expected to be affected. Dubbed in advertisements as the "UK's number one personal injury compensation specialist", the "no win, no fee" giant listed profits of £17 million in 2002.

3. Employee reactions

Many employees at TAG, which has in the past been accused of aggressive selling methods, *spoke of their anger* [emphasis added] after they learnt of their fate by text message. The message asked recipients to call a number at head office, which contained the voice message from administrators PricewaterhouseCoopers (PwC). It said: "All staff who are being retained will be contacted today. If you have not been spoken to you are therefore being made redundant with immediate effect."

4. Company reactions

A spokeswoman for PwC confirmed that text messages were used in some cases of redundancy, and conceded that the situation was "not ideal".

(Retrieved from: http://www.dailymail.co.uk/news/article-182944/Claims-workers-sacked-text-message.html#ixzz55ZaBIS3B)

As this example illustrates, the controversial delivery of the dismissal via a short text message is exacerbated by the absence of further communication during the dismissal process. The information structuring of this and other similar texts is reasonable when one considers that narratives (a) are not 'objective', that is, they deliver meta-evaluations of the alleged inappropriacy either explicitly or implicitly, and (b) that their aim is to trigger further involvement (metapragmatic participation), i.e., to generate interest and, ideally for the writer of the news report, moral uproar. In Example 7.10, the employer reacts defensively to the accusation of unethical behaviour. However, it is relevant here to recall that in some other cases, such as Example 7.5, the employer reacts to criticisms with appeals to an alternative *competing* moral order (i.e., it is proper to abruptly dismiss a 'problematic' employee), usually by realising the speech act Justify. Since such appeals tend to occur late in the reports, it is clear that – insofar as one interprets moral order to be a discursive construct – it can be of secondary importance to the default moral order featured in the report of the incident.

While the above is a recurrent structure of foregrounding in the narratives, nine of the 112 narratives adopt a different structure in that they present the employer's perspective first. However, the reason behind such alternative choices is normally not that the narrators approve the employer's behaviour, but rather that they follow an 'anecdotal' line of storytelling (see Georgakopolou 1997), as shown by the following example:

Example 7.11   The first time he fired someone, one manager explained, it took him two hours and the process was excruciatingly painful for both himself and the affected employee. Over time, he got 'so good' at firing employees that somewhere between the time they entered his office and walked across to take a chair, they were fired. 'We brought you in to discuss some difficult matters. We know you are not happy here, that you are not happy with your performance … We are not happy with it either, and feel you can do better elsewhere. So today we are going to part company and we are going to wish you good luck. Here is a severance check and a letter of recommendation we want you to have, along with what we owe you. We want you to take the rest of the day off on us, and here are twenty bucks so you can treat yourself to a nice lunch.' What goes around comes around, and this same manager reports that when it was his time to be fired he found 'the box' on his desk. Everyone knew the dreaded box was given to dismissed employees to fill it with their personal belongings. This manager did not have the courtesy of facing his supervisor, he received a phone call seconds after entering his office: 'See that box on your desk? Get your belongings, report to payroll … We'll give you a ride home.' And if you think that was tasteless, it seems someone can always top your story. I recently read about a host of people being dismissed, … via E-mail!
The words firing and dignity hardly belong together. Nevertheless, there are a few principles we can keep in mind that will help preserve a certain amount of dignity to that employee we are ready to let go.

(Retrieved from: http://nature.berkeley.edu/ucce50/ag-labor/
7article/article19.htm [last accessed 7 June 2023])

While the anecdotal approach of this text does not foreground the employee's evaluation, this does not mean that the reader is intended to empathise with the employer. In this case, the Principle of Tact (Leech 1983) underlies the perceived moral order of the irreversible rite of dismissal: the text claims that the employer dismissed the employee in an abrupt and, as such, 'tactless' fashion.

7.3.3   Study of the Second Sub-corpus

The study of reader evaluations of pragmatically unambiguous and ambiguous dismissals has shown a noteworthy difference between how readers evaluate such perceived 'inappropriately' realised rituals. Table 7.4 shows this evaluative difference:

Table 7.4 *Evaluation of unambiguous and ambiguous cases*

	Negative evaluations (273 online evaluative comments)	Positive evaluations (68 online evaluative comments)

Pragmatically unambiguous cases:
Eight narratives, with three narratives
    featured on sites with no commenting
    option		

TOTAL: 61 comments	59 (96.7%)	2 (3.3%)[5]

Pragmatically ambiguous cases:
111 narratives, with thirty narratives
    featured on sites with no commenting
    option		

TOTAL: 280 comments	197 (70.4%)	83 (29.6%)

The figures here are problematic in the sense that not all the websites in the corpus possessed a commenting option. Yet, Table 7.4 shows that members of the public almost always evaluate unambiguously inappropriate rites of dismissal negatively – which comes as no surprise – while pragmatically ambiguous rites of dismissal are more divisive: the ratio of negative comments is 70.4 per cent (197) in comparison with 29.6 per cent (eighty-three) for positive comments.

Regarding positive evaluations, it would be overly ambitious to attempt an interpretation of the motivation behind each case when a commenter disagrees with the evaluation of the narrator of a dismissal, or that of the dismissed employees quoted in the narrative. However, in many cases, such evaluative discrepancies are based on some personal experience either in the given company or with the 'archetype' of employees associated with those being dismissed. The following excerpt illustrates such evaluations:

Example 7.12   We visited this pub several times in December/January to find the bar staff rude and disinterested; as a group I commented on that several times so probably better if they didn't work in a service industry. It may not be the most professional way to be told that you are dismissed but the cash-in-hand nature of the position is an indication of its transient nature.

(Retrieved from: www.mirror.co.uk/news/uk-news/boss-justifies-sacking-shocked-staff-11833113 [last accessed 7 June 2023])

This commenter evaluates the behaviour of the employer positively and pre-scriptively endorses the moral order of abruptly dismissing certain types of employees. This evaluation is based on the alleged unprofessional behaviour of the staff. If a person serves the customers inappropriately, she appears to lose her right to be treated with specific deference at the given workplace, i.e., the dismissed employee is morally sanctioned (see Nwoye's 1992 insightful prag-matic discussion of moral sanctioning). In some other cases, commenters align[6] themselves with the employer on the grounds that, having fulfilled managerial functions themselves or having worked at companies, they regard written notice as 'unavoidable' in certain settings and relationship types.

However, because a significant majority of the commenters (70.4 per cent) align themselves with the person being dismissed, it is reasonable to argue that the cluster of lay observer evaluations that surround such incidents are anchored in a default moral order underlying the rite of dismissal with a strong sense of irreversibility, which triggers a need to be tactful under all circumstances. Comments reflect a broad array of appeals to this moral order: some are quasi-religious in nature (e.g., 'that is one huge God complex by the Manager'), others are quasi-scientific (e.g., 'Capitalism is the extraordinary belief that the nastiest of men for the nastiest of motives will somehow benefit for all'), while still some others simply state the emotions of the person posting the comment (e.g., 'that company is absolutely pathetic', 'bit of a coward').[7]

7.4   Conclusion and Summary of Part II

This final chapter of Part II of the present book has examined the phenomenon of liminality, which is a typical characteristic of more complex rituals. While in anthropology the concept of liminality is often used to describe anti-structural rites of passage, and 'liminoid' refers to theatrical performances, for the pragma-tician, liminality occurs in any ritual which even temporarily brings the participants into an interactional setting that differs from their ordinary life. At the same time, liminality is scalar, and it manifests itself in a fully-fledged fashion in rituals with a sense of irreversibility, such as workplace dismissals studied in this chapter, representing a typically structural ritual. Irreversibility unavoidably triggers a strong sense of metapragmatic awareness: notwithstanding whether a rite of dismissal, marriage proposal, invitation to join an important society or another ritual is taking place, the participants and observers of the ritual are likely to notice if something goes amiss with the interactional flow simply due to the importance of the ritual for at least the recipient, and in other occasions also for some others – as a typical example one may refer to the devastating impact of a mismanaged marriage proposal on the families involved in many societies. Therefore, the pragmatician can pin down liminality by focusing on cases when a pragmatic issue occurs in a liminal ritual, by focusing on metapragmatic evaluations.

In this chapter, I once again avoided interpreting the phenomenon under investigation through the lens of politeness. While breaches of the expected flow of events in liminal rituals are no doubt relevant to impoliteness, as the analysis of the main corpus of the case study has shown, many participants, reporters and commenters do not interpret the events purely in terms of impoliteness but go much further, by referring to moral norms, values and other grand notions. This is logical if one considers that violations of the expected ritual flow and the underlying moral order are not simply 'impolite' in the strict sense of the word but often they are 'civil' and 'inhumane' and have a devastating impact on the recipient. Putting such violations under the umbrella of 'impoliteness' would, in my view, overstretch this term. While impoliteness conventionally involves causing offence, here one witnesses more than simple offence due to the impact of the liminal ritual on people's lives.

The case study has shown that even in pragmatically ambiguous dismissals, evaluations follow certain tendencies. Such tendencies also apply for cases when those who are responsible for the perceived breach of the moral order may simply intend to be cautious rather than offensive by realising the dismissal in a succinct way. In turn, the existence of such tendencies reveals the existence of a default moral order which underlies any liminal ritual, even if it is not codified like workplace dismissal. Table 7.5 summarises evaluative tendencies in the case study:

Table 7.5 *Evaluative tendencies in the case study*

Participant evaluations:	In the majority of cases (85/120 narratives, i.e., 70.8%) even the employer expresses some form of regret over a pragmatically ambiguous dismissal
Observer reflective evaluations:	The news items reporting the incidents align themselves with the employee
Lay observer evaluations:	A significant majority (197/280 comments, i.e., 70.4%) of the commenters explicitly align themselves with the dismissed person

These tendencies show that while there may be two competing moral orders in such conflictive cases – including expectations towards a tactful dismissal versus tolerance for the employer to abruptly dismiss an employee if this abruptness is morally endorsed – there is ultimately a default moral order that influences the evaluations which are made in a set of different participant statuses.

Part II of this book has discussed the three key features of mimesis, (self-) displaying behaviour and liminality, which characterise interactionally and relationally complex rituals. While these features have been somewhat neglected in pragmatics, I argued that they are important to consider because they provide insight into what happens in many interaction rituals.

In the following and final Part III of the book, we will discuss various units of analysis through which interaction ritual can be studied, by devoting special attention to the methodological considerations outlined in Chapter 2.

7.5   Recommended Reading

Kádár, D. (2017) *Politeness, Impoliteness and Ritual: Maintaining the Moral Order in Interpersonal Interaction*. Cambridge: Cambridge University Press.

In the book featured as recommended reading here, I examined the relationship between ritual and politeness in much detail, by focusing on how these two phenomena can be interconnected rather than distinguished. I also discussed the concepts of 'liminal' and 'liminoid', by analysing a case study of liminoid theatrical performance. In the excerpt below I provide a rather simple definition of liminality, which however may complement what has been covered in the present chapter:

Liminality manifests itself in the following operational characteristics of ritual:

- Ritual, unlike some other activity types, operates with clearly formalised and recurrent linguistic/language behavioural elements that the participants perform each time (or which are clearly recognisable as ritual elements, if a ritual occurs as a one-off event). As ritual sticks out from the ordinary flow of events, it is meant to gain a distinct form in operandi.
- Participants invest emotions to participate in a ritual because ritual as a liminal action brings them into an altered state of mind (e.g., Collins 2004). Such emotive investment may not characterise every pragmatic phenomena.

While all activity types reflect moral orders, the liminal operation of ritual is heavily bound to the maintenance of these orders. Consequently, evaluators that reflect moral orders tend to be more heavily present in ritual than in other phenomena. (Kádár 2017: 12–13)

Part III

Methodological Issues

Synopsis

Part III of this book focuses on methodological issues in the pragmatic study of ritual. Here 'methodology' does not so much involve questions such as how one can record and transcribe naturally occurring rituals, such as military training studied in Chapter 5 and related ethical considerations. While such practical methodological issues are no doubt important, they have been discussed already in various chapters of Part I and Part II; in addition, procedures of data collection and transcription in the pragmatic study of ritual are not saliently different from other areas of pragmatics. The main focus in this part is rather on how one can study interaction ritual in two major methodological routes. As was mentioned in Chapter 2, the concept of ritual frame is so important in the study of interaction ritual that it is ever-present in the way in which one can methodologically approach the pragmatic units of expressions, speech acts and discourse in ritual research. Let us here refer again to Figure 2.2:

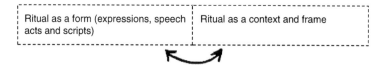

Figure 2.2 The role of ritual frame in research on interaction ritual.

Figure 2.2 includes two major methodological takes on ritual. The first one is the following: the ritual pragmatician can depart from the study of pragmatic units of analysis like expressions and speech acts because manifestations of such units are often ritually relevant. That is, a pragmatic study of ritual may interpret ritual as a form as a starting point. Archetypical examples to consider here are 'ritual expressions' such as 'Amen' and 'please' and (typologically) ritual speech acts such as Greet. Yet, this book has shown that the ritual–form interface needs to be approached critically because expressions and speech acts tend to gain a ritual pragmatic function in actual ritual frames rather than having a ritual value *per se*, i.e., one can only study their ritual function in a rigorous and replicable way if one considers their conventional use(s) in interaction. The arrow in the figure shows that the ritual function of such forms of language use can be reliably studied if their use is considered through the more abstract concept of ritual frame.

An exception to this may include expressions and realisations of certain speech acts which are very closely associated with 'ritual' in the popular sense, as well as scripts of ceremonies. One may argue that such forms of language use have such a strongly conventionalised ritual use that they are always ritual. However, even in the study of such expressions, speech acts and scripts, one cannot fully ignore the frame in which they are used if one wants to tease out exactly how they are used in interaction and how they evolve over time.

As regards the second methodological take on ritual, there are many complex ritual phenomena which can only be studied from a pragmatic angle in a replicable way if one attempts to interpret them through pragmatic units of analysis. For example, while military training studied in Chapter 5 has many ritual elements, from the pragmatician's point of view it can only be interpreted as a ritual (rather than a context) if one captures its recurrent pragmatic features, e.g., by studying the expressions and speech acts frequented by the trainers.

Part III presents these two methodological takes in ritual research. Chapter 8 considers the relationship between expressions, the smallest unit of pragmatic analysis, and ritual. The chapter will provide a bottom–up, corpus-based and replicable approach through which expressions associated with structurally or functionally ritual speech acts are used in different contexts. It will be argued that the relationship between expressions and interaction ritual can be best captured through a contrastive pragmatic lens because the contrastive view allows the researcher to consider how strongly a pragmatically important expression tends to indicate a functionally and/or structurally ritual speech act when pitted against a comparable expression in another (preferably typologically distant) linguacul-ture. The chapter will provide a case study of Chinese and English expressions associated with the ritually performed speech act Apologise.

Chapter 9 will continue discussing the first methodological take in the pragmatic research of ritual proposed above, by examining how speech acts associated with ritual can be examined in a replicable way. The chapter will argue against 'identifying' new 'ritual speech acts' *ad libitum* because such a procedure shuts the door on studying speech acts through which ritual is realised in a replicable way. Instead, the pragmatician should identify their subject of analysis with the aid of a finite typology of speech acts. The next task is to consider how a particular ritually relevant speech act is realised in a particular ritual frame. Chapter 9 will present a case study of the ritual phenomenon of 'admonishing' in a corpus of ancient Chinese texts. Admonishing represents a ritual realisation type of the Attitudinal speech act category Suggest (do-x)/(not-to-do-x).

Chapters 10 and 11 discuss how the second methodological take on ritual can be put to practice. There are many complex ritual phenomena which can only be studied from a pragmatic angle in a replicable way if one attempts to interpret them through pragmatic units of analysis. Here complexity means that
a) a particular phenomenon is either too broad to be discussed as a single ritual, i.e., it represents a form of ritual behaviour which spans across many different ritual contexts and frames, or
b) like military training it represents a particular context and related ritual frame which triggers ritual behaviour but cannot be subsumed under a single ritual heading from the pragmatician's point of view.
In the study of such phenomena, it is advisable for the researcher to depart from interpreting ritual in a bottom–up way by first considering the frame or frames in which the ritual under investigation occurs and then systematically studying how ritual manifests itself in (and indicates awareness of) such frames. Chapters 10 and 11 will propose a replicable methodological framework for the study of such complex rituals.

Chapter 10 will focus on the first of these cases: it explores the ritual phenomenon of self-denigration in Chinese. Self-denigration occurs in a broad variety of Chinese interaction rituals and ceremonies, and if one attempts to describe its pragmatic features by relying on data drawn from a single context, one unavoidably risks oversimplifying it. Rather, in the study of such an interaction ritual phenomenon one should consider how it is used in different interpersonal scenarios with varying power and intimacy and in different phases of an interaction, which both imply varying ritual frames with differing rights and obligations.

Chapter 11 will use elements of the framework in a discourse-analytic way, in order to study language use in a single complex ritual frame in a replicable way. As a case study, the chapter will examine ritual bargaining in Chinese markets.

8 Methodological Take-1A: The Relationship Between Expressions and Ritual

8.1 Introduction

This chapter considers the relationship between expressions, the smallest unit of pragmatic analysis, and ritual. By so doing, it illustrates how the first methodological take outlined in the synopsis of Part III can be put into practice.

While verbal rituals are often popularly associated with certain formal expressions, from an academic point of view such an association can be very problematic because it is the interactional context – i.e., the ritual frame – which provides a ritual pragmatic function to pragmatically important expressions, i.e., an expression *per se* is neither ritual nor 'mundane'. To provide a simple example, 'Amen' can be said to be a 'ritual expression' – and it *is* by default in the language use of many millions of Christians! However, this expression may as well be used in non-ritual conversation in phrases like 'Amen to that' where its ritual function is only referential. Further, 'Amen' may also be used in very mundane contexts such as in the utterance 'Who the heck gave his Amen to this madness?' For the ritual pragmatician the question is therefore not so much whether a formal expression is ritual or not, but whether it has a comparably stronger or weaker relationship with interaction ritual. In the case of 'Amen' this question is of course clear due to its religious origin and use. However, since interaction ritual involves a complex cluster of day-to-day interactions, the pragmatician needs to consider whether pragmatically important quotidian expressions such as 'please', 'sorry', 'hello' and so on have a stronger or weaker relationship with ritual. Such expressions tend to be often described as 'ritual' and associated with politeness. Furthermore, many such expressions are either associated with speech acts which tend to be performed in ritual ways, such as Request and Apology (see Blum-Kulka et al. 1989) or others which normally occur in ritual parts of an interaction such as Greet and Leave-Take (see Edmondson & House 1981; Edmondson et al. 2023). Figure 8.1, drawn from Edmondson and House (1981: 98), illustrates the relationship between speech acts and ritual:

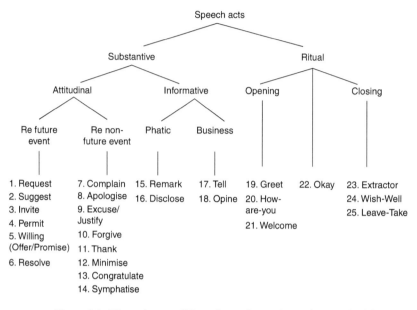

Figure 8.1 Edmondson and House's typology of speech acts (cited from Edmondson & House 1981: 98).

As Figure 8.1 shows, there is a cluster of structurally ritual speech acts occurring under the 'Ritual' label in the typology. Other Substantive speech acts, such as Apologise, gain a ritual function when they are realised by following ritual interactional conventions (see more in Edmondson et al. 2023).

Following Figure 8.2 quoted in the synopsis of Part III, in the study of the relationship between expressions and ritual, the literal definition of ritual as a form normally serves as a departure point: the rationale of looking at one or more expressions is that the analyst may assume that expression x is likely to have a ritual value. Following a Popperian take in pragmatic research (see Edmondson & House 2011), one however should not set out to prove the validity of such an assumption, but rather investigate whether it is true or not, and if yes, how a particular expression relates to ritual in a more abstract sense, i.e., as a context where rights and obligations are preset. If the relationship between a particular expression and ritual turns out to be relatively weak, the original assumption that expression x is 'ritual' in the popular sense needs to be critically revisited. The procedure of research here is thus the following:

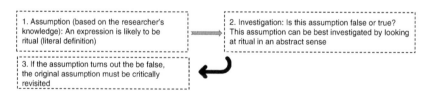

Figure 8.2 Procedure of research in the ritual study of expressions.

The relationship between expressions and interaction ritual can be best captured through a contrastive pragmatic lens because the contrastive view allows the researcher to consider how strongly a pragmatically important expression tends to indicate a functionally or structurally ritual speech act when pitted against a comparable expression in another (preferably typologically distant) linguaculture.

In this chapter, I present a case study which I conducted with Juliane House where we contrastively examined comparable expressions associated with the Attitudinal speech act Apologise[1] in the typologically distant Chinese and English linguacultures, in order to examine whether they are more strongly or weakly associated with ritual in an abstract sense.

The structure of this chapter is as follows. In Section 8.2, I revisit the ritual perspective – which has already been discussed in different chapters of this book – by arguing that it provides a more accurate view on the pragmatic use of pragmatically important expressions like 'sorry' than the politeness perspective. In Section 8.3, I present a methodological framework through which expressions associated with ritual – which are called 'ritual frame indicating expressions' (RFIEs) in this book – can be studied in a bottom–up, corpus-based and contrastive way. Section 8.4 presents the case study, and finally Section 8.5 provides a conclusion.

8.2   Expressions and Interaction Ritual: Retrospection

I believe that – as with various other pragmatic phenomena – the ritual view can provide a particularly reliable insight into the ordinary and conventionalised use of pragmatically important expressions. The use of such expressions has often been approached through the lens of politeness, which however has been a rather controversial area. Once again, I do not intend to pit ritual against politeness, which would be a futile and unhelpful train of thought because these phenomena are complementary and they have a lot in common: ritual at one end of a pragmatic scale represents the realm of communally oriented behaviour, while politeness and impoliteness at the other end of the same scale represent individually oriented pragmatic behaviour. Indeed, politeness and impoliteness are relevant for the study of pragmatically important expressions – however, I believe that they are less relevant than ritual.

A brief retrospection may prove the validity of this argument. Expressions like 'sorry' popularly tend to be associated with politeness, and in the field of pragmatics, various scholars have described them as 'politeness markers'[2] (see e.g., Sifianou 1992; Van Mulken 1996; Aijmer 2009). Yet, the association between form and politeness has been the source of much academic debate. In one particular body of research, which includes, among others, Fraser and Nolen (1981), House (1989), Eelen (2001) and Watts (2003), it has been argued that linguistic politeness, impoliteness and expressions are only loosely, if at all, related, and it is primarily through conventionalisation that their relationship can be identified. In Brown and Levinson's (1987) seminal work, forms occur as subsets of politeness 'strategies'; this implies that in their view forms are of secondary importance for politeness theory. Outside of politeness theory, the expression 'politeness marker' has continued to be frequently used: in areas such as language socialisation and language learning it is of little importance whether these forms are technically 'polite' or not, and researchers engaged in applied linguistics and other areas have often used the concept of 'politeness marker' in a rather liberal way (see e.g., Gleason et al. 1984; Byon 2003). In addition, various politeness scholars such as Pilegaard (1997), Yeung (1997) and Ogiermann (2009) have used this notion to categorise and quantify their data. In a recent paper, Schlund (2014) has provided a comprehensive overview of the debates surrounding the concept of 'politeness marker' and has also proposed a model which – she claims – provides an approach to study the interface between 'politeness marker' and politeness itself. Regretfully, Schlund's research is not fully empirical in scope and, to date, the relationship between expressions associated with polite behaviour and linguistic politeness itself has not been sufficiently captured.

One may argue that the lack of a comprehensive study of the expression–politeness interface is not a coincidence because ultimately an expression *per se* only becomes polite or impolite if its use (or lack) is interactionally noticed, i.e., if something extraordinary happens in the flow of the interaction. On the other hand, since the Speech Act Realisation Project (Blum-Kulka et al. 1989) it has been largely agreed that pragmatically important expressions tend to have a relatively straightforward relationship with speech acts, contextual rights and obligations and, consequently, also with ritual. 'Straightforward' here does not mean simple: as House and Kádár (2021a) pointed out, there are many different types of relationship between expressions and speech acts, well beyond the scope of what is discussed in the current chapter. However, it can be argued that due to the strongly conventionalised relationship between certain speech acts and ritual outlined above (see Figure 8.1), it is less ambitious to study the use of expressions by considering their ritual speech act indicating function than by attempting to consider their relationship to politeness and impoliteness.

8.3   Analytical Framework: The Ritual Frame Indicating Expressions Theory

In this book, pragmatically important expressions are referred to as 'ritual frame indicating expressions' (RFIEs). RFIE theory emerged in Kádár and House (2020a, 2020b) in which, with Juliane House, we established an approach for the contrastive pragmatic analysis of expressions, which are pragmatically important and commonly associated with structurally or functionally ritual speech acts. In Kádár and House (2020a), we defined the concept of a RFIE as follows: such expressions associated with speech acts are not necessarily polite, but rather are markers of standard situations and they indicate awareness of a 'ritual frame' underlying standard situations. Our definition of 'standard situation' originated in House's (1989: 115) seminal work – to facilitate the reader's work, here I quote this definition again:

> The notion of a standard situation involves participants' rather fixed expectations and perceptions of social role. Role relations are transparent and predetermined, the requester has a right, the requestee an obligation, the degree of imposition involved in the request is low, as is the perceived degree of difficulty in realizing it. In a nutshell, the participants know where and who they are. Clearly, the distinction between a standard and a nonstandard situation is not clear-cut. For example, in an interaction where a policeman is reprimanding a car owner, when, for instance, the policeman utters a request to move the car, it is evident that the expression please takes place in a standard situation and thus has been formulated with the goal of indicating this situation.

The concept of a standard situation includes any situation in which rights and obligations prevail. Due to the prevalence of rights and obligations in any standard situation, such situations are ritual in nature. With Juliane House we use the notion of 'ritual frame', which has already been thoroughly discussed in this book, to describe pragmatic rights and obligations associated with each standard situation. It is worth noting that the way in which ritual frame is applied in the present bottom–up and corpus-based study of expressions in this chapter differs from how 'frame' has been used in a particular body of cognitive research which has been conducted by, for example, Schank and Abelson (1977), Tannen (1979), Fillmore (1982), Barsalou (1992), Chafe (1994), Terkourafi (2005) and Bednarek (2005). This is because, in such cognitive research, 'frame' has often been used in a top–down way, i.e., it was applied in the study of the use of expressions in contexts selected by the researcher. Unlike such research, RFIE theory pursues an interest in the variety of frames a particular RFIE can indicate.

Ritual frame, as the concept is interpreted in RFIE theory, clearly correlates with conventionalisation (Terkourafi 2001). In other words, the more conventional the meaning of a particular RFIE becomes, the less directly related it will be to individualistic politeness (House 1989; Wichmann 2004; Terkourafi 2011), and the more open it is to being deployed as an indicator of a ritual frame.

In the following, I provide an overview of the contrastive pragmatic analytical framework through which one can analyse RFIEs and the resulting standard situational spread of ritual behaviour, in a bottom–up fashion, illustrated by Figure 8.3:

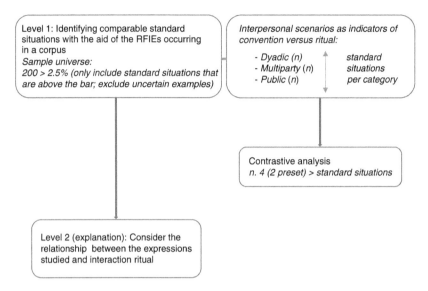

Figure 8.3   Analytical model used in RFIE research.

The procedure depicted in Figure 8.3 consists of two levels. On the first level, the initial task is to identify RFIEs in the linguacultural data that one is intending to compare. Various criteria can be used to identify comparable RFIEs – in the case study reported in this chapter, the criterion was simply to find the simplest and most standard expressions associated with the speech act Apologise according to two panels of five native speakers. Based on such native speaker feedback, it was evident that 'sorry' in English is on a par with 'duibuqi' 对不起 in Chinese: according to the respondents, these are the most 'universal' RFIEs in the two linguacultures.

After the RFIE groups were chosen, a sample corpus needs to be collected. In the case study reported below, a sample of 200 examples featuring a particular RFIE was collected. The next criterion in the first level of analysis is to identify the standard situations which are indicated by a particular RFIE. To ensure that a manageable number of such standard situations were obtained, a threshold of five was applied for 200 examples. In other words, a minimum 2.5 per cent rate of occurrence threshold was used to ensure that a particular standard situation was sufficiently recurrent.

There are various ways in which one can collect a sample dataset of 200 examples. For instance, in the case study, twenty hits were collected by randomly sampling batches of five examples in the corpora. Invalid examples, such as metareferences to a RFIE, were excluded from the data. Due to this approach, the data sampling took place in two stages, firstly by collecting an initial dataset, and then by replacing the invalid examples with valid ones that occurred before the batches of five examples in the corpus.

The following should be noted regarding the use of the concept of 'standard situation' in interaction ritual research involving RFIEs. First, it is advisable for such analysis to operate with two preset standard situations, namely 'institutional with power-salience' and 'informal with now power-salience'. The reason why such standard situations are useful is that the sociolinguistic parameter of power attracts ritual behaviour (see Kádár 2013), and so featuring formal versus informal standard situations as general categories helps the researcher observe variation in the use of RFIEs. Second, the number of standard situations and the size of the dataset are meant to correlate. In the case study reported below, the four standard situations are in proportion with the dataset of 200 utterances. Third, when using the analytic category of 'standard situation' one should remember that any standard situation triggers a sense of awareness of rights and obligations and the underlying ritual frame. So, even in cases when a particular RFIE is used in a non-ritual way, it usually continues to indicate the ritual frame itself, as the case study below will also show.

Let us now discuss the top right-hand box in Figure 8.3, which illustrates the application of the variables of the participatory framework that are used to analyse each RFIE, before a contrastive pragmatic analysis is performed. The analytic model outlined here uses three categories, defined as 'interpersonal scenarios', including (1) 'dyadic', (2) 'multiparty' and (3) 'public':

• Dyadic: Interactions in private where there are no overhearers.
• Multiparty: Any interaction involving two participants with either over-hearers or situated in a scenario in which dyads are part of a broader relational network. Multiparty interactions tend to feature complex participatory frameworks.
• Public: Interactions which are designed to be accessible to unratified participants (see also Goffman 1981).

In order to ensure that the dataset representing one RFIE is comparable with another, it is advisable to create a cluster of interpersonal scenarios and standard situations by breaking down the occurrences of each standard situation that a particular RFIE indicates across the interpersonal scenarios. The trifold categories of 'dyadic', 'multiparty' and 'public' are useful because they can throw light on the relationship between a particular RFIE and its speech act-anchor. This speech act-anchor, in turn, is relevant to the study of whether a particular RFIE has a stronger or weaker relationship with ritual (see Figure 8.1), considering that if an expression loses its speech act-indicating function, it also often loses from its interaction ritual value.

After completing the preparatory work, the next step is to engage in contrastive pragmatic analysis, as per the bottom right-hand box of Figure 8.3. The focus of this investigation is the relationship between the RFIEs contrasted and their 'speech act-anchor', as well as the related strong weak/strong relationship between RFIEs and interaction ritual. As part of investigating this issue, it is relevant to quantitatively compare 'speech act anchored' and 'non-speech act anchored' uses of an RFIE. In the case study below, the number of non-speech act anchored occurrences of an expression will be indicated in the tables by underlining and bracketing the figures.

Finally, the bottom left-hand box in Figure 8.3 shows that on the basis of the framework outlined here, one may reach a general view about the relationship between particular RFIEs and interaction ritual. I would caution against making linguacultural conclusions on the basis of such outcomes, e.g., by making arguments alongside the 'East–West' dichotomy.

A relevant issue to consider in the RFIE-based study of ritual is performativity. There is a strong correlation between ritual and speech act. Austin (1962) in his now classical work has predominantly used performative utterances which are ritual in nature, such as 'I appoint you Consul' (1962: 23), or 'I welcome you' (1962: 24). In addition, in ritual research (e.g., Hollywood 2002), performativity is often mentioned as a key criterion for defining an utterance as ritual. Thus, it is logical to argue that the performative function is prevalent in ritual, while non-speech act-anchored uses of an RFIE also lack performative value.

8.4   Case Study

The present case study explores the relationships between the RFIEs 'duibuqi' and 'sorry' and ritual. The data of this case study is based on Mandarin Chinese and English corpora of comparable size and comprehensiveness. The Chinese corpus was collected from the Balanced Chinese Corpus (BCC; http://corpus .zhonghuayuwen.org/CnCindex.aspx). The English corpus is the British National Corpus (BNC).

8.4.1   The Ritual Frame Indicating Expression 'Duibuqi'

Table 8.1 shows the spread of the RFIE 'duibuqi' across various interpersonal scenarios:

Table 8.1 *Occurrences of the ritual frame indicating*
expression 'duibuqi' across different interpersonal scenarios

Overall number	Dyadic	Multiparty	Public
200	19 (9.5%)	126 (63%)	55 (27.5%)

This spread indicates that the use of 'duibuqi' strongly leans towards 'multiparty' and 'public' scenarios, suggesting that there is potentially a strong relationship between this RFIE and the use of RFIEs in the Chinese linguaculture. However, this initial finding needs to be further elaborated upon.

The second most frequently observed interpersonal scenario in which the RFIE 'duibuqi' operates is the public scenario. Here I mention this use of 'duibuqi' first because it is straightforward from the perspective of ritual, considering that the public interpersonal scenario triggers a ritual load, as the following example of a public Apologise illustrates:

Example 8.1   对不起, 我道歉并且更正。

   I am sorry, I apologise and will change my attitude.

While Example 8.1 only represents an utterance-level public Apologise, it includes various key features of ritual already mentioned in various chapters of this book. First, it is self-explanatory that this utterance is communally oriented and liminal in nature. Second, the Apologise here is clearly excessive: the RFIE 'duibuqi' in the example is followed by the expressions *daoqian* 道歉 ('I apologise') and *gengzheng* 更正 ('I change my attitude'), which increase the seriousness of the apology.

'Duibuqi' is most frequently used in multiparty interpersonal scenarios in the corpus of this study. Similar to the public setting, multiparty represents a complex interpersonal scenario, which tends to trigger ritual language use, as illustrated by the following example:

Example 8.2   对不起, 有关我们厂的情况资料都已经全部分发给记者了。

   I am sorry, I already distributed all material relating to our factory to the journalists.

This formal Apologise realisation takes place in a formal setting, which has a multiparty character because it is situated in an institutionalised and hierarchical interaction (the interaction is multiparty rather than public because only 'ratified' participants can hear the utterance in its original context, whereas if it took place in public it would be accessible to everyone; see Goffman 1981 on 'ratification').

As Table 8.1 shows, there are also dyadic cases in the corpus of this case study, although they are relatively small in number. The following example illustrates the use of the RFIE 'duibuqi' in a dyadic setting:

Example 8.3   对不起, 我说得太过份了。

   I am sorry, I was very rude.

This dyadic use of 'duibuqi' is formal and the RFIE indicates a genuine Apologise. Due to the formality of the way in which 'duibuqi' is used, Example 8.3 also represents a speech act-anchored and ritual use of the RFIE.

In terms of the standard situations across the various interpersonal scenarios in the corpus, the analysis has revealed the following:

Table 8.2 *Occurrences of the ritual frame indicating expression 'duibuqi' across standard situations and interpersonal scenarios*

Standard situation	Dyadic (19)	Multiparty (126)	Public (55)
Ceremonial	8	21	23
Informal (no power-salience)	11	20	n/a
Institutional (power-salience)	n/a	85	n/a
Political	n/a	n/a	32

As Table 8.2 shows, 'duibuqi' often occurs in ceremonial settings, particularly (but not exclusively) family ceremonies. What is worth noting is that this RFIE is often used not so much to express an *ad hoc* or strictly interpersonal Apologise, but rather it is applied in a ceremonial and performative fashion:

Example 8.4   对不起, 太太, 我失了手啦!

I am sorry, wife, I made a mistake!

In the present dataset, the RFIE 'duibuqi' tends to be used in itself if there are two speakers, whereas if the Apologise is realised in multiparty settings within families, language users may also use a 'duibuqi + object' format. This latter – syntactically more complex – RFIE form is not on a par with 'sorry' and, as such, it is not studied in detail here (readers with interest are advised to consult Kádár & House 2021a).

'Duibuqi' is not limited to family in ceremonial standard situations: outside of family scenes, it is also often deployed in ceremonial multiparty settings, as Example 8.1 has illustrated. Example 8.5 represents another ceremonial situation, in which the language user acknowledges his hiring (rite of passage) with a symbolic Apologise indicated by the RFIE 'duibuqi' uttered in a performative way:

Example 8.5   对不起, 我觉得象我这样的一个外乡人, 很难说能为您效劳。

I am sorry, I feel that a countryside bumpkin like myself may not be able to work for you in an effective way.

The next standard situation category to be analysed is 'informal', i.e., cases in which interpersonal or institutional power is relatively absent. The following examples are indicative of the use of the RFIE 'duibuqi' in this standard situation:

Example 8.6   <u>对不起</u>, 从零开始, 真气人那！

Apologies, we need to start from scratch, this is really frustrating!

Example 8.7   <u>对不起</u>, 博士。

Apologies learned colleague (lit. 'doctor').

What these examples show is that even in the 'informal' standard situation with no salient power involved the RFIE 'duibuqi' tends to indicate a real Apologise in a formal and ritual way.

'Duibuqi' is most frequently deployed to indicate the 'institutionalised' standard situation in the corpus of this case study, i.e., it is used in contexts in which power is clearly salient. Such standard situations take place in multiparty interpersonal scenarios. If one examines the use of the RFIE 'duibuqi' in such cases, it becomes evident that, without exception, it is used in a speech act-anchored and ritual fashion, as illustrated by the following example:

Example 8.8   富欣林却尖声尖气地叫了起来：'同志们, <u>对不起</u>, 我看错了, 我拉了一个数字啦。'

Fu Xinlin cried out in an agitated manner: 'Comrades, I am sorry, I missed a digit.'

What becomes immediately obvious when one examines this example is that the producer of the utterance is highly emotive, which gives salience to the utterance. Further, 'duibuqi' fulfils a (quasi-)performative ritual function here.

Finally, 'duibuqi' can be used in the 'political' standard situation (often texts from the 1950s in the Chinese corpus), which are all public. The following example illustrates the use of the RFIE 'duibuqi' in this standard situation:

Example 8.9   <u>对不起</u>, 党, 也对不起, 老战友陈宏奎呀！

I am sorry, Party, and I am also sorry, my old comrade, Chen Hongkui!

It goes without saying that such uses of RFIEs are clearly ritual, without exception.

8.4.2   The Ritual Frame Indicating Expression 'Sorry'

Table 8.3 shows the spread of the RFIE 'sorry' across various interpersonal scenarios in the corpus:

Table 8.3 *Occurrences of the ritual frame indicating expression 'sorry' across different interpersonal scenarios*

Overall number	Dyadic	Multiparty	Public
200	78 (39%)	91 (45.5%)	31 (15.5%)

An immediately interesting pragmatic feature of 'sorry' shown in Table 8.3 is the high frequency of dyadic settings in which it is used, compared to the Chinese dataset. The fact that this expression leans towards dyadic and multiparty scenarios already indicates that it may have a comparably weaker relationship to ritual.

In terms of the standard situations across the various interpersonal scenarios in the corpus, the analysis has revealed the following:

Table 8.4 *Occurrences of the ritual frame indicating expression RFIE 'sorry' across standard situations and interpersonal scenarios*

Standard situation	Dyadic (78)	Multiparty (91)	Public (31)
Classroom	n/a	26	n/a
Informal (no power-salience)	49	28	n/a
Institutional (power-salience)	29	37	n/a
Political	n/a	n/a	31

A standard situation which clearly distinguishes 'sorry' from 'duibuqi' is 'classroom'. The following examples illustrate the use of the RFIE 'sorry' in this multiparty scenario:

Example 8.10   How many tens in one hundred? Oh <u>sorry</u>, ten.

Example 8.11   We will start to think about Nick. No, <u>sorry</u>, you've got notes on Nick.

Such uses of 'sorry' are clearly casual, i.e., non-ritual. Although, in theory, classroom interaction can be highly ritual, as in the case of examinations, and an Apologise RFIE would indicate real apologies in such a setting, there are no such uses in the English corpus.

Moving on to the 'informal' standard situation – i.e., informal interactions between friends or colleagues – the RFIE 'sorry' occurs either in dyadic or multiparty scenarios in the English corpus. The following examples illustrate such uses of 'sorry':

Example 8.12   Here you are, darling. Whoops, <u>sorry</u>, couldn't poison you.

Example 8.13   So, who goes for Trudy? <u>Sorry</u>? Who goes for Trudy?

Example 8.14   Anybody gonna want to get up tomorrow? <u>Sorry</u>? Nobody wanna get up tomorrow.

The RFIE 'sorry' in these instances is only weakly linked to the speech act Apologise because it is used in a casual way, and consequently cannot adopt a performative ritual function.

Regarding the 'institutional' standard situation, 'sorry' can be employed in both dyadic and multiparty scenarios, as the following examples illustrate:

Example 8.15   Lorna, sorry, I thought you have some more questions.

Example 8.16   Oh, yes, sorry, I thought that mine was a copy.

Example 8.17   Chairman, sorry, on correspondence there was this letter.

Example 8.18   Sorry, I want to make two more points.

These examples represent casual rather than ritualised language use because there is a weak relationship between 'sorry' and the speech act Apologise, particularly when contrasted with its Chinese RFIE counterpart. While the first two Examples 8.15 and 8.16 occur in multiparty settings, the RFIE 'sorry' in them does not become interactionally salient, and neither does it fulfill a performative pragmatic role.

The last category to be analysed here is 'political', which is restricted to interpersonal scenarios taking place in public. The following example illustrates the use of 'sorry' in this standard situation:

Example 8.19   The planning process would imply, and, sorry, while I am speaking I am left a little confused.

Despite the complexity of the interpersonal scenario involved here, such a use of the RFIE 'sorry' also has a weak relationship with ritual.

8.4.3   Contrastive Analysis and Explanation of the Differences

As part of the framework outlined in Section 8.3, let us now compare the standard situations that the RFIEs 'duibuqi' and 'sorry' have indicated in the sampled corpora:

Table 8.5 *Comparing standard situations in the Chinese and English corpora*

Chinese RFIE ('duibuqi')	English RFIE ('sorry')
Ceremonial	n/a
Informal (no power-salience)	*Informal (no power-salience)*
Institutional (power-salience)	*Institutional (power-salience)*
Political	*Political*
n/a	*Classroom*

The 'ceremonial' standard situation is salient in the Chinese corpus, unlike its English counterpart. This indicates that it is in ceremonial scenarios (rather than *ad hoc* conversation) that this RFIE is needed. In the case of 'classroom', the lack of this standard situation in the Chinese dataset might only be an anomaly, and in fact there were two examples of such use in the sampled corpus, i.e., the indication of this standard situation by the RFIE 'duibuqi' might simply be below the bar that was established earlier. However, the situation may be more complex than this. It is worth considering that Chinese classrooms tend to prompt deferential and, as such, ritual language, compared to their English linguacultural counterparts. Thus, it is logical that the RFIE 'duibuqi' is less frequent in this standard situation than the pragmatically 'weaker' 'sorry', at least as far as the language use of teachers is concerned – note that in the two datasets, all classroom utterances are made by lecturers and not students.

In the following, let us examine in greater detail the differences between the RFIEs in the Chinese and English corpora, by investigating their pragmatic ability to fulfil a performative ritual function. This, in turn, also triggers a focus for the research into whether these RFIEs can indicate the speech act Apologise or not. The frequency of these forms to indicate 'dyadic', 'multiparty' or 'public' scenarios correlates with their pragmatic capacity (or lack of such capacity) to fulfil a performative ritual function, and their related ability to indicate speech acts – in the present case, Apologise.

In the case of the Chinese RFIE 'duibuqi', there are only 16 of the 200 occurrences (8 per cent) in the sampled corpus which do not fulfil the speech act Apologise. The distribution of such cases (as underlined below) is illustrated in Table 8.6:

Table 8.6 *The number of non-speech act-anchored uses of the ritual frame indicating expression 'duibuqi' in the Chinese corpus*

	Dyadic (19)	Multiparty (126)	Public (55)
Ceremonial	8 (2)	21 (1)	23
Informal (no power-salience)	11 (3)	20 (4)	n/a
Institutional (power-salience)	n/a	85 (6)	n/a
Political	n/a	n/a	32

Importantly, all these non-speech act anchored uses of the RFIE 'duibuqi' represent attention-getting, as the following examples illustrate:

Example 8.20   对不起, 请开壶龙井！

   Apologies, please open this jar of Longjing tea!

Example 8.21   对不起, 这位同志, 有什么服务不周的地方请您给我提出来。

   Apologies, comrade, if you are dissatisfied with any service, could you point it out?

The first example takes place in a 'ceremonial' setting in a family, and the second one is from an 'institutional' meeting. What is interesting in both these cases is that the contexts in which the RFIE 'duibuqi' occurs are ceremonial and ritual, but the RFIE itself is used to get the other's attention and so it loses from its ritual value. It is worth noting that, in the Chinese corpus, none of the attention-getting uses takes place in public interpersonal scenarios. This may correlate with the fact that there is a *strong* relationship between the RFIE 'duibuqi' and the speech act Apologise, unlike in English. In other words, Chinese language users clearly prefer to apologise when they use 'duibuqi', and this RFIE has a sense of pragmatic gravity.

The examination of the English RFIE 'sorry' shows that it is often used to express the two non-speech act-anchored pragmatic functions of attention-getting and self/other-repairing (for such uses of 'sorry', see also Kitao & Kitao 2013; Arizavi & Choubsaz 2018). This implies that 'sorry' has a comparatively weaker relationship with ritual and the speech act Apologise. If one considers the frequency of the use of 'sorry' to indicate attention-getting and repair in the English dataset, it becomes evident that it differs substantially from its Chinese counterpart, as Table 8.7 illustrates:

Table 8.7 *The number of non-speech act-anchored uses of the ritual frame indicating expression 'sorry' in the English corpus*

	Dyadic (78)	Multiparty (91)	Public (31)
Classroom	n/a	26 9 attention-getting 12 repair	n/a
Informal (no power-salience)	49 19 attention-getting 22 repair	28 17 attention-getting 9 repair	n/a
Institutional (power-salience)	29 10 attention-getting 13 repair	37 15 attention-getting 19 repair	n/a
Political	n/a	n/a	31 17 attention-getting 14 repair

The RFIE 'sorry' seems to occur most frequently in multiparty scenarios, which would afford ritual language use. However, since 'sorry' is very often not meant to be an apology but rather something else, in many such cases it indicates attention-getting and, to an even greater degree, repair. As a related characteristic, it very rarely adopts a performative function. The following examples illustrate these conventional uses in multiparty scenarios ('classroom', 'informal' and 'institutional'), as well as in the 'political' standard situation.

Example 8.22   Sorry, I can't hear you.

(multiparty classroom – attention-getting)

Example 8.23   That just means that x is 7. Sorry, it's 3.

(multiparty classroom – repair)

Example 8.24   If you use the toilet roll. Sorry, why do you want it to glow?

(multiparty informal – attention-getting)

Example 8.25   I thought it joined up on Mozambique. Sorry, I thought the border was on Mozambique.

(multiparty informal – repair)

Example 8.26   Sorry, just remind us what proportion is a flat pack.

(multiparty institutional – attention-getting)

Example 8.27   The contractor is very specific. Yes, the contract, sorry, is very specific.

(multiparty institutional – repair)

Example 8.28   Sorry, my other point is about riot.

(political – attention-getting)

Example 8.29   Five nos. No, no, no, no, no. Yes, I, sorry, I mean that may be a cut-off point.

(political – repair)

It is evident from these examples that the RFIE 'sorry' has a comparatively weaker relationship with ritual than 'duibuqi', even though standard situations, such as 'public debate', could trigger ritual behaviour. Importantly, even in such contexts the RFIE continues to indicate the ritual frame, i.e., awareness of rights and obligations, as otherwise no attention-getting or self-correction would take place. That is, a relatively weaker relationship between and RFIE and ritual does not imply that the RFIE ceases to operate as an indicator of the ritual frame itself, which underlies any standard situation.

8.5   Conclusion

This chapter has considered how the ritual pragmatician can capture the relationship between expressions and ritual, hence illustrating how the first methodological take of pragmatic research on ritual proposed in this book can be put to practice. I argued that while verbal rituals and expressions have a stereotypically assigned relationship, it is problematic to claim that there are 'ritual expressions' – rather, one should examine the relationship between pragmatically important expressions and interaction ritual by considering how such expressions are related to speech acts. Such a study of the relationship between expressions and speech acts provides a gateway to ritual research, considering that some speech acts are structurally ritual as the seminal work of Edmondson and House (1981) has shown, while certain Attitudinal speech acts such as Apologise tend to be realised in ritual ways. I argued that examining the pragmatic features of expressions through the lens of ritual provides a more reliable insight into them than the politeness perspective.

I proposed a framework for the ritual study of pragmatically important expressions, which are called RFIEs in this book. This framework is centred on the relationship between RFIEs and speech acts, and it approaches the relationship between RFIEs and interaction ritual through the concepts of standard situation and interpersonal scenario. This framework is contrastive in scope because the relationship between expressions and ritual is never absolute: RFIEs are always related to ritual to some degree, and the nature of this relationship can be characterised as 'stronger' or 'weaker' if one looks at the use of such expressions from a contrastive pragmatic angle.

I argued that one should avoid making linguacultural overgeneralisations on the basis of the framework proposed in this chapter. For example, I believe it would be an error to hop on the 'East–West dichotomy' bandwagon on the basis of what the case study of this chapter has shown, by arguing that in 'Eastern' languages expressions in general are more ritualised than their 'Western' counterparts. Such an argument would be very problematic because ultimately interaction ritual manifests itself in such diverse forms of expressions, including expletives studied by Labov (1972; see Chapter 2) that one simply may not be able to make conclusive statements about the expression–ritual interface.

In the following Chapter 9, we will continue discussing the first methodological take of pragmatic research on ritual, by examining how speech acts associated with ritual can be examined from a pragmatic point of view.

8.6   Recommended Reading

House, J., Kádár, D. (2021a) *Cross-Cultural Pragmatics*. Cambridge: Cambridge University Press.

In the current chapter I only presented how one can use RFIE theory for the study of the relationship between expressions and speech acts. Readers with further interest in the RFIE theory may wish to consult the above book where my colleague Juliane House and myself discussed this framework in more detail. In the following section quoted from the above-mentioned book, we discuss the concept of 'pragmatically important expressions', a notion which has also been widely used in this chapter, by arguing that RFIEs only represent a particular type of such expressions:

We can cross-culturally study expressions from a cda [cross-cultural discourse analytic] point of view in both single-source and multiple-source discourse data. In such investigations, a key area of research includes the study of linguaculturally and metapragmatically significant expressions. The study of such forms is different from the examination of other expressions such as RFIEs, in that many of those expressions which we define here as 'linguaculturally and metapragmatically significant' may not belong to the realm of RFIEs but are rather cultural descriptors of language use. Two key types of such expressions are the following:

1. *Pragmatically important abstract terms, such as 'face', 'civility', 'considerateness' and 'politeness' itself, which language users frequently refer to in reflective discourse;*
2. *Descriptions of pragmatically relevant forms of behaviour such as 'heckling', 'scolding', 'condemning', 'warning', 'encouraging', and so on.*

Various of such forms of behaviour are often, in our view, mistakenly associated with major speech act categories. (House & Kádár 2021a: 139)

9   Methodological Take-1B: The Relationship Between Speech Acts and Ritual

9.1   Introduction

In this chapter we continue discussing the first methodological take in the pragmatic study of ritual proposed in this book, by examining how speech acts associated with ritual can be examined in a replicable way. A key issue in the study of such speech acts is the following: there are many so-called 'speech acts', like 'blessing', 'praying', 'challenging' and so on, which are popularly associated with ritual. However, it is very problematic to define such phenomena as 'ritual' because that would imply that the ritual pragmatician can 'identify' new speech acts *ad libitum*, just like an anthropologist finding new ritual practices with no equivalent when visiting 'exotic' countries and cultures. In House and Kádár (2023: 1), Juliane House and myself discussed the problematic nature of proliferating speech acts in detail, and here I cite an argument from this study:

> As regards the case of freely inventing new speech acts, *ad hoc* categories such as 'confessing' and 'admonishing' are unhelpful if our goal is to undertake replicable research based on speech acts ... [in] pragmatics. ... The idea of only working with comparable and similarly conventionalised units of analysis clearly precludes proliferating speech acts *ad libitum*. Here, we refer to the invention of new speech acts whenever it suits the researcher's agenda. This has been such a common academic practice that we cannot provide a comprehensive overview of so-called 'speech acts' invented for ... pragmatic purposes owing to space limitation. While we find it difficult to pin down exactly where the idea of freely invented speech act categories originates, we believe that it appeared in the pragmatic literature at least as early as Wierzbicka's (1985) study, which triggered a wealth of 'innovative' speech act categories, such as that of 'self-sacrifice' (for a most recent L2 example see Allami & Eslamizadeh, 2022). Proliferating speech acts ad libitum precludes the desired replicability of any research.

This is exactly why there are no so-called 'ritual speech acts' (cf. e.g., Rota 2022) in my view, only speech acts used in a ritual practice or in a ritual context.[1] The task of the pragmatician is to rely on a finite and interactional typology of speech acts – in this book I propose using the one outlined in Figure 8.1 in Chapter 8 because it is a radically minimal and finite typology of speech acts which approaches speech acts as interactional phenomena.

The idea of finiteness of speech acts is not without controversy. In House and Kádár (2023: 5) we argued as follows regarding this point:

The question may rightly emerge: is a particular set of interactionally embedded speech acts 'sufficient' and can others not rightly identify new speech acts? Also, can we 'reserve the right' of insisting that only our speech act categories legitimately exist? These would be fair questions to ask, and our response would be that the speech acts we propose are 'minimal' in the Chomskyan sense – that is, they are designed to represent the basic pragmatic unit of speech act which is meant to be smaller than units of interaction ... This is also why such speech act categories are not 'ours', in that a radical finite typology of speech acts needs to include only those speech acts that are such simple and basic constituents of language use that they can easily be replicated in the study of interaction across languages and datatypes.

In ritual research focusing on speech acts, the first task of the researcher is therefore to consider how a particular 'ritual speech act' can be pinned down with the aid of a replicable typology of speech acts. As part of considering this issue, it is also important to make sure that one does not overinterpret speech act, which is an utterance-level phenomenon by default.[2] For example, it would have been clearly wrong in Chapter 3 to argue that ritual trash talk in MMA events represents a 'speech act'! Such phenomena, in my view, can only be studied through speech act analysis if one observes recurrent speech act types through which trash talk and the like are realised.

Once we identify our subject of analysis with the aid of a finite typology of speech acts, the next task is to consider how this speech act is realised in a particular ritual frame. In this chapter, I do this by proposing a replicable methodology which examines realisations of the speech act under investigation through the lens of the units of expressions and discourse.

I investigate the ritual phenomenon of 'admonishing' as a case study. Admonishing represents a ritual realisation type of the Attitudinal speech act category Suggest (do-x)/(not-to-do-x) (see Edmondson & House 1981; Edmondson et al. 2023). While ancient Chinese admonishing has many distinctive pragmatic characteristics that sets it apart from other everyday realisation modes of Suggest, it is reasonable to subsume admonishing under the illocutionary category of Suggest. When one realises admonishing, he engages in a performative ritual act, often in an unmitigated fashion. Unlike many other forms of Suggest, admonishing is historically embedded (see Bax 1981). The act of admonishing is apparent in historical forms of discourse in a number of linguacultures: in many parts of the world, including China, Egypt (Lichtheim 1976), ancient Europe (see an overview in Dauphinais & Levering 2005), Renaissance Italy (e.g., Tasca 2004) and suchlike, admonishing was a culturally important act. In historical European linguacultures, for instance, there was a particular theological genre – ecclesiastical discourse – associated with this ritual, whereas in China admonishing was a key part of ancient literary discourse on state governance.

As the case study below will demonstrate, admonishing is a ritual worth investigating because the ritual frame in which admonishing in the case study occurs often not only affords but even triggers paradoxical pragmatic behaviour. This paradox stems from the fact that, in many historical linguacultures, admonishing was directed at a recipient – most typically a ruler – who was more highly ranked than the admonisher himself. The case study consists of data drawn from sources dating from before the second century BC, i.e., the ancient period of Classical Chinese. In Chinese, the subject of our research is called *jian* 諫, a Chinese expression used for 'admonishing' in political and governance contexts.

The structure of Chapter 9 is as follows. Section 9.2 provides a brief overview of previous research on ritual admonishing to further point out why it is advantageous for the ritual pragmatician to study such phenomena with the aid of a finite and replicable set of speech acts. Section 9.3 presents the data and methodology of the case study, Section 9.4 includes the analysis, while Section 9.5 provides a conclusion. Note that while similar to Chapter 8, the present chapter reports on a case study, the analytic framework outlined in the methodology section is replicable in other speech act-anchored ritual investigations.

9.2   The Study of Ritual Admonishing as a Speech Act Suggest: Retrospection

Previous research in pragmatics mainly defined 'admonish(ing)' as a specific 'speech act'. Such research includes, for example, Reinach (see an overview of Reinach's early work in DuBois 2002), as well as various studies on Chinese pragmatics (e.g., Chen 2011). A key problem with such research is what has already been described in this chapter: it is of little use to identify an 'exotic' speech act with no linguacultural or contemporary equivalent because such an approach shuts the door on replicability.

Some other researchers considered admonishing outside of the speech act paradigm. In historical pragmatics in particular, a limited number of studies have analysed the act of admonishing in various linguacultural settings, including Chinese (Shen & Chen 2019), Old English (Green 1995), Middle English (Hostetler 2012), the French classical period (Kerbrat-Orecchioni 2011) and, of course, the Bible (e.g., Houston 1993). While various scholars, such as Hostetler (2012), have drawn attention to the face-threatening nature of admonishing, the majority of previous research has focused on admonishing in family contexts where the admonisher is higher ranked than the admonished (for an exception, see e.g., Shen & Chen 2019). Admonishing powerful political actors, such as rulers, was also quite common in many historical linguacultures, as the following extract indicates:

Trajanus called his senate his father; for as the father doth foretell his son of the good or ill that may befall him, so ought the senate to admonish the king of things profitable, and unprofitable, to him and the state. (*Cobbett's Parliamentary History of England, Volume 1*, 1049)

Of all the examples from 'Western' linguacultures, it is perhaps the Bible which most clearly illustrates the historical importance of admonishing because it includes numerous cases in which the kings of ancient Israel were admonished by the prophets (see an overview in Petersen 2002). Notwithstanding the important contribution the above-outlined research has made for pragmatics, from a ritual point of view it has failed to conduct replicable research. Such a replicability could have been achieved if these scholars had attempted to consider how the phenomenon under investigation relates to replicable speech acts. The same problem applies to those previous scholars who have considered admonishing directed at those in power. For instance, McCabe (2008: 233) distinguishes the speech act category 'Divine Judgement' in the context of the Bible – although setting up such a separate speech act category is clearly an unnecessary terminological proliferation. In a similar fashion, Houston (1993) focuses on prophetic 'judgements' when describing face threats in the Old Testament.

The current case study follows the previously introduced approach to admonishing by subsuming it under the speech act category 'Suggest'. It should be noted that while some scholars such as Kallia (2005) made a distinction between the speech act categories 'Suggest' and 'Advise', they have been more often used interchangeably in pragmatics. I agree with this latter view, and in order to integrate the present research into the speech act typology used in Edmondson and House (1981) and House and Kádár (2021a), I only use the term 'Suggest'. The definition of Suggest is based on Edmondson and House (1981: 124) who define this speech act as follows:

The Suggest as an illocution is analysed as the case in which a speaker communicates that he is in favour of H's [i.e., the hearer's] performing a future action as in H's own interests, while in the case of the Request, the future action to be performed by H was claimed to be in the interests of the speaker. . . . Thus, while we intend that the distinction between our terms Request and Suggest reflect a semantic distinction between the terms REQUEST and SUGGEST as lexical items, we may well find a Requestive term such as BEG used in the making of a Suggest, and the term SUGGEST used to make what would seem quite clearly to be a Request: – Do go and see a doctor about it, I beg you – I suggest you let me get on with my work now

What makes certain forms of admonishing difficult to study resides in the paradoxical feature of this ritual phenomenon, i.e., that admonishing may not only be provided from a power position but also by the non-powerful side (see more below). In Ancient Chinese studied in this chapter, the relevance of power relations in admonishing is indicated beautifully at the lexical level because Classical Chinese uses two distinct characters for 'admonishing', namely:

- *xun* 訓: a term used to describe an instance of admonishment which is delivered by a person in power, such as a father admonishing his child;
- *jian* 諫: a term which describes an instance of admonishment delivered by a minister to a ruler, or a lower-ranking person towards a higher-ranking one.

Jian, as a culturally embedded ritual, has been widely studied in Chinese academia, albeit primarily outside the realm of pragmatics: Chinese scholars have approached the study of *jian* principally in the fields of literature and political science. Those linguists who have explored *jian* have mainly focused on its stylistic (see Han 2018; Ke 2012; Ning 2012) and rhetorical characteristics (see He 2003; Mao & Hou 2007). These studies reveal that, in ancient China, admonishing the ruler on matters of governance had long been regarded as a moral obligation of loyal officials and, therefore, became an institutionalised form of ritual behaviour. For instance, during imperial China, an institutional official rank (*jianguan* 諫官 'admonishing official') was created: officials fulfilling this role were dutybound to critically admonish the ruler when this was perceived to be necessary. Consequently, in historical China, admonishments were not *ad hoc* in nature, but were conducted in the form of ceremonies. Admonishing the ruler was not without its dangers: just as various Speakers of the British Parliament were executed over the centuries (see Bull, Fetzer & Kádár 2020), various outspoken Chinese officials were also executed, lost their careers, or were exiled to remote parts of the empire (see Zeng 2019). As a result of the dangers that were associated with admonishing, ritual customs were designed to 'purify' the participants. Officials performing the act of admonishing wore a special ceremonial robe which differed from the ordinary, highly adorned clothes that officials normally wore in court. Both the ruler and the officials fasted before the rite of admonishing commenced (Cai 2009).

As this review of previous sinological research shows, it is definitely worth studying admonishing, which represents a complex ritual, from a pragmatic point of view. In the following, let us discuss the data and methodology through which the present case study aims to achieve this goal. As already mentioned, the methodological take proposed here is replicable in other speech act-anchored ritual inquiries.

9.3   Data and Methodology

The corpus of this case study includes 362 occurrences of admonishing which were chosen on the basis of the above-outlined definition of admonishing, as a realisation type of Suggest. In order to test whether ancient Chinese realisations of admonishing suit this definition, before engaging in a corpus investigation of a large scope, the research team which I led conducted a small pilot study by examining the ancient Chinese Classic *The Commentary of Zuo* (*Zuozhuan* 左传). We focused only on cases in which admonishing is made to a ruler. The pilot study revealed that instances of admonishing not only include cases in which the Chinese character occurs as a metapragmatic reference to the act of admonishing, but all other cases in which a Suggest is realised in a face/power-threatening sense (see Shen & Chen 2019).

The corpus of this case study consists of the following sources:

Table 9.1 *Overview of sources of the present corpus*

Source	Summary	Number of admonishments
1. *Zuozhuan* 左傳 *The Commentary of Zuo*	An ancient chronicle of thirty chapters covering a period from 722 to 468 BC, which focuses primarily on political, diplomatic and military affairs from that era. This work was composed during the fourth century BC.	157
2. *Yanzi Chunqiu* 晏子春秋 *Annals of Master Yan*	An ancient Chinese text from the Warring States period (475–221 BC). This text contains a collection of stories, speeches and remonstrations that have been attributed to Yan Ying, a famous official from the State of Qi.	74
3. *Shiji* 史記 *Records of the Grand Historian*	The history of ancient China that was completed around 94 BC.	51
4. *Guoyu* 國語 *Discourses of the States*	An ancient Chinese text that consists of a collection of speeches which have been attributed to rulers and other men from the Spring and Autumn period (771–476 BC).	37
5. *Lüshi Chunqiu* 呂氏春秋 *Master Lü's Spring and Autumn Annals*	An encyclopaedic, classical Chinese text that was compiled around 239 BC.	21
6. *Zhan Guo Ce* 戰國策 *Annals of the Warring States*	An ancient collection of anecdotes of political manipulation and warfare during the Warring States period.	10
7. *Guanzi* 管子 *Master Guan*	An ancient Chinese political and philosophical text that is named after and has traditionally been attributed to the philosopher and statesman, Guan Zhong who lived in the seventh century BC.	12

The corpus consists only of multiple-source – rather than single-source – manifestations of *jian*, i.e., this case study focuses on instances in which the admonishment is made in the form of a dialogue between a minister, or a philosopher, and the ruler of a kingdom. As mentioned before, all the sources studied date from before the second century BC, i.e., the ancient period of Classical Chinese. During this time, i.e., before China was united by the Qin Dynasty in 221 BC, various countries fought for hegemony over the empire. *Jian* flourished during this tumultuous period because it was regarded as a minister's sacred duty to help his ruler overcome perils and secure victory over other countries by admonishing him if an error in governance had occurred/was perceived to be looming (see e.g., Galvany 2012).

Since Classical Chinese was essentially a written language. it is likely that the instances of admonishing that are studied here were reconstructed and edited after the actual events had taken place – which could, potentially, be quite some time later. However, since ancient *jian* can only be accessed by using sources that are similar to the ones we are employing, I do not think that the present corpus is somehow 'imperfect' as that would raise broader concerns regarding the validity of historical pragmatic data in general (see Jacobs & Jucker 1995). Also, this case study does not examine whether a particular historical event in the corpus actually took place, as this aspect is of secondary importance to the historical pragmatic study of the realisation of admonishing.

The present case study is anchored in the historical pragmatic analysis of the ways in which the unit of speech act is embedded in interaction. Brinton (2001) defines this approach as 'diachronically oriented discourse analysis', while Jacobs and Jucker (1995) refer to it as 'diachronic pragmatics'. It is important to emphasise here again that, according to House and Kádár (2021a), speech act is inseparable from discourse, and as part of studying the unit speech act we need to focus on both of its realisation through expressions and the ways in which it is embedded in discourse. Accordingly, this case study pursues the following replicable procedure of looking at two different aspects of a ritual phenomenon like admonishing when studying it through the lens of speech act:

– Lexical expressions which indicate the standard situation and the related ritual frame of ceremonial admonishments. As already noted in this book, standard situations tend to have a ritual character, and expressions that indicate standard situations can be referred to as ritual frame indicating expressions (RFIEs). It is important to note here that while communicating in standard situations is normally meant to be easier than interacting in other contexts, standard situations can also trigger painfully laborious facework: for instance, highly ritual ceremonies in which facework is of great import-ance are also standard for those who participate in them. In methodological terms, the departure point for the analysis of expressions in the present corpus is the following: if an expression is found to frequently occur in face-threatening admonishments, then it is very likely that this expression, in some way, indicates that the given admonishment is part of a ritual, i.e., the official or philosopher who realises admonishing as a form of Suggest has a certain sense of right or is even obliged to perform it.

– On the discourse level, the methodology proposed here involves identifying recurrent – and, as such, conventionalised – patterns by which instances of a ritual like admonishing are realised. In the present case study, the team of researchers involved defined these means as 'discursive practices' to avoid using the term 'strategy' as employed by Brown and Levinson (1987) because, as part of the aforementioned paradox, the discursive practices that are being studied here increased, rather than decreased, the face threat that admonishing normally implied.

Figure 9.1 illustrates the operation of the analytic procedure outlined here:

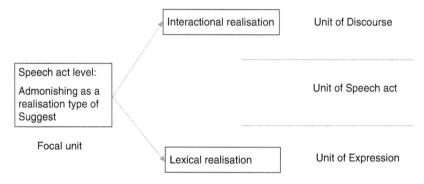

Figure 9.1 Proposed analytic procedure.

Figure 9.1 embodies the argument of House and Kádár (2021a) that different pragmatic units cannot be studied in a separate way: when it comes to the unit of speech act, we need to systematically consider its lexical and interactional (discourse level) realisations. In the case of studying admonishing, such realisations are highly conventionalised, considering the admonishing triggers a ritual frame, in which rights and obligation and related pragmatic conventions are very clear to all participants involved.

It is worth noting in passing that similar to what has been argued elsewhere in this book, the framework proposed here captures the ritual phenomenon under investigation outside of the conventional politeness paradigm. While issues such as face threat are politeness-relevant, in understanding the paradox identified in the present case study it is of little use to consider politeness in an individualised sense. This is because the face threats involved in admonishing are *meant to happen* according to the interactional and moral order of the ritual, i.e., they do not represent individual choices but rather ritual rights and obligations. Also, as already noted above, RFIEs and other pragmatic inventories of admonishing often increase rather than decrease face threat, i.e., they do not represent 'politeness tools' in the conventional sense.

9.4   Analysis

9.4.1   Setting the Scene: Admonishing as a Paradoxical Phenomenon

As it has been already noted on various occasions, the ritual of admonishing manifests itself as a paradox. In other circumstances, any situation in which a clear hierarchy applies would prevent threatening the face of the higher-ranking participant; criticising a ruler who was invested with absolute power and sacred celestial-like status would thus have had serious consequences. However, as the current analysis will show, the act of admonishing operated within a ritual frame, which facilitated the crossing of the boundary between sacred ruler and his subordinate. By following the conventions of this ritual frame, the admonishing official could express a view which, according to him, best served the interest of the ruler. This is where the paradox resides, at least from a modern etic perspective; that is, unlike in ordinary circumstances, within a ritual frame of admonishing, the admonisher had specific rights and obligations that allowed him to use language in ways that would have normally transgressed the status-related boundaries between himself and the ruler. Of course, this was subject to the fact that an admonishment was realised in an institutionalised ceremonial fashion and was not *ad hoc* in nature. This paradox meant that an admonishment was conducted by using conventionalised tools to express directness, and this seems to contradict – from a present day perspective – the face threat that the admonishment might create.

It is important to bear in mind that not all forms of admonishment include this sense of paradox. That is, the paradox only emerges if we examine admonishing in a ruler–subordinate relationship.

9.4.2   Ritual Frame Indicating Expressions Indicating the Ritual Frame of Admonishing and Expressions Downgrading Their Force

The examination of the present corpus shows that when ministers and philosophers admonished their rulers, they frequently deployed a limited inventory of RFIEs to indicate that the admonishment was part of an institutionalised ritual practice. These RFIEs were often embedded in the conventionalised interactional practices that facilitated the realisation of admonishing, and they indicated awareness of the ritual situation holding for the participants, and the related rights and obligations. By deploying an RFIE conventionally associated with admonishing as a realisation type of the speech act Suggest, Chinese officials not only indicated their awareness of the ceremonial situation holding for the participants, but also framed admonishing as a conventional realisation of a ritual Suggest.

Classical Chinese is a heavily formulaic, written medium: classical Chinese texts not only frequent formulaic prose (e.g., four-character units) but they also tend to be heavily loaded with honorifics and other formal expressions. The frequency with which certain formulae are used to realise admonishing as a ritual Suggest is therefore particularly important in the current research: if a particular formulaic expression is frequently used when a ritual Suggest is performed, then this expression indicates a ritual frame. Table 9.2 summarises the RFIEs that were found to indicate the ritual frame of admonishing in the corpus:

Table 9.2 *Types and frequency of ritual frame indicating expressions in the corpus*

Ritual frame indicating expression	Number of occurrences in the corpus	Relative frequency
jin 今 'in present times'	122	33.7%
xi 昔 'in ancient times'	27	7.5%
gu ... jin ... 古 ... 今 ... 'in old times ... presently ... '	20	5.5%
buke 不可 'no, you should not'	65	18.0%
weike 未可 'no, you should not'	2	0.5%

The figures in Table 9.2 represent relative and not absolute frequencies, that is, the table shows the number of instances of admonishment (out of a total of 362 in the corpus) in which RFIEs were deployed. As the figures in the table indicate, two RFIEs – which are highlighted in grey – are particularly frequent in the corpus, while the remaining three RFIEs are their variants. Even if a particular expression qualifies as an RFIE, this does not mean that it somehow 'belongs' to a specific ritual setting. Rather, its frequency indicates that a particular speech act realisation pattern is ritual.

In terms of pragmatic use, the RFIEs in Table 9.2 can be divided into two different but interrelated groups. The first group which includes *jin* 今 'in present times' and its variants *xi* 昔 'in ancient times' and *gu ... jin ...* 古 ... 今 ... 'in old times ... presently ... ' refer to a precedent, from which the speech act Suggest can be deduced. Referring to precedents is a common practice in many ceremonial and institutionalised standard situations, spanning courtrooms to church ceremonies, and so it is evident that, in the ritual of admonishing, these RFIEs indicate that the Suggest is not *ad hoc* in nature but rather is part of a ceremony. In a highly face-threatening situation, such as admonishing a sacred ruler, it is fundamentally important to 'disarm' any face threat by deindividuating (see Garcés-Conejos Blitvich 2015) the admonisher. By so doing, the admonisher's realisation of Suggest is more likely to be interpreted within a ritual frame. Example 9.1 illustrates the use of the RFIE *jin*:

Example 9.1   晏子曰：'臣聞明君必務正其治，以事利民，然后子孫享之。 詩雲：'武王豈不事，貽厥孫謀，以燕翼子。' 今君處佚怠，逆政害民有日矣，而猶出若言，不亦甚乎！' 《晏子春秋》

Master Yan[3] said, 'This minister (i.e. "I") heard that a wise monarch governs the state with appropriacy, implements policies favourable to the people, in order to benefit future generations.' The *Book of Odes* says, 'King Wu of the Zhou Dynasty[4] took his role as a king very seriously, so his deeds were passed down to later generations and benefitted his descendants.' At present (*jin*), you, my lord, are loitering and care for nothing. You have violated the rules of governance and have harmed the people for a long time. How can you speak like this [referring to the words of the ruler that triggered the admonishment]? Is this not highly inappropriate? (*Annals of Master Yan*)[5]

Many present-day readers might well be surprised by the harsh tone of the admonishment in Example 9.1. In ancient China, admonishing could in fact be very direct, although this directness was mitigated in a number of ways, most notably by honorific 'downgraders' (see Edmondson 1981 on downgrading) which were used as deferential forms of address and self-reference.[6] Table 9.3 indicates the two most frequently occurring downgraders in the corpus of this case study:

Table 9.3 *Frequently used honorific expressions in the corpus*

Expression	Number of admonishments which included the expression (out of a total of 362)	Relative frequency
1. *jun* 君 'you, my lord'	288	79.6%
2. *chen* 臣 'I, this minister'	109	30.1%

As Table 9.3 illustrates, in the majority of cases in the corpus the admonisher deploys downgrading forms of address or self-reference. What is important here is the high frequency with which these downgraders occur. One could justifiably argue that these forms of address and self-reference were used in many different settings outside of the ruler–official relationship. However, in such settings these expressions were generally used much less frequently for admonishing purposes. This tendency is logical when one considers that, in historical linguacultures such as ancient Chinese, being disrespectful towards a ruler was a deadly sin. Thus, it is evident that the harshness witnessed in the admonishment was only possible because the setting was institutionalised, and honorifics reinforced this sense of institutionalisation, as the following example illustrates:

Example 9.2   晏子曰: '昔文王不敢盤於游田, 故國昌而民安。楚靈王不廢干溪之役, 起章華之台, 而民叛之。 今君不革, 將危社稷, 而為諸侯笑。臣聞忠臣不避死, 諫不違罪。君不聽臣, 臣將逝矣。' 《晏子春秋》

Master Yan said, 'In ancient times, King Wen[7] knew that he should not squander his time by indulging in hunting, and his kingdom was prosperous, and the people enjoyed peace. King Chuling,[8] however, led his country into the War of the Creek of Gan and during the war he even built the Palace of Zhanghua at very high cost, and it was not surprising that his people finally revolted. If today you, <u>my lord</u> (*jun*), fail to implement reforms, the kingdom will be at a great risk and you will be mocked by the dukes. <u>This minister</u> (*chen*) heard that faithful ministers are not afraid of death, and advisers are not afraid of being punished. If <u>you, my lord</u> (*jun*), do not take the advice of <u>this minister</u> (*chen*), <u>this minister</u> (*chen*) is ready to step down' (*Annals of Master Yan*)

In Example 9.2, the honorific term *jun* occurs twice and *chen* three times. It is important to note here that historical Chinese honorifics were very strongly indexical in nature (Agha 1998), that is, each honorific indicated a very specific relationship between the speaker and the recipient (see Kádár 2007). For example, the above honorifics were used exclusively by state ministers who had the institutional right to admonish the ruler in ancient China. This had a fundamental consequence for the role of these honorifics as downgraders. That is, in a context in which the face and power of the ruler was threatened, uttering these terms, and hence indexically showcasing awareness of the relationship holding for the situation and the related authority of the ruler, ensured that the situation became safer for the admonisher.

Another RFIE group which is salient in the present corpus is *buke* 不可 (lit. 'you cannot') and its variant *weike* 未可, both of which indicate strong moral opposition when the speaker realises Suggest in the form of an admonishment. These expressions are very direct, and therefore it is evident that they could only ever be deployed as part of an institutionalised ritual practice:

Example 9.3   伍員曰: '不可。臣聞之:樹德莫如滋, 去疾莫如盡....' 《左傳》

Wu Yuan[9] said to the king: '<u>No, you should not (*buke*)</u>'. This minister heard the following: 'Morality should be nurtured at all times, until all evil is eradicated. . . . ' (*Zuozhuan*)

In the corpus of this case study, the RFIE *buke* almost always occurs at the beginning of an admonishment, and any mitigation, including the aforementioned honorifics, tend to follow it. The fact that this RFIE was deployed as an introductory move in the admonishment implies that it operated as a ceremonial form at the start of the admonishment.

Other expressions in the corpus function as boosters of the directness expressed by the RFIE *buke*. Most significantly, various officials deploy the imperative adverb *qi* 其 in their admonishments:

Example 9.4   公曰：'魯可取乎?' 對曰：'不可, 猶秉周禮。周禮, 所以本也。臣聞之, 國將亡, 本必先顛, 而后枝葉從之。 魯不棄周禮, 未可動也。君其務寧魯難而親之。...' 《左傳》

The lord asked: 'May we seize the state by force?' The advisor said: '<u>No, you cannot</u> (*buke*). For the state of Lu continues to follow the rites of Zhou and these rites are the foundation of any state.[10] This minister has heard the following: a state's destruction is like a tree. The trunk falls down first, and the twigs and leaves follow it. We cannot destroy Lu because it has its sacred rites. You, my lord, <u>must</u> (*qi*) help Lu to resolve its inner turmoil and form an alliance with it. . . . ' (*Zuozhuan*)

Following this overview of RFIEs and other expressions through which admonishing as a realisation type of Suggest operated according to the corpus of this case study, let us now examine two interactional practices in which admonishing was embedded.

9.4.3   Interactional Practice 1: Referring to Historical Figures

An important interactional practice that was used to realise the admonishing was the practice of referring to historical figures. In the present corpus of 362 instances of admonishment, making reference to historical figures occurs in seventy-one cases, i.e., this represents a conventionalised ritual practice with a frequency of occurrence of 19.6 per cent. While this ritual interactional practice can significantly increase the length of the admonishment and, as such, it may seem to be an interactional 'detour', it appears to have functioned as justification for the admonishment by providing a precedent. Here the length of the admonishment does not correlate with indirectness, and therefore it would be inappropriate to refer to this practice as a 'mitigatory strategy'.

Contrasting the Ruler with an Ancient Sovereign

A standard form of the aforementioned interactional practice includes those cases where the admonishing official contrasted the current ruler with an ancient mythical king, in the form of an open criticism. The following example illustrates the realisation of this type of admonishment:

Example 9.5   御孫諫曰：‘臣聞之：‘儉，德之共也；侈，惡之大也。’先君有共德而君納諸大惡，無乃不可乎！’《左傳》

Yu Sun advised: 'This minister (*chen*) has heard that frugality is the greatest moral virtue and extravagance is the greatest evil. The ancient kings were endowed with this greatest of all virtues, but you, my lord (*jun*) indulge yourself in the greatest evil. How can this be appropriate? (*Zuozhuan*)

Despite its directness, this interactional practice of unfavourably comparing the ruler with a highly respected predecessor was considered to be a conventional ritual realisation of admonishing due to the paradox mentioned above. In other words, the minister who deployed this interactional practice simultaneously realised a rather direct Suggest as an admonishment and downgraded it with honorifics, thereby indicating that he accepted the king's authority.

Contrasting the Ruler with His Father

While Example 9.5 is already face-threatening in nature, this sense of face threat appears to be further exacerbated when the admonisher refers to the ruler's immediate predecessor, by claiming that the latter was a better leader than his son. The following example illustrates this interactional practice:

Example 9.6   (晏子)對曰：‘...昔者先君桓公之地狹於今，修法治，廣政教，以霸諸侯。...今君不免成城之求，而惟傾城之務，國之亡日至矣。君其圖之！’《晏子春秋》

Master Yan said: 'In the past, the former lord, Duke Huan,[11] governed a state which was smaller than your kingdom today. However, he changed the law, hence dominating the princes. . . . Now, you, my lord (*jun*), failed to rule the land and engage in actions that could overturn the state. Thus, this country is doomed. You must (*qi*) consider this, my lord (*jun*).' (*Annals of Master Yan*)

In this example, the contrast between the current ruler and his father is made in an even more forceful manner when the official uses the previously discussed imperative adverb *qi* to urge the ruler to reform. In a similar way to the previous Example 9.5, the extreme directness of admonishing is paradoxically counterbalanced by the use of honorifics to indicate acceptance of the ruler's authority.

Providing Both Good and Bad Examples for the Ruler

Another way to realise the interactional practice being studied here is to simultaneously provide good and bad examples for the ruler. This is illustrated in the following example:

Example 9.7   楚子示諸侯侈，椒舉曰：'夫六王二公之事，皆所以示諸侯禮也，諸侯所由用命也。夏桀為仍之會，有緡叛之。商紂為黎之蒐，東夷叛之。周幽為大室之盟，戎狄叛之。皆所以示諸侯汰也，諸侯所由棄命也。今君以汰，無乃不濟乎?' 《左傳》

King Ling of Chu showed arrogance towards the princes of other states. His minister Jiao Ju said: 'The former Kings and Dukes treated the sovereigns of other states with courtesy, which is why their wish was respected. However, when King Jie of the Xia Dynasty[12] held the Assembly of Reng, the state of You Min revolted against him; when King Zhou of the Shang Dynasty held the Military Parade of Li, the tribe of East Yi betrayed him; when King You of the Zhou Dynasty made the Covenant of Taishi, the tribes of Rong and Di betrayed him. In all these cases, the princes revolted against the kings because they were treated most arrogantly. Now, <u>you, my lord</u> (*jun*) also show an arrogant manner towards your princes. How can this be appropriate?' (*Zuozhuan*)

In this case, while the historical precedent is lengthy and includes both positive and negative examples, it does not make the admonishment any less direct, and it is worth noting that negative precedents form the larger part of such narratives. Again, the paradox is particularly visible here because the official realising this direct form of admonishment is, at the same time, indicating that he accepts the authority of the ruler by deploying the honorific form of address *jun*. In addition, as he closes his admonishing, he adds a rhetorical question which downgrades the force of this ritual Suggest.

9.4.4   Interactional Practice 2: Quoting Ancient Sources

As Stanley (2004) argues, using quotations as a form of rhetoric is a fundamental pragmatic device in *Paul's Letters* and other ancient European sources. One can observe a similar interactional practice in the Chinese corpus of this case study: here the admonisher often uses one or more archaic sources to frame the admonishment. The most important of these sources is the *Book of Odes* (*Shijing* 詩經) and, to a lesser degree, the *Book of Documents* (*Shangshu* 尚書). The former is the oldest existing collection of Chinese poetry which comprises 305 works dating from the eleventh to the seventh century BC, while the latter is an ancient collection of prose attributed to mythical figures. Soon after these two works were complied, they were already considered to be 'classical' works in Ancient China and, as we will discuss in more detail below, they were believed to be sacred (see also e.g., Chen 2017). Table 9.4 summarises the number and frequency with which ancient sources were quoted in the corpus:

Table 9.4 *The frequency with which ancient sources were quoted in the corpus*

Source	Number of quotes	Frequency
Book of Odes, *Daya* 大雅 (*Major Court Hymns*) *Section*	11	3%
Book of Odes, *Xiaoya* 小雅 (*Lesser Court Hymns*) *Section*	11	3%
Book of Odes, *Zhou Song* 周頌 (*Eulogies of Zhou*) *Section*	6	1.7%
Book of Odes, *Guofeng* 國風 (*Airs of the States*) *Section*	3	0.8%
Book of Documents	15	4.1%
Other sources	10	2.8%
Total	56	15.5%

As Table 9.4 shows, quoting ancient sources – occurring fifty-six times in the present corpus – was a standard interactional practice in ancient China. This practice is similar to the previously discussed interactional practice of referring to historical figures and events.

When one examines the figures in Table 9.4, a notable historical pragmatic pattern emerges: when ministers and philosophers admonished their rulers, they preferred to quote sources regarded as 'reference material' by royalty and the aristocracy. According to Table 9.4, the *Book of Odes* was by far the most commonly quoted reference, and admonishers referred most frequently to the *Daya* 大雅 (*Major Court Hymns*) and *Xiaoya* 小雅 (*Lesser Court Hymns*) sections of this source. Both the *Daya* and *Xiaoya* belonged to the *Court Hymns* section of the *Book of Odes*, which included ceremonial poems that were used by the aristocracy to pray for good harvests each year, worship gods and venerate their ancestors. These sections were regarded as sacred in ancient China, and when deployed for admonishing purposes, they reinforced the ritual frame by which the paradoxical admonishing Suggest was realised. The importance of this interactional practice becomes particularly noticeable when one compares the frequency with which the *Daya* and *Xiaoya* quotes occur in the present corpus with the respective size of these sections in the *Book of Odes*:

Table 9.5 *The size of the sections of the* Book of Odes *quoted in admonishing*

Section	Number of poems
Guofeng Section	160
Xiaoya Section	74
Zhou Song Section	40
Daya Section	31

Guofeng – which constitutes by far the largest section of the *Book of Odes* according to Table 9.5 – was very rarely used in admonishing, as shown in Table 9.4. Although the *Guofeng* section formed part of the sacred classical text, the *Book of Odes*, and was therefore revered in ancient China, it only included poems which detailed the lives of ordinary people and, as such, was arguably irrelevant in the context of an admonishment. As the corpus of this case study shows, the admonisher most frequently criticised the ruler by referring either to a sacred poem which ritually represented the appropriate ceremonial behaviour of ancient aristocracy or, in a similar fashion, to the *Book of Documents* which included sacred prose about the deeds performed by ancient rulers.

Returning to the ritual pragmatic paradox in this case study, the quoting of sacred texts appears to be a particularly powerful way to criticise the ruler. By referring to such a sacred text, which was regarded, unanimously, to be authoritative and was in contrast with the admonished ruler's behaviour, the admonisher unavoidably challenged the ruler's authority. It is thus not a coincidence that, in those examples which feature the interactional practice of quoting, the admonisher almost always rather robustly downgraded the impact of this challenge, in both linguistic and non-linguistic ways. The following example illustrates this point:

Example 9.8   士蒍稽首而對曰：'臣聞之，無喪而戚, 憂必仇焉。無戎而城, 仇必保焉。寇仇之保, 又何慎焉!守官廢命不敬, 固仇之保不忠, 失忠與敬, 何以事君?《詩》雲：'懷德惟寧, 宗子惟城。' 君其修德而固宗子, 何城如之?三年將尋師焉, 焉用慎?' 《左傳》

Shiwei prostrated himself in front of the king and said: 'I, this minister (*chen*), have heard that if one mourns with no reason, trouble is certain to approach. Also, if one builds city walls without a war looming, the enemy is certain to occupy these walls. Now, as our city walls will be occupied by our enemies, why should we attempt to finish and fortify them? [I was criticised by my superior for the quality of the walls, saying that] I have not been following orders to build the wall, and also saying that I have been disrespectful to the sovereign. But if I fortify our walls just to profit our enemy, this would be lack of loyalty to our state. If respect and loyalty are lost, how can I serve you, my lord (*jun*)? The *Book of Odes* says: "Being kind to people brings peace to the state, and the family of the ruler will be as firm and strong as a wall." If you, my lord (*jun*) must cultivate your morality and reinforce your family's position, is this not much better than erecting walls? I believe that it will be three years before we need to wage war, so why are we now troubled about the walls?' (*Zuozhuan*)

As shown in Example 9.8, not only does the admonisher use some of the RFIEs, but he also indicates his utmost reverence to the ruler by kowtowing in front of him and realising the admonishment from the floor of the audience room. Although it was the custom for admonishing officials to kowtow in front of their ruler, the fact that the text mentions this deferential act appears to be salient, considering that the source *Zuozhuan* in which the example occurs does not in each case mention kowtowing. It is also important to note that the quote in the above example is taken from the sacred *Daya* section of the *Book of Odes*, and this gives strong ritual power to the admonishment.

In a number of examples in the present corpus, the person realising an admonishing appears to 'overwhelm' the ruler with his use of historical quotes. Example 9.9 illustrates this 'overwhelming' practice:

Example 9.9   對曰：'舜之罪也殛鯀, 其舉也興禹。管敬仲, 桓之賊也, 實相以濟。《康誥》曰："父不慈, 子不祗, 兄不友, 弟不共, 不相及也。"《詩》曰：'採葑採菲, 無以下體。' 君取節焉可也。' 《左傳》

> Jiu Ji replied: 'Formerly, Shun[13] put Gun to death according to the law, but he raised Yu, son of Gun. Guan Jingzhong[14] was an enemy of Duke Huan of Qi, but the duke appointed him as his Minister and he served the duke with loyalty. The Kanggao[15] says: "If one's father lacks kindness, a son lacks reverence, an elder brother lacks friendship and a younger brother lacks respect, it is them and not their kin who should be punished." The *Book of Odes* says: "When you gather the turnips and the radishes you do not throw away the roots and eat only the leaves." When you, my lord (*jun*), appoint a person, you must make use of his strength.' (*Zuozhuan*)

In this case, the admonisher only expresses his own opinion in the very last sentence of the admonishment, with the body of the admonishment being either quotations or references to historical figures.

9.5   Conclusion

In this chapter, we have continued discussing the first methodological take in the pragmatic research of ritual proposed in this book, by examining how speech acts associated with ritual can be examined in a replicable way. A key issue in the ritual study of such speech acts is the following: there are many seeming 'speech acts', like 'blessing' and 'admonishing' itself, which are popularly associated with ritual. However, it is highly problematic to define such phenomena as 'ritual speech acts' because that would imply that the ritualist can 'identify' new speech acts *ad libitum*. In order to avoid this pitfall, in the present chapter I have proposed to use a finite and replicable typology of speech acts to capture phenomena associated with ritual. As a case study, the chapter looked at ritual admonishing as a manifestation of the replicable illocutionary category Suggest. I have argued that admonishing is a historically embedded phenomenon, i.e., it is a realisation type of Suggest which existed in an institutionalised, ceremonial form in ancient China and other historical linguacultures.

The case study of the present chapter has pursued a replicable methodological take through which ritual can be approached through the lens of speech acts (see Figure 9.1), by focusing on the RFIEs and interactional practices through which this speech act realisation type operated. I argued that the pragmatic features of admonishing in ancient China are seemingly paradoxical when viewed from a modern etic perspective. The paradox is the following: in many historical linguacultures, an admonishment was directed at a recipient of significantly higher ranking than the admonisher himself. In perhaps no other circumstances was it acceptable to criticise the ruler because of the absolute power and sacred, celestial-like status with which ancient rulers were invested. Certain historical systems of governance, like that of ancient China, permitted admonishing, insofar as this act occurred within a ceremonial ritual frame of interaction, which created a protected interactional environment for the safe operation of the admonishment without challenging the ruler's authority beyond what was absolutely necessary. This 'protection' did not necessarily mean that it was always safe to admonish the ruler, because the admonisher could be executed or demoted. The ritual frame indicated by conventionalised realisations of admonishing Suggest helped to reduce the dangers associated with admonishing, as these dangers would have been considerably greater if the admonishing had unfolded as a non-ritual *ad hoc* act.

After having illustrated how the first methodological take in the pragmatic research of ritual proposed in this book operates in Chapters 8 and 9, in the following let us move onto the discussion of the second methodological take.

9.6   Recommended Reading

Xygalatas, D. (2022) *Ritual: How Seemingly Senseless Acts Make Life Worth Living*. London: Profile Books.

The phenomenon of paradox very often emerges in the context of ritual because ritual behaviour involves seemingly unnecessary aspects of life, which are however compulsory and important across societies and cultures. A certain sense of paradox is also present in the typology of Edmondson and House (1981) that I have referred to throughout this book, which associates ritual with seemingly 'empty' but interactionally important speech acts like Greet. The present chapter has discussed a specific paradox, which is encoded in the DNA of the ritual under investigation. Readers with interest in ritual paradoxes are advised to consult the recent authoritative study of Xygalatas, which discusses this topic in detail. The following excerpt is from the work of Xygalatas:

Rituals are central to virtually all our social institutions. Think of a judge waving a gavel or a new president taking an oath of office. They are held by militaries, governments and corporations, in initiation ceremonies, parades and costly displays of commitment. They are used by athletes who always wear the same socks in important games, and by gamblers who kiss the dice or cling on to lucky charms when the stakes are high. And in our everyday life they are practised by each and every one of us when we raise a glass to make a toast, attend a graduation ceremony or take part in a birthday celebration. The need for ritual is primeval, and, as we shall see, may have played a pivotal role in human civilisation.

But what drives us all to engage in these behaviours, which have tangible costs without any directly obvious benefits? And why are these activities often held to be so deeply meaningful, even as their purpose is so often obscure? (Xygalatas 2022: 2–3)

10 Methodological Take-2A: Capturing Ritual Practices

10.1 Introduction

The remaining two chapters of Part III will discuss how the second methodological take on ritual can be put into practice. As was argued before, there are many complex ritual phenomena which can only be studied from a pragmatic angle in a replicable way if one attempts to interpret them through pragmatic units of analysis. Here complexity means that

1. a particular phenomenon is either too broad to be discussed as a single ritual, i.e., it represents a form of ritual behaviour which spans across many different ritual contexts and frames, or
2. like military training, it represents a particular context and related ritual frame which triggers ritual behaviour but cannot be subsumed under a single ritual heading from the pragmatician's point of view.

In the study of such phenomena, it is advisable for the researcher to depart from interpreting ritual in a bottom–up way by first considering the frame or frames in which the ritual under investigation occurs and then systematically studying how ritual manifests itself in such frames.

The present chapter focuses on the first of these cases: it explores the ritual phenomenon of self-denigration in Chinese, which has already been touched on in Chapter 6. Self-denigration occurs in a broad variety of Chinese interaction rituals and ceremonies, and if one attempts to describe its pragmatic features by relying on data drawn from a single context, one unavoidably risks oversimplifying it. This is why, in Chapter 6, self-denigration was mentioned as part of a broader ritual competition, rather than a 'ritual' on its own. In the study of such an interaction ritual phenomenon the arguably best academic practice is to consider how it is used in different interpersonal scenarios with varying power and intimacy and in different phases of an interaction, which both imply varying ritual frames with differing rights and obligations.

Similarly to other chapters in Part III of this book, this chapter provides a case study. This case study will illustrate the operation of a replicable and strictly language-based analytic procedure through which pragmatic phenomena representing the first type of complex ritual outlined above can be studied. The procedure described here can be used for various goals, largely depending on the agenda of the researcher. For example, one may first describe the contextual spread of an interaction ritual to identify differences between its use in contexts dominated by power versus others where the power variable is absent, and then consider how social hierarchy influences language use. In this chapter, I will use the proposed procedure to distinguish purely deferential ritual uses of self-denigration from cases when this phenomenon lubricates the flow of an interaction, which is a relevant issue to consider because this book has a vested interest in the ritual and politeness perspectives.

As was noted before in this book, the notion 'self-denigration' refers to the act of humbling oneself, one's family member, or one's property/belonging. Self-denigration is often realised in combination with elevating the other, and it is a phenomenon popularly associated with East Asian languages.[1] Self-denigration is an essentially ritual phenomenon: all participants involved in an act of self-denigration usually know that humbling themselves is not necessarily genuine, and also forms of self-denigration tend to ritually reinforce or define the rights and obligations holding for a particular context. Self-denigration therefore has a predominantly social meaning through which the speaker expresses deference by default and indicates both her own social status and that of her interlocutor. For example, in historical Chinese, the self-denigrating expression *wansheng* 晚生 ('late born') was often used by young officials, and by uttering this expression the speaker not only humbled himself but also indicated that he belongs to the elite. While Chapter 6 already described the types of expressions through which self-denigration was realised in Chinese, in the following I outline again the most important types of such expressions:

- Adjective+noun compound expressions, such as *xiaoren* 小人 (lit. 'small man'), an expression used by speakers of any rank;
- Verbal forms, such as *guigao* 跪告 (lit. 'announcing on kneel'), an expression used when a lower-ranking speaker tells a piece of news to a higher-ranking hearer.

There are also more complex realisations of self-denigration in Chinese (Kádár 2007; see also Chapter 6), but as this list shows, unlike in Japanese and Korean, self-denigration in Chinese is not part of morphology, and in historical Chinese in particular, self-denigration was realised by a rich repertoire of expressions. The case study of this chapter focuses on self-denigration in vernacular Chinese novels written between the mid-fourteenth and the twentieth centuries.

While self-denigration in Chinese has been extensively studied in pragmatics, previous research has often examined this phenomenon in a lexico-semantic way, i.e., through zeroing in on self-denigration by studying the pragmatic function of expressions selected by the researcher at the very outset of the research. As has already been noted, rather than following a top–down approach where one first identifies expressions of self-denigration and then interprets their use, the present chapter relies on a bottom–up model through which self-denigration can be captured in sampled data in phases of interactions, as well as speech acts occurring in these phases.

The structure of this chapter is as follows. Section 10.2 provides a review of relevant literature on self-denigration in Chinese, including previous politeness-anchored research on this phenomenon. The discussion will show that when it comes to self-denigration, once again we have a phenomenon on hand which can be more accurately understood through the ritual perspective than through the politeness one, even though politeness may also have to be considered in the study of certain manifestations of this phenomenon. Section 10.3 introduces our methodology and data. Section 10.4 presents the analysis and results of the case study. Finally, Section 10.5 provides a conclusion.

10.2   The Study of Self-denigration in Chinese: Retrospection

In pragmatics, and in linguistic politeness research in particular, the study of 'self-denigration' has a long history, starting with Gu's (1990) seminal work. Gu presented self-denigration as a form of politeness, characterised by a strongly ceremonial style. He argued that self-denigration is an essentially Chinese form of pragmatic behaviour, and he used his study of this phenomenon to criticise Brown and Levinson's (1987) renowned universalist approach to politeness. Gu's research prompted academic interest in self-denigration in Chinese. Since historical Chinese, unlike its modern counterpart, was honorific-rich, some scholars have examined this phenomenon in historical data including, for example, Kádár (2007, 2010, 2012), Pan and Kádár (2011), Xu (2013) and Li (2022). However, many more scholars have studied this phenomenon in modern Chinese including, for example, Chen (1993), Huang (2008), Chen (2010), Ren and Woodfield (2016), Chen (2019), Mai et al. (2021) and Zhou (2022), to mention some representative examples. An important insight achieved by this latter group of researchers is that they have clarified how self-denigration in the 'honorific-poor' modern Chinese linguaculture differs from its historical counterpart. This clarification is important because Gu (1990) mainly used historical forms of self-denigration to illustrate his views on modern Chinese. Like Gu, many scholars have approached self-denigration in a lexico-semantic way: they first determined which expressions they wanted to study in their data before examining the data itself. An exception to this trend includes the research of Chen (1993, 2020) who studied self-denigration both as it emerges in interactional responsive moves and as a strategy in academic writing. Some others approached self-denigration in particular speech acts, without however considering their embeddedness in inter-action (see e.g., Tang & Zhang 2009). Such approaches fall short of the full picture of the operation of self-denigration.

Self-denigration has also been studied outside of the Chinese linguacul-tural context, including, for example, the use of English as a lingua franca on the Internet (see e.g., Walkinshaw et al. 2019; Page 2019), academic English writing (e.g., Itakura & Tsui 2011), academic discussions (e.g., Mayahi & Jalilifar 2022; Jalilifar & Mayahi 2022) and natural conversation (e.g., Boxer & Cortés-Conde 1997), to mention some representative examples. A funda-mental merit of such research is that it has made it clear that 'self-denigra-tion' is certainly not an exclusively 'Chinese' or even 'East Asian' phenomenon.[2] Many such studies on self-denigration were based on dis-course analysis, supposedly because self-denigration in 'Western' lingua-cultures tends to be somewhat less formulaic than self-denigration in East Asian linguacultures (see Kádár 2007). The current case study aligns itself with this research strand, in that I conceptualise the use of Chinese self-denigrating expressions from an interactional point of view. However, the model proposed will also take one step further: instead of limiting research to the unit of discourse only, I approach the interactional use of self-denigrating expressions in Chinese through the lens of speech acts and larger units of interaction, by integrating the analysis into interaction ritual theory. Examining self-denigration by looking at the building blocks of discourse allows one to consider conventionalised and recurrent uses of self-denigra-tion beyond the use of individual expressions, which is fundamental if one considers that self-denigration in Chinese is an interaction ritual widely present in everyday civilities.

The present case study of self-denigration – and the analytic framework proposed – also allows considering again why the ritual perspective can be particularly useful in the study of the conventionalised use of phenomena associated with politeness. Since self-denigrating expressions in Chinese are honorifics, their research is relevant to previous pragmatic debates on Ide's (1989) notion of 'discernment', i.e., the idea that honorifics in Japanese and other honorific-rich languages are by default not used in a strategic way in Brown and Levinson's (1987) sense (see also Chapter 2). For example, according to Ide, when Japanese students talk about their lecturer, they cannot freely decide whether to 'strategically' use honorifics or not because the use of honorifics in such a context is prescribed by the situation. Ide's criticism of Brown and Levinson was very close to what Gu (1990) argued about Chinese self-denigration: both Ide and Gu pro-vided critical views on universalistic definitions of politeness. However, several scholars argued that while honorifics in languages such as Japanese tend to indicate social hierarchies, they may also be used strategically. O'Driscoll (1996) was one of the first scholars who raised this issue in general, and Okamoto (1999), Usami (2002) and Pizziconi (2003, 2011) have also all shown that the usage of honorifics can be strategic in Japanese. In Kádár (2007), I argued that the same strategic use of honorifics can be observed in historical vernacular Chinese data.[3] Many of these scholars have also argued that honorifics are not always used to show politeness, i.e., they can fulfil other interactional functions as well, such as indicating irony, aesthetics, or social distance. In addition, failure to normatively apply honorifics does not inherently entail a face threat: interactants in Japanese and other honorific-rich languages tend to make (often seemingly random) switches between honorific and non-honorific styles (see Cook 1998, 2005). In other words, honorifics afford a dual use: on the one hand they can indicate social hierarchies as described by Ide, while they can also fulfil other interactional goals. I argue that defining self-denigrating honorifics as manifestations of interaction ritual, instead of using the concept discernment – anchored in the politeness paradigm – helps us to capture the above-outlined dual use of honorifics. The concept of interaction ritual implies that self-denigration essentially indicates social hierarchies and related rights and obligations, while at the same time it can help the speaker to lubricate the machinery of interaction. As Chapter 9 has already shown, ritual affords strategic pragmatic behaviour such as downgrading, even though such strategic language use may not overrule the potentially non-strategic nature of a ritual (e.g., the admonishing of a ruler). Lubricating the flow of an interaction is clearly an interactional strategy in the conventional sense of the word.[4]

10.3   Methodology and Data

10.3.1   Methodology

In the following, I outline a methodology that in my view can be used in a replicable way for the study of ritual phenomena like self-denigration in Chinese, which manifest themselves in many different contexts and in the form of different frames, i.e., which are abstract from an analytic point of view.

In this framework, one approaches ritual phenomena through three inter-related units: expressions, speech acts and discourse (see also Chapter 9), with the middle-sized unit of speech acts being at the centre of the analysis. One first collects data from various corpora (see more below) by sampling dialogues which include realisations of the ritual under investigation – in the present case, self-denigrating expressions. During this procedure, one first needs to relate verbal manifestations of the ritual to their interactional context of occurrence, by considering the Type of Talk in which they occur. The concept of 'Type of Talk' was proposed in Edmondson and House (1981) and Edmondson et al. (2023): it consists of conventionalised episodes which are the building blocks of any interaction. This notion is pragmatic rather than conversation analytic, in that it has been developed to describe recurrent and coherent sequences of interaction from the point of view of speech acts. Type of Talk typically include the following categories: Opening, Core and Closing, with Core consisting of many different sub-types, such as Business, Corrective and Patch-Up Talk. Since each Type of Talk typically consists of certain speech act types, such as the speech act Apologise in Patch-Up Talk to provide a simple example, the study of expression level manifestations of a ritual embedded in Type of Talk also allows us to systematically consider the conventionalised relationship between expressions and speech acts. In House and Kádár (2021a), Juliane House and myself argued that such a study of the conventionalised relationship between expressions and speech acts in Type of Talk necessitates using a finite and interactional typology of speech acts. The proposed methodological framework is based on Edmondson and House's (1981) finite typology of speech acts, which I already presented in Chapter 8:

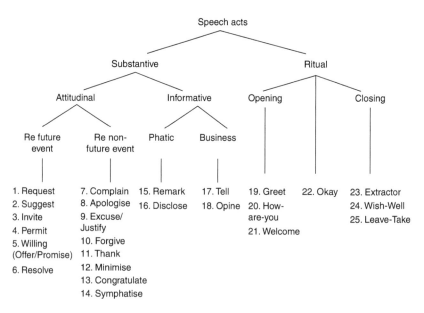

Figure 10.1 Edmondson and House's typology of speech acts (cited from Edmondson & House 1981: 98).

The above typology is finite, consisting of twenty-five strictly interactionally defined speech acts. This means that often-used labels such as 'refusal' or 'agree' are not speech acts in this system because they only have an interactional but no illocutionary value, unlike the speech acts in this system which all have both interactional and illocutionary values.[5] As was noted previously in this book, finiteness is a key of this system because – to refer to Willis Edmondson's seminal thought – it is no use introducing illocutions rather like a conjuror producing rabbits out of a hat, such that nobody knows where they come from, how many more there might be left in, or whether, indeed, the whole procedure is an illusion.[6] Importantly, the argument here is not that one should make a division between illocution and interaction because the two are inherently interconnected. Rather, illocutions become interlinked through interactional moves, which either Satisfy or Counter/Contra a previous move (see more in Edmondson et al. 2023; see also Chapter 11). For example, a Remark ('Your sweater is beautiful') can be Countered by a Minimise ('It's not at all'), and ritual self-denigration apparently comes into operation here as a speech act stepping into reaction with an Initiating speech act through an interactional move. The following Chapter 11 will outline how to use the above system of speech acts in the study of interactional moves in more detail.

In annotating ritual data according to the approach proposed here, one first needs to define the Types of Talk in which a given verbal ritual phenomenon – in the present case, self-denigrating expression – occurs, and then also annotate the type of speech act in which it is embedded, and also other speech acts co-occurring with that particular speech act.

As was already noted, a key advantage of the approach proposed here is that it allows the scholar to conduct a ritually anchored investigation. For example, in the present case study we will consider how a ritual phenomenon – self-denigration – is related to both interaction ritual conventions and individual strategies, in order to continue considering the relationship between the ritual and politeness perspective. As was already pointed out in this book, certain types of talk are essentially ritual in nature: Opening and Closing Talk (as well as Small Talk, although it is not present in the corpora studied in this chapter) trigger ritual engagement, with strictly defined conventions of language use. This implies that, in such Types of Talk, interaction ritual language use usually fits with what is contextually required and may not serve individual interactional (strategic) agendas by default.[7] In Business Talk and various other forms of Core Talk, however, interaction is generally goal-oriented and so one cannot usually predict whether an interaction ritual such as self-denigration only serves its conventional role, or rather an individual agenda. It is the above speech act system which helps the researcher to interpret whether such an individual interactional agenda is involved in the realisation of self-denigration, or not. The typology of speech acts in Figure 10.1 includes speech acts which are ritual in nature, such as Greet, Welcome and Leave-Take. Such speech acts tend to occur in ritual interaction, and so they are less relevant for the analysis of whether ritual phenomena like self-denigrating expressions are used strategically or not. However, if there is another speech act involved, and a self-denigrating expression operates as a lexical tool to increase the pragmatic effect of the particular speech act, then it is clear that the given expression is used beyond what is simply necessary.

As part of the methodology proposed here, one also needs to consider how an utterance containing a ritually used expression can be classified according to the standard sociolinguistic parameters Social Distance and Power [+/–SD, +/–P]: variation in such parameters implies variation in the ritual frame holding for a particular interaction. In pragmatics, it was the Cross-Cultural Speech Act Realization (CCSARP) Project (Blum-Kulka et al. 1989) which first used the variables of [+/–SD, +/–P] on a large scale. Later on, scholars such as Cohen (2008) and McConarchy (2019) introduced other variables, and recently Nilsson et al. (2020: 2) argued that 'age, gender, participant roles, medium and venue affect speakers' choice of greeting form.' Notwithstanding the importance of such additional variables, the proposed framework relies on the basic [+/–SD, +/–P] variables because they provide insight into the above-outlined question of whether a particular self-denigrating expression is used in a strategic way, or not.

The proposed methodological framework is both qualitative and quantitative. When quantifying data, one needs to count each self-denigrating expression separately.

10.3.2   Data

The corpora of this case study include the following three Chinese novels:

1. *Shuihu zhuan* 水浒传 ('Outlaws of the Marsh'): one of the best-known Chinese novels, which was compiled sometime between the fourteenth and sixteenth centuries.[8]
2. *Sanxia-wuyi* 三侠五义 ('Three Heroes and Five Knights'): a nineteenth-century novel written by Shi Yukun 石玉昆 (ca. 1798–1871).
3. *Shediao yingxiong zhuan* 射雕英雄传 ('The Legend of the Condor Heroes'): a historicising novel written by Jin Yong 金庸 (1924–2018), published in 1957.

The first two novels represent historical language use, while the third one is an early modern novel, which however imitates the style of historical novels, and so it features many traditional manifestations of self-denigration. I chose these novels for two reasons. Firstly, they are generically comparable (see the pragmatic Principle of Comparability in House & Kádár 2021a): they are all Chinese 'heroic' novels, featuring conversations between martial artists, rebels and other interactants. They also include interactions between such speakers and high-class language users, and so they provide useful data to study self-denigration according to the various social role relationships involved in the proposed methodology. Also, all these novels include many dialogues, so they can provide insight into the interactional use of self-denigration, although they are not 'authentic' interactions in the strict sense of the word but rather quasi-authentic ones. Secondly, the novels represent self-denigration in Chinese across a long timespan. Studying diachronically different sources helps us to avoid cherry-picking one particular source or time period to study self-denigration. I believe that the fact that the third novel is an early modern piece of Chinese literature is an important asset because it provides examples of early modern Chinese interpretations of historical self-denigration. It should be noted that the author of the third novel, Jin Yong, is often regarded as a modern master of the historical Chinese vernacular style.

The corpus for analysis consists of three times thirty-five occurrences of self-denigration (105 in sum), with the dialogues studied having an overall length of approximately 4,000 Chinese characters in total. I chose these interactions through random sampling: I randomly picked dialogues featuring instances of self-denigration from the novels, and then categorised each instance of self-denigration by following the methodology outlined in the previous section, i.e., by categorising instances of self-denigration according to the units of types of talk, speech acts and social role relationships.

10.4   Analysis

10.4.1   First Corpus: Shuihu Zhuan

Table 10.1 below summarises the findings in the first corpus from a quantitative point of view.

The following analysis will proceed by following the frequency of the three Types of Talk Opening, Core and Closing. Table 10.1 shows that self-denigrating expressions in the first corpus occur most frequently in Business Talk (sixteen out of thirty-five uses of expression), which is not conventionally a ritual Type of Talk. However, as Example 10.1 illustrates, the use of self-denigrating expressions in Business Talk often follows ritual pragmatic conventions, while such expressions can at the same time help the speaker to achieve individual interactional goals:

Example 10.1   对高俅说道：“小人家下萤火之光, 照人不亮, 恐后误了足下。我转荐足下与小苏学士处, 久后也得个出身。足下意内如何？” 高俅大喜, 谢了董将士。

> He said to Gao Qiu, "My, this humble commoner's family burns in the fire like fireflies, and we do not get noticed by others. So, I'm afraid you will miss the chance to have a bright future if you stay with me. I'll recommend you to the Scholar Su, and you will have a bright future under his patronage. Would you accept this, sir?" Gao Qiu was overjoyed and thanked Dong.[9]

Here the speaker is higher ranking than the addressee while at the same time the interactants are already familiar with each other, so this interaction represents

Table 10.1 *The pragmatic features of self-denigrating expressions in the first corpus: A quantitative summary*

	Tell	Opine	Disclose	Apologise	Complain	Request	Remark	Willing	Invite
Business Talk (16)	2 [+P,+SD]	4 – 2 [+P,+SD] 1 [+P,–SD] 1 [–P,+SD]		1 [+P,+SD]	2 – 1 [+P,+SD] 1 [+P,–SD]	2 – 1 [+P,+SD] 1 [–P,+SD]	1 [–P,–SD]	2 [–P, SD]	2 [–P,+SD]
Opening Talk (14)	5 – 3 [+P,+SD] 2 [+P,–SD]		6 – 3 [+P,+SD] 3 [+P,–SD]	2 – 1 [+P,+SD] 1 [–P,+SD]			1 [–P,–SD]		
Patch-Up Talk (5)		3 – 2 [+P,+SD] 1 [+P, –SD]		2 – 1 [+P,+SD] 1 [–P,+SD]					
Total (35)	7	7	6	5	2	2	2	2	2

Business Talk in a [+P, −SD] role relationship. The fact that it is a higher-ranking person who uses a self-denigrating expression might indicate that self-denigration here is simply a 'ritual'. This may also be due to the fact that the self-denigrating expression *xiaoren* 小人 (lit. 'little man', i.e., 'humble commoner') is realised as a phrasal downgrader in a broader metaphoric ritual speech act Complain. However, self-denigration is here followed by an Opine,[10] a Suggest and Request (for information) through which the speaker suggests to the interactant that the latter is advised to leave the speaker's house to stay with another patron. While this cluster of speech acts ultimately benefits the hearer, as also shown by the hearer's reaction, it could imply a lack of hospitality on the speaker's part. So, self-denigration is not entirely 'innocent' in this case because it mitigates the speaker's message.

The same pragmatic function of self-denigration can also be observed in Example 10.2:

Example 10.2   高太尉出班奏曰：“...微臣不胜惶惧。伏乞我皇圣断。”天子闻奏大惊, 随即降下圣旨...

Gao Taiwei went out, saying, "... I, this humble official am overwhelmed with fear. I humbly beg my emperor to decide on this matter."

When the emperor heard this, he was frightened, and immediately issued the imperial edict ...

In this [+P, +SD] situation, the speaker is an official who aims to persuade the emperor to take a particular course of action against a group of rebels. In the first utterance, he denigrates himself by using the expression *weichen* 微臣 ('humble official'), embedded in the Informative speech act Tell, in order to prepare the ground for his subsequent Request (to-do-x) where he uses again a self-denigrating expression, namely the verbal phrase *fuqi* 伏乞 ('prostrate and humbly beg'). Similar to Example 10.1, the use of these expressions is highly conventionalised and ritualised: when speaking to the emperor, Chinese officials had the ritual obligation to heavily denigrate themselves and elevate the emperor. At the same time, self-denigration in this instance of Business Talk[11] also paves the way for the speech act Request, which can be said to have a predictable effect on the emperor, as the reaction of the latter also shows.

The above-outlined potentially strategic use of self-denigration does of course not apply to all instances of self-denigration in the corpus – it is important here to reiterate the point that interaction ritual *can* but not always does actually fulfill personal agendas, i.e., ritual self-denigration by default always serves to symbolically uphold relationships as one or more of the interactants humble themselves. Such a default use is prevalent in [−P] relationships where the interactants have less incentive to strategically 'package' their utterances. Example 10.3 illustrates such use of self-denigration in Business Talk:

Example 10.3   史进那里肯放, 说道: "师父, 只在此间过了。 小弟 奉养你母子二人, 以终天年, 多少是好!"
王进道: "贤弟, 多蒙你好心, 在此十分之好。 ..."

Shi Jin refused to let them leave, saying, "Master, I've lived here. I, this younger brother of yours will support your mother and yourself for the rest of my life as much as you need!"

Wang Jin said, "Dear younger brother, thanks to your kindness, it's very nice to be here. . . . "

Here, the first speaker Shi Jin denigrates himself by using the quasi-familial expression *xiaodi* 小弟 (lit. 'little younger brother'). While this expression indicates that he is of a relatively lower social status than his interactant, quasi-familial expressions like this also indicate relational closeness between the interactants. This self-denigrating expression occurs in a speech act Willing,[12] which is a hearer-oriented speech act that clearly benefits the other as the speaker communicates that he is in favour of performing a future act, as in the interests of the hearer. So, self-denigration here simply *cannot* fulfil any personal agenda in the strategic sense of the word.

Along with Business Talk, the only other Type of Talk in the first corpus which is not conventionally ritual is Patch-Up Talk, i.e., interactional episodes where one or more of the interactants aim to repair their relationship with the other after a major offence, mostly by realising the speech acts Apologise, Excuse/Justify in response to the realisation of the speech act Complain. In Patch-Up Talk in the present corpus, one can again observe strictly conventional and ritual pragmatic behaviour, in particular realisations of self-denigration embedded in the speech act Apologise, which strictly serve what is expected in the given context. In other cases, ritual self-denigrating expressions and the speech acts in which they are embedded may serve the speaker's individual goal along with restoring the relationship between the interactants following an offence. Consider Examples 10.4 and 10.5:

Example 10.4   太尉说道: "我是朝廷中贵官, 如何教俺走得山路... 下官 !"
真人复道: "贫道 等怎敢轻慢大臣? 这是祖师试探太尉之心。本山虽有蛇虎, 并不伤人。"

Qiu Wei said, "I'm an official, how would you expect me to walk by myself on a mountain road like this? It is too dangerous to walk on this road... Why are you teasing me, this simple official!?"

> The Taoist priest replied, "How would I, this humble Taoist priest dare to despise you, great official? It is the Grandmaster's intention to test you [by asking you to walk on this road]. Although there are snakes and tigers in this mountain, they do not hurt people."

Example 10.5　太公起身劝了一杯酒, 说道: "师父如此高强, 必是个教头。小儿有眼不识泰山。"

> The lord stood up and offered the guest a glass of spirit, saying, "You, Master, are so strong, and must be a martial arts coach. My worthless son has no eyes to see a person of great ability."

In Example 10.4, the first speaker Qiu Wei is an official who feels offended by the messenger of his host (a Taoist leader), as the messenger tells him that he needs to follow a dangerous mountain path to get to the Taoist shrine he wishes to visit. Qiu Wei gives voice to his frustration by realising the speech act Complain, in which the self-denigrating form *xiaguan* 下官 ('this simple official') is embedded. As noted previously, historical Chinese self-denigrating expressions very often indicate the social status of the speaker in a particular context. While *xiaguan* expresses ritual humbleness in the current [+P, +SD] role relationship, it also alerts the other about the important social status of the speaker, which would normally preclude being forced to walk on a mountain path. In response, the messenger realises a speech act Apologise, followed by an Excuse/Justify. He uses the self-denigrating expression *pindao* 贫道 (lit. 'poor Taoist priest') to refer to himself in the speech act Apologise as lower ranking than his interlocutor. Since Apologise and ritual self-denigration embedded in the Apologise are simply expected in this instance of Patch-Up Talk, it is difficult to argue that they serve any personal strategic agenda.

Example 10.5 is different from Example 10.4, in that through engaging in Patch-Up Talk the speaker also hopes to recruit the insulted addressee as a martial arts trainer for his son. Prior to this interaction, the speaker's son insulted their guest who is a famous martial arts expert, and the speaker suggested they fight with each other, in order for his son to be taught a lesson. The martial arts instructor easily defeated the speaker's son, and that is the point when the utterance featured in Example 10.5 occurs. In this interaction, the speaker realises two subsequent speech acts Opine, and he also denigrates his son by referring to him with the expression *xiao'er* 小儿 (lit. 'worthless son'). As previously noted, referring to someone's family member in a denigrating way also qualifies as an act of self-denigration in the Chinese linguaculture. The speech act Opine, in which the speaker expresses appreciation, hence pleasing the addressee, is not conventionally part of Patch-Up Talk. Considering that the speaker wishes to recruit the interactant as a trainer for his son, one can reliably argue that self-denigration is potentially 'non-innocent' here.

As Edmondson and House (1981) and Edmondson et al. (2023) argue, Opening Talk is characterised by much ritual and often phatic communicative activity. Typical speech acts for this Type of Talk are Greet, How-are-you, Welcome, Disclose and Remark. The speech act Disclose essentially gives biographical information, such that through this information the hearer 'knows one better'. A Remark is essentially phatic in nature, and hearer-supportive in intent. In making a Remark, a speaker shows himself favourably disposed towards his hearer. Due to the ritual nature of this Type of Talk, pragmatic behaviour including self-denigration tends to follow strict conventions in Opening in the corpus studied. Examples 10.6 and 10.7 show how self-denigrating expressions are realised in Opening Talk in [+P, +SD] and [–P, +SD] relationships.

Example 10.6 宋江…便唤那老妇人问道："你姓甚么？那里人家？如今待要怎地？"

那妇人道："不瞒官人说，老身 夫妻两口儿，姓宋，原是京师人。…"

Song Jiang called the old woman, asking her, "What is your name? Where do you come from? Where do you want to go now?"

The woman said, "My husband and myself do not want to fool you, noble official. We, this old commoner couple, bear the surname Song, and we are originally from the capital. …"

In Example 10.6, the elderly female speaker utters the expression *laoshen* 老身 (lit. 'old body') to denigrate herself and her husband, indicating that they are both commoners (see Kádár 2007). Interestingly, in the first corpus the speech act Greet is largely absent from Opening Talk. While this phenomenon may be partly due to the fact that the present data were drawn from novels, the speech act Greet is not compulsory in many contexts also in the modern Chinese linguaculture (see House et al. 2022). This means that Greet is often substituted by How-are-you and other Phatic speech acts. However, such other Phatic speech act types like How-are-you are also often absent in Opening in the present corpus, and it emerges that it is ritual self-denigration embedded in Attitudinal rather than Phatic (Ritual) speech acts which is frequented in Opening Talk (see Figure 10.1).[13] This phenomenon is particularly evident in [+P, +SD] scenarios like the one featured in Example 10.6: through self-denigrating expressions one or more interactants indicate or clarify their relationship, which behooves opening an interaction, at least as far as the present data is concerned. For instance, in the current example, the first speaker Song Jiang is an official who interacts with an old commoner couple. According to his higher rank, he directly starts the interaction with a barrage of Requests (for information). In response, the female member of the couple first realises the speech act Willing, also by using the above-mentioned self-denigrating expression *laoshen*. By so doing, she ritually confirms the unequal relationship between herself, her husband and Song Jiang, which one may argue also ritually Satisfies the way in which Song Jiang's utterance was realised. Following this speech act, the elderly female speaker provides the information Requested by Song Jiang, by realising a speech act Tell. While the speech act Willing could be said to serve as a 'preface' for the subsequent speech act Tell, this Willing is not demonstrably strategic because the elderly female speaker is ritually expected to sound as deferential as possible when interacting with an official.

Example 10.7 represents Opening Talk in a [–P, +SD] relationship:

Example 10.7   正在那里劝不住，只见屏风背后转出老管营来，叫道："义士，老汉听你多时也。今日幸得相见义士一面，愚男 如拨云见日一般。且请到后堂少叙片时。"武松跟了到里面。老管营道："义士且请坐。"
武松道："小人是个囚徒，如何敢对相公坐地。"
老管营道："义士休如此说。愚男万幸，得遇足下，何故谦让？"

The old manager came out from behind the screen and said, "Chivalrous man, I, this old commoner, have been listening to you. Fortunately, I, this foolish person met you today, which felt like seeing the sun through the clouds. May I humbly ask you to follow me to the back hall for a talk?"

Wu Song followed him. The old manager said, "Please sit down, chivalrous man." Wu Song said, "I, this humble commoner is a prisoner. How would I dare to sit with you?"

The old manager said "Please don't speak like this. I, this foolish person, am unbelievably fortunate to meet you, so why are you so humble?"

Here the interactants once again do not realise a Greet or any other Phatic speech act. However, unlike in Example 10.6, the interactants symmetrically use many self-denigrating expressions embedded in the Informative speech acts Tell and Opine. In so doing, both of them use self-denigrating expressions frequented by commoners. While one of the speakers, Wu Song, used to be a military official, in the scenario featured here he does not hold this rank any longer, and so the self-denigrating expressions used by the interactants simply ritually indicate that they are commoners who are not familiar with each other. This example again illustrates that it is often through self-denigration that the interactants manage to clarify their social status relative to one another, in particular in [+SD] relationships.

Interestingly, in the present corpus, ritual self-denigration plays a paramount role in Opening Talk in [–SD] relationships as well, as Example 10.8 shows:

Example 10.8   那人道："小人却才回来，听得浑家叫唤，谁想得遇都头！..."

"I, this humble person just came back", the man said. "I heard my ugly wife calling me. I wouldn't have thought I will bump into you!"

In this [–P, –SD] scenario, the speaker Opens the interaction through a chain of Remarks, denigrating both himself and his wife. A key difference between this example and the previous Examples 10.6 and 10.7 is that here a Phatic speech act is used in Opening, which accords with the [–P, –SD] nature of the interaction. Yet, the fact that such casual and phatic Remarks are loaded with self-denigrating expressions shows that self-denigration was by default associated with the ritual Opening of an interaction in the historical Chinese lingua-culture. In [–P, –SD] scenarios, self-denigration can be said to uphold or stabilise rather than clarify or negotiate interpersonal relationships. As such, once again one can argue that self-denigration does not (and cannot) fulfil salient individual strategic agendas in Opening Talk.

10.4.2   Second Corpus: Sanxia-Wuyi

As Table 10.2 shows, in the second corpus of this case study the use of self-denigrating expressions is relatively similar to what one can observe in the first corpus. Further, as becomes clear from Table 10.2, in the second corpus of this case study, self-denigrating expressions also most frequently occur in Business Talk, and they tend to be used in various role relationships as well. In spite of such relative similarity between the second and first corpora, there is also a noteworthy difference between them, in that in the second corpus there is also an occurrence of the speech act Greet in Opening Talk:

Example 10.9   包公见了，不慌不忙，向前一揖，口称："大人在上，晚生 拜揖。"
李大人看见包公气度不凡，相貌清奇，连忙还礼，分宾主坐下，便
问："贵姓? 仙乡? 因何来到 敝处?"

When Bao Gong saw him, he moved forward composedly, saying, "Your Excellency, I, this worthless junior official hereby bows in front of you."

Seeing Bao Gong's extraordinary bearing and strange appearance, Li hurriedly returned his courtesy: he respectfully made him sit down and asked him, "What's your noble name and precious hometown? Why did you come to my humble abode?"

In this [+P, +SD] interaction, the first speaker realises a Greet in a formal way, by using the other-elevating verbal expression *baiyi* 拜揖, literally meaning 'bowing with hands crossed in front of someone'. In Austin's (1962) terms, this is a typically performative utterance where the above-described verbal expression realises the speech act Greet in a very explicit way. As part of this formal greeting, the speaker also uses the self-denigrating expression *wansheng* (lit. 'late born'), indicating that he is a younger speaker who holds the rank of an

Table 10.2 *The pragmatic features of self-denigrating expressions in the second corpus: A quantitative summary*

	Tell	Opine	Request	Apologise	Willing	Remark	Invite	Greet
Business Talk (18)	5 – 2 [+P,+SD] 2 [+P,-SD] 1 [-P,+SD]	3 [+P,+SD]	4 – 2 [+P,+SD] 2 [-P,+SD]	1 [+P,+SD]	2 – 1 [+P,+SD] 1 [-P,-SD]	1 [+P,-SD]	2 – 1 [+P,+SD] 1 [+P,-SD]	
Opening Talk (13)	3 – 2 [+P,+SD] 1 [-P,+SD]	3 [+P,+SD]	2 [+P,+SD]	2 [+P,+SD]		2 – 1 [+P,+SD] 1 [-P,-SD]		1 [+P,+SD]
Patch-Up Talk (4)				3 – 2 [+P,+SD] 1 [+P,-SD]	1 [+P,+SD]			
Total (35)	8	6	6	6	3	3	2	1

official of lower social status than his interactant. In response, the other speaker realises a chain of deferential Requests (for information), and in the last of these Requests he also embeds the self-denigrating expression *bichu* 敝处 ('humble place').

While Example 10.9 is interesting because it shows that in [+P] relationships in particular the speech Greet *can* occur, in the majority of the data featuring Opening Talk, this speech act tends to be substituted by other speech acts, and self-denigrating expressions play a central role in such Openings, as the following example illustrates:

Example 10.10   口中说道："小人冒犯钦差大人, 实实小人该死。"
                 包公连忙说道："壮士请起, 坐下好讲。"
                 那人道："钦差大人在此小人焉敢就座。"

He said, "I, this humble person offended your highness, I, this humble person genuinely deserve to die."

Bao Gong said quickly, "I beg you, noble knight, to get up, let us sit down and have a talk."

The man said, "How would I, this humble person dare to sit with you?"

In this [+P, +SD] scenario, the first speaker opens the interaction by realising a strong Apologise: here he uses the self-denigrating expression *xiaoren* ('I, this humble person') twice (plus once more later in the interaction). This is a real rather than a ritual Apologise: prior to this interaction, the speaker insulted the other by not recognising that he is a famous judge and district official. Interestingly, as he addresses the other deferentially, there seems to be no pressure on him to formally Greet the other before realising the Apologise. This again confirms the point that the speech act Greet does not seem to be compulsory at least as far as the present data is concerned. Rather, Greet realisations can be 'bought out' by self-denigrating expressions embedded in various speech acts in the Opening phase, through which the speakers who realise Opening ritually work out or maintain their relationship.

10.4.3   Third Corpus: Shediao Yingxiong Zhuan

Table 10.3 summarises the pragmatic features of the third corpus of this case study. As Table 10.3 shows, in the third corpus of the present case study, self-denigrating expressions also most frequently occur in Business Talk, and they tend to be used in various role relationships as well. A distinctive feature of the third corpus is, however, that it includes instances of Closing Talk. The following examples illustrate how Closing Talk tends to be realised in the corpus:

Table 10.3 *The pragmatic features of self-denigrating expressions in the third corpus: A quantitative summary*

	Tell	Opine	Request	Willing	Apologise	Remark	Suggest
Business Talk (19)	5 [+P,+SD] 1 [+P,–SD] 1 [–P,+SD]	5 – 3 [+P,+SD] 2 [–P,+SD]	2 [+P,+SD] – 1 [+P,+SD] 1 [–P,+SD]	3 – 2 [–P,+SD] 1 [+P,–SD]	2 [+P,+SD]	2 [+P,+SD]	
Opening Talk (7)	3 [+P,+SD]	2 [–P,+SD]	2 [+P,+SD]				
Closing Talk (7)	2 [+P,+SD]		2 [+P,+SD]	2 [–P,+SD]			1 [+P,+SD]
Patch-Up Talk (2)					2 [–P,+SD]		
Total (35)	10	7	6	5	4	2	1

Example 10.11   郭靖道: "小可坐骑性子很劣, 还是小可亲自去牵的好。"
那渔人道: "既是如此, 在下在寒舍恭候大驾。"
Guo Jing said, "This humble person's horse has a bad temper, so it's better for this humble person to lead it by himself."

The fisherman said, "In that case, this humble one will be waiting for you in my humble house."

Example 10.12   陆冠英道: "小弟这就告辞。两位他日路经太湖: 务必请到归云庄来盘桓数日。"
Lu Guanying said, "I, this little brother of yours is leaving now. The two of you will be passing through Taihu Lake, and at that time please come to Guiyun to visit me for a few days."

Example 10.11 represents a [+P, +SD] scenario: while the first speaker has a higher social status than his interlocutor, the other helps him out by providing him accommodation for the night. The interaction featured here represents a case of temporary farewell, and the first speaker Closes the interaction by realising a Tell and then a Suggest. In both these speech acts he embeds self-denigrating expressions. Similar to cases of Opening that were studied in the analysis of the second corpus, what one can see here is that the speaker does not realise the speech act Leave-Take in Closing. In a similar fashion, his interactant realises a Willing rather than a Leave-Take, and in this speech act he also embeds a self-denigrating expression in reference to his home. In Example 10.12, the speaker realises a Tell which includes the deferential expression *gaoci* 告辞 ('announcing leave'). While this use resembles a Leave-Take, there is no actual speech act Leave-Take realised here because this Tell is followed by another Tell and an Invite. As Table 10.3 also shows, the speech act Leave-Take tends to be absent in Closings, and the interactions are concluded by other speech acts and self-denigrating expressions embedded in these speech acts.

10.4.4   Findings and Discussion

Table 10.4 summarises the pragmatic features of self-denigrating expressions in the three corpora of this case study, according to the types of talk, speech acts and role relationships in which they occur. The following features of Table 10.4 are relevant for the study of the particular question pursued in the current case study: By far, the type of talk in which self-denigrating expressions occur most frequently is Business Talk. The frequency of self-denigrating expressions in this type of talk already indicates that such ritual expressions tend to be often used beyond the ritual phases of an interaction, pursuing potentially different interactional agendas. An important related feature of self-denigrating expressions in the corpora relates to the fact that these expressions are most frequented in Informative speech acts, i.e., Tell and Opine, followed by

Table 10.4 *The pragmatic features of self-denigrating expressions in the three corpora of the case study: A quantitative summary*

	Tell	Opine	Apologise	Request	Willing	Remark	Disclose	Invite	Complain	Suggest	Greet
Business Talk (53)	*12* – 7 [+P,+SD] 3 [+P,–SD] 1 [–P,+SD] 1 [–P,+SD]	*12* – 8 [+P,+SD] 3 [–P,+SD] 1 [+P,–SD]	*4* [+P,+SD]	*8* – 5 [+P,+SD] 3 [–P,+SD]	*7* – 3 [–P,–SD] 2 [–P,+SD] 1 [+P,+SD] 1 [–P,–SD]	*4* – 2 [+P,+SD] 1 [–P,–SD] 1 [+P,–SD]		*4* – 2 [–P,+SD] 1 [+P,+SD] 1 [+P,–SD]	*2* – 1 [+P,+SD] 1 [+P,–SD]		
Opening Talk (34)	*11* – 8 [+P,+SD] 2 [+P,–SD] 1 [–P,+SD]	*5* – 3 [+P,+SD] 2 [–P,+SD]	*4* – 3 [+P,+SD] 1 [–P,+SD]	*4* [+P,+SD]		*3* – 2 [–P,–SD] 1 [+P,+SD]	*6* – 3 [+P,+SD] 3 [+P,–SD]				*1* [+P,+SD]
Patch-Up Talk (11)		*3* – 2 [+P,+SD] 1 [+P,–SD]	*7* – 5 [+P,+SD] 1 [+P,–SD] 1 [–P,–SD]		*1* [+P,+SD]						
Closing Talk (7)	*2* [+P,+SD]			*2* [+P,+SD]	*2* [–P,+SD]					*1* [+P,+SD]	
Total (105)	25	20	15	14	10	7	6	4	2	1	1

various Attitudinal speech acts, such as Apologise, Request and so on. While all such speech acts may be realised in a ritual way, they do not conventionally belong to the Ritual cluster of speech acts, unlike Greet which is however very infrequent in the data. Another related general characteristic of self-denigrating expressions in the corpora of this case study is that they tend to be used in various social role relationships, but they are most frequently used in [+P, +SD] relationships. This tendency, along with the frequency of such expressions in Informative and Attitudinal speech acts indicates that the use of self-denigrating expressions may serve individual strategic goals, while at the same time indicating awareness of the relationship between the interactants. This dual function of the expressions studied, which was also illustrated through the analysis of individual examples, accords with the ritual nature of these expressions.

10.5   Conclusion

This chapter has considered how the second methodological take on ritual can be put to practice. As was argued before, there are many complex ritual phenomena which can only be studied from a pragmatic angle in a replicable way if one attempts to interpret them through pragmatic units of analysis. Specifically, the chapter has studied cases when a particular phenomenon is too broad to be discussed as a single ritual, i.e., it represents a form of ritual behaviour which spans across many different ritual contexts and frames. The chapter proposed a replicable and pragmatics-anchored analytic procedure through which the use of such ritual phenomenon can be studied. This procedure can be used in many ways, depending on the goal of the researcher. The case study of this chapter illustrated one of such uses: I considered how this model can be used to distinguish default deferential ritual uses of self-denigration from cases when this phenomenon lubricates the flow of interaction, i.e., its use becomes strategic. This sense of strategic use bears relevance to politeness research in which the relationship between honorifics and politeness has been broadly discussed. In my view, ritual provides a more accurate framework to consider the default and strategic uses of honorifics as manifestations of ritual behaviour than if one approaches honorifics merely through the politeness paradigm, i.e., through debates on whether honorifics afford strategic (polite) uses or not.

   Having argued thus, politeness is certainly not irrelevant for the present case study. As the analysis has shown, in dialogues drawn from historical and historicising Chinese novels, self-denigration very often serves to smooth the flow of an interaction or mimimise offence, along with expressing deference. One would have less likely identified this interactional function of self-denigration had one not used an interactional speech act framework like the present one, by looking at the Type of Talk and speech act types in which self-denigrating expressions occur, hence avoiding departing from the semantic meaning of self-denigrating expressions. This outcome, in turn, shows that politeness becomes relevant for the study of interaction ritual phenomena like self-denigration in Chinese whenever a particular ritual serves the personal agenda of the speaker.

The following Chapter 11 will consider another aspect through which the second methodological take on ritual can be put to use, by looking at a context which triggers ritual behaviour but cannot be subsumed under a single ritual heading from the pragmatician's point of view.

10.6   Recommended Reading

Ide, S. (2005) How and why honorifics can signify dignity and elegance: The indexicality and reflexivity of linguistic rituals. In Lakoff, R., Ide, S. (eds.), *Broadening the Horizon of Linguistic Politeness*. Amsterdam: John Benjamins, 45–64.

The present chapter has discussed how the use of honorifics can be considered through the lens of interaction ritual in general, and the second methodological approach proposed in this book in particular. It was noted that in previous research, honorifics were often approached from a politeness point of view. However, the politeness-anchored study of honorifics has raised various problems: many scholars have pointed out that honorifics only have a casual relationship with politeness because they can express many other contextually embedded meanings. One of the key figures in the pragmatic study of honorifics is Sachiko Ide who pointed out the importance of ritual in her work, even though she tried to capture Japanese honorifics from a politeness angle. The following is an excerpt from one of Ide's studies:

One day, a journalist from The Financial Times, *who had a Ph.D. in sociology from Cambridge University, came to my office for an interview. She felt that, if the honorific system were abolished from the Japanese language, this messy economical confusion could be resolved. She believed that language supports the infrastructure of a society. She presumed that the point of the system of honorifics was to ensure distance between interactants and it is also a system geared toward making information ambiguous and complicating its transmission. Therefore, if the system of honorifics were to be abolished from the society, it would make it easier for the Japanese to transmit information. This in turn would solve the complicated societal problems and economic crisis. . . .*

How and why can honorifics signify dignity and/or elegance? It has been shown that honorifics are formal linguistic forms that cannot be used independent of the context. They are basically ritualistic linguistic forms chosen to fit to the particular situational context. The use of honorifics function as linguistic politeness because the fitting of the proper linguistic forms to the contextual factors makes the interactants feel secure in the interaction and the situation.

What does using honorifics accomplish? The use of honorifics expresses, or more precisely indexes, the appropriate relationship between the speaker and the hearer. It also indexes the formality of the situation. But honorifics do more than that. Honorifics can index the speaker's attributes. (Ide 2005: 46, 60, 61)

11 Methodological Take-2B: Describing Ritual Contexts

11.1 Introduction

This final chapter of Part III will consider how the second methodological take on ritual can be used to study a context and a related ritual frame which trigger conventionalised ritual behaviour but cannot be subsumed under a single ritual heading from the pragmatician's point of view. The foundations of the model proposed are similar to what was discussed in the previous chapter. However, in the study of ritual in specific contexts, one has a different starting point of inquiry than in the study of a ritual phenomenon spanning across many different contexts. That is, instead of collecting sampled manifestations of a ritual phenomenon and then considering their conventionalised uses in different ritual frames, here one examines data occurring in one particular ritual frame in a bottom–up manner. This difference implies a more discourse-analytic and less corpus-based take on language use, which also influences how the elements of the model proposed in the previous chapter are put to use.

To illustrate the operation of this model, I examine ritual bargaining in Chinese markets. Bargaining is a process by which the seller and the buyer of a product negotiate the price of the item on sale. In many parts of the world, bargaining is a conventionalised ritual practice. And in China bargaining is such an important 'tradition' that failing to bargain often triggers negative feelings about the buyer, while successful bargaining may become a source of public entertainment and a way of 'gaining face' in front of others. While bargaining is therefore definitely a ritual in the popular sense, it is problematic from the pragmatician's point of view to refer to bargaining *per se* as a ritual, without considering whether and how it manifests itself in recurrent patterns of ritual language use.

The chapter has the following structure. Section 11.2 discusses how the framework discussed in Chapter 10 should be extended for a discourse-analytic inquiry. Section 11.3 describes various interpretations of the term 'bargaining', in order to position the current ritual anchored research, then outlines previous research on bargaining in Chinese markets, and finally introduces the corpus used to investigate Chinese market bargaining in the case study. Section 11.4 is devoted to the data analysis and, finally, a conclusion is provided in Section 11.5.

11.2   Extending the Framework

The model outlined in Chapter 10 approaches ritual language use by examining the phases of an interaction, speech acts, as well as expressions. The model is centred on the finite, replicable and interactionally defined set of speech acts outlined before, through which one can annotate and interpret one's data. In the present chapter, the framework is applied in a discourse-analytic way. That is, the focus of the analysis is on how speech acts fill certain slots in the structure of a ritual interaction – through this it becomes possible to capture seemingly erratic interactions through a ritual lens. This interactional approach to speech acts is based on Edmondson (1981), Edmondson and House (1981) and Edmondson et al. (2023). In this approach, the most basic unit in the inter-actional structure is an exchange, in which the interactants together co-construct an outcome through individual moves. The terms 'move' and 'exchange' are based on Goffman (see e.g., Goffman 1981). These terms differ from conversation-analytic terms, such as 'adjacency pair', although they are not in contradiction with them; as House and Kádár (2023: 5) argue,

The reasons why we do not use the CA [i.e. conversation analytic] notions of 'adjacency pair' and 'preference organisation' is the following: as Paul Drew and his colleagues explained (Drew, 2013; Drew & Walker, 2010), convincingly in our view, conversation analysts use speech act theory to interpret particular conversationally relevant turns-at-talk in their data. They also study how speech acts are co-constructed in interaction, hence taking a relatively 'broad' view on speech acts. We believe that this view is valid and important. Yet, in our approach we use speech act categories to interpret EVERY turn in any data as a speech act or cluster of speech acts, and also unlike conversation analysts we do not operate with the notion of extended speech act. Because of this, we also interpret the turn-by-turn relationship between speech acts and attempt to capture and quantify pragmatic conventions of this relationship by using the above-outlined non-CA terminology.

Adopting the concept of 'move' means that the second move of the simplest two-part exchange complements or 'fulfils' the first (see also Chapter 10). Edmondson (1981) and Edmondson and House (1981) call these two moves in the simplest structural unit of exchange *Initiate* and *Satisfy*. For example, a speech act of Request that Initiates an interaction may be either fulfilled or rejected, in everyday terms. Only the 'fulfilling' move constitutes a Satisfy of the initiating Request, whereas a rejecting move may itself need to be fulfilled by the speaker making the original Request before an interactional outcome is reached. Remaining with the speech act Request, if a Request is turned down, this move does not 'Satisfy' the initiating Request: this is termed a *Contra* move. Given an Initiate, an interactant may Satisfy or Contra it. A further possible move is a *Counter*. A Counter is essentially similar to a Contra but has different potential consequences. Firstly, if a Counter is satisfied, the speaker who produced the Satisfy may nevertheless continue to uphold the position which was Countered. That is, a Contra is essentially something final, whereas a Counter is similar to an objection that leads to further negotiation. It goes without saying that the concept of Counter is particularly relevant for understanding the interactional dynamics of the bargaining case study.

The following is an example to illustrate how this structural approach operates:

Example 11.1   A: I think we should invite the whole family.
               B: Oh God, their kids are so loutish.
               A: Yeah, I agree, they're pretty horrible, but you know, they did put
                   up with our lot last time.
               B: Oh God, all right, invite them then, and the bloody dog.
                   (Edmondson & House 1981: 41)

The central point here is that A 'agrees' with B's first statement but does not change his opinion about inviting the whole family. In fact, immediately after agreeing with B, A 're-presents' his initial suggestion, i.e., A indirectly states the necessity to invite the family in question because the ritual reciprocation of an invitation is highly conventional. This move is a new Initiate, which is then satisfied by B who accepts the validity of A's argument of the necessity to reciprocate the invitation.

It is worth noting that in the above example there is only a Counter move but no Contra move. An example featuring a Contra move is as follows:

Example 11.2   A: Like to come to my party tomorrow night?
               B: Can't, I'm afraid – I've got something else on.
               A: Oh, never mind, some other time perhaps.
                   (Edmondson & House 1981: 39)

In this case we have an Initiate–Contra–Satisfy exchange, in which the outcome is said to be negative.

The structural unit of exchange can be integrated into the larger unit of phase – a procedure which we will follow during the data analysis. Phases consist of the Opening, Core and Closing parts of an encounter, with the latter representing the entire interaction. The unit of phase, which also encompasses Types of Talk discussed in Chapter 10, helps the scholar to systematise the different interactional dynamics which hold for various stages of an encounter. Figure 11.1 summarises the various units in the interactional model:

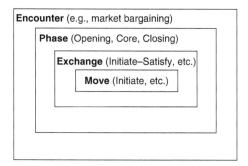

Figure 11.1 The interactional units in the model.

As shown in Figure 11.1, an encounter can be divided into phases, and phases are realised through exchanges. Exchanges themselves are realised through moves, and moves are approached in this study from the perspective of speech acts, interpreted through the typology of speech acts which was discussed in detail in the previous Chapter 10. While most of the illocutionary categories in the typology are self-explanatory, less frequently used categories will be briefly introduced when they occur in the case study analysis below. Along with speech act categories the model also uses the category 'Supportive Move', in order to capture a form of language use which facilitates the interactional success of a particular speech act (see also Blum-Kulka et al. 1989). The most typical form of a Supportive Move, which will recur in the analysis presented later, is the 'Grounder', a move which provides a reason for one's actions (see Edmondson & House 1981: 46).

Figure 11.2 describes how the above-outlined extended model can be put to use in the study of ritual contexts like market bargaining:

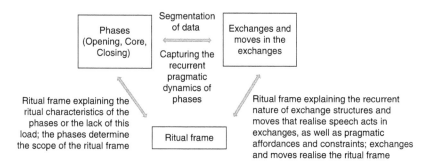

Figure 11.2 The extended analytical model.

The larger interactional units, phases, and their smaller components, exchanges and moves, are in a twofold relationship with one another. Identifying the phases of an encounter helps to segment the data, hence allowing a more systematic and in-depth examination of how exchanges and moves are realised. Examining exchanges and moves through a speech act lens, on the other hand, allows one to capture the recurrent pragmatic dynamics of the phases.

Ritual frame is also in a twofold relationship with both the larger unit, phases, and the smaller units, exchanges and moves. Ritual frame helps the scholar to interpret the pragmatic features of phases, e.g., how Opening and Core Phases are related to one another in terms of their ritual characteristics or the lack of such characteristics. The interactants, on the other hand, talk a ritual 'into being' as they follow an interactional ritual pattern that is associated with the various phases. Regarding the smaller units, exchanges and moves, the ritual frame explains why such units are recurrent and conventionalised in the seemingly erratic data. The notion of ritual frame also helps to explain the constraints and affordances of the pragmatic realisation of exchanges and moves, such as why certain speech act sequences that realise ritual aggression are tolerated in a particular ritual exchange (consider the concept of anti-structure discussed in Parts I and II). Ritual frame explains why such aggression is generally not perceived as proper aggression, as the following analysis will also demonstrate. On the other hand, ritual frame comes into operation through the recurrent units, exchanges and moves.

Considering that the proposed extended version of the analytic framework is discourse analytic in scope, the case study outlined below is essentially qualitative, i.e., pragmatic recurrence in the data is not quantified in the strict sense but is rather used to identify patterns of ritual behaviour. While using a proper quantitative analysis is not at all in contradiction with the approach proposed here, audio-recorded interactional corpora like the one used in this case study are often too small to do meaningful quantification in them.

11.3   Positioning the Case Study

The aim of this section is to position the current case study. The section will first discuss two different interpretations of the word 'bargaining', in order to discuss exactly how this concept is interpreted in the present ritual-anchored research. It will then outline previous research on bargaining in Chinese markets. Finally, the section will introduce the corpus used to investigate Chinese market bargaining in the case study.

11.3.1 Bargaining

In previous research, the term 'bargaining' has been used in two different, albeit not incompatible, ways:
1. As a broader concept encompassing negotiation in many different types of transactions;

2. As a more specific concept referring to business transactions in which the parties involved negotiate the price of goods or services by following conventionalised ritual patterns.

The former, broader interpretation of bargaining is typically applied in areas such as legal and economic studies (e.g., Muthoo 1999), in which 'bargaining' has become the foundation of a major 'bargaining theory' (e.g., Iyer & Villas-Boas 2003). In this body of research, ritual bargaining is only one form of negotiation captured under the umbrella term 'bargaining'. For example, in his discussion of bargaining theory, Lebow (1996: 73) defines ritual bargaining as follows:

People sometimes open the bargaining with inflated demands. "Tailpipe Harry" hopes to realize $2,300 for a 1987 Toyota on his lot, but puts a $3,000 sticker price on it. He is prepared to come down as much as $700 to give the appearance of making a meaningful concession. By doing so, he hopes to convince a customer that the car is a "steal." With any luck, he may have to drop only $500 from the price to clinch the deal. A prospective buyer can play the same game and offer Harry $1,500, fully expecting to pay more to get the car. ... Bargaining of this kind is characteristic of the bazaars of the Middle East. Everybody in the market knows the tactic of inflated bids and participates in the ritual.

The second, narrower definition of bargaining – the one adopted in this case study – is limited to business transactions in which the participants rely on conventionalised patterns of language use. Such bargaining practices tend to be ritual. Previous pragmatic research on bargaining has mostly adopted this definition (but see Sally 2003; Holzinger 2004). For example, in his now classic contrastive pragmatic research, Fillmore (1980: 139) describes bargaining as a ritual form of behaviour which is often realised with the conventionalised formulaic utterance "I'll tell you what" in American linguaculture:

Formula: I'LL TELL YOU WHAT
  Setting: A and B are negotiating some issue, X, and have so far not been able to reach an agreement
  Antecedent event: –
  Speaker's attitude: what A is about to say will solve the impasse
  Function of utterance: to introduce a compromise proposal
  Usage notes: commonly associated with a bargaining context
  Prototype example: A and B have been haggling over the price of a watch; B has offered $10, A has been insisting on $50; A says: 'I'll tell you what. I'll let you have it for $30'. ...
  Similar formulas: I'LL TELL YOU WHAT I'M GONNA DO/HERE'S MY FINAL OFFER
  Miscellaneous observations: 'I'll tell you what' could be used by either party in a bargaining setting; 'I'll tell you what I'm gonna do' would be used only by the salesperson. I associate these expressions only with males.[1]

11.3.2   Bargaining in Chinese Markets

Bargaining in China is an ancient ritual practice: the first written source describing it dates back to the fourth century AD (see *Hou Han Shu* 后汉书 [*The History of Later Han*]). Various linguists have explored Chinese bargaining practices from the perspectives of speech act theory and discourse analysis. For example, Tao (2012) examined the use of different speech acts in instances of bargaining, and both Chen and Yao (2015) and Xie and Zhan (2018) approached bargaining from a discourse-analytic perspective. However, no attempt has been made to systematically combine speech acts, interaction and interactional ritual to study Chinese bargaining practices.

When studying Chinese ritual bargaining, it is particularly useful to rely on the finite set of speech acts constituting the backbone of the proposed framework. The replicability of the aforementioned typology lies in the level of abstraction of the speech act definitions, which lends itself to contrastive pragmatic analysis (for more detail, see House & Kádár 2023). In previous research on bargaining, various scholars have identified 'new' speech act categories to describe linguaculturally embedded bargaining practices. For example, Chakrani (2007) investigated bargaining in Arabic from a speech act point of view, by describing it as a practice that he considers to be very different in Arabic than its 'counterpart' in other linguacultures:

The following exchange shows how bargainers invoke and mobilize salient concept of their cultural knowledge to win the bargaining duel.
(1) Setting: an electronic store
Interactants: a young salesman and an old buyer
Situation: the older man wants to buy a cell phone battery
Buyer: ħij:əd xamsi:n ħij:əd. ħij:əd xamsi:n La:ħ jərḍi: ʕla: wuldi
'Take off 50 (dirhams), take it off. Take off 50 may God be pleased with my son'
Seller: ra:ħ tsajbna: mʕa:k
'I have given you the right (good) price'
Buyer: ja: nʕ al ʃ :iṭa:n ma tkunʃ qa:səħ
'Just curse the Satan, do not be hard'
The H-oriented speech act *La:ħ jərḍi: ʕla: wuldi* (May God be pleased with my son), performed by the seller is successful in fulfilling the necessary SA ingredients governing the felicitous performance of any given action. The literal meaning of this speech act is an expressive, namely, a blessing. (Charkrani 2007: 47)

A key problem with such an analysis is that it unnecessarily proliferates speech act categories (see the speech act of so-called 'blessing' in the above analysis). Such proliferation shuts the door on replicable cross-cultural pragmatic research on bargaining practices (see also House & Kádár 2023). While there is, undeniably, linguacultural variation in the realisation of bargaining practices, such variation should not prevent contrastability. This, in turn, implies that one is well advised to analyse bargaining by using speech act categories which are important and conventionalised in many linguacultures. For example, the replicable speech act 'Wish-well' (see Edmondson & House 1981: 196) would be analytically more appropriate than 'blessing' in the context of bargaining. This is not only because 'blessing' is one particular realisation type of the superordinate category 'Wish-well', but also because 'Wish-well' is equally important in many different linguacultures.

11.3.3   Data

The corpus of the present case study consists of approximately four hours of audio-recorded interactions which took place in five different Chinese markets in Dalian, a city located in the northeast of China. To collect the data, a group of advanced graduate students first asked permission to audio-record conversations at a number of stalls and market shops. They then alerted the customers that they were going to be audio-recorded and requested their consent to do so. This procedure obviously entailed a sense of observer's paradox (see Labov 1972) but due to research ethical considerations we had to accept this paradox. During the transcription process all personal information was removed and both the audio-recorded and the transcribed data were stored in an anonymised form, in order to follow the standard ethics procedure of pragmatic research. Due to ethical considerations, the team who conducted this research was not able to videorecord interactions because videorecording would have required us to obtain permission of any person who happens to pass through the physical space of the stall where bargaining takes place.

The team of researchers with whom I conducted this case study transcribed the data in a simple and accessible way, that is we refrained from using conversation-analytic conventions. A particular convention in this study includes the use of annotation boxes on the right-hand side of the transcripts. These boxes indicate the speech acts inside their interactional structural slots. Our team annotated the corpus manually, and so broader speech act annotation issues relevant for the study of large corpora are not relevant to the current investigation (see Weisser 2014). Readers with an interest in this annotation convention can find more information in House and Kádár (2023).

The transcripts in the case study below apply the following convention: the seller is abbreviated as 'S' and the buyer as 'B' (if there are more buyers, they are numbered as 'Bn'.

11.4   Analysis

Let us begin the data analysis by examining patterns of the Opening Phase of the Chinese bargaining encounters. As the analysis will demonstrate, Opening is not part of the ritual of bargaining. However, it is relevant to include this phase in the investigation because its analysis provides a more comprehensive description of the data.

11.4.1   Opening

In casual interpersonal encounters, the Opening Phase is standardly ritual (see also Chapter 10). As Edmondson and House (1981: 201) argue,

The Opening of a conversation is characterized by much ritual or phatic communicative activity. Typical illocutions for this type of talk are the Greet, the How-are-you, the Welcome, the Disclose, and the Remark.

Paradoxically, in ritual bargaining encounters it is exactly the Opening Phase which is *not* ritual, and it is no coincidence that practically all speech act types frequented in this phase are substantive rather than ritual ones (see the typology in Figure 10.1). This paradox dissolves when one considers that the aim of ritual phatic talk (see Malinowski 2002 [1935]), which generally characterises the Opening Phase, is to help interactants to either get to know one another or to break the embarrassment of a silence. In the Chinese linguaculture, there is conventionally no need for strangers to attempt to engage in any form of ritualised phatic talk (see Pan & Kádár 2011; House et al. 2022) and bargaining between seller and buyer in a marketplace typically represents the relationship between strangers who are, by default, supposed to remain strangers. This claim about Chinese should definitely not be regarded as an essentialist one. While a contrastive examination of market bargaining is beyond the scope of the present case study, it is very likely that in the 'West' the pragmatic dynamics of market bargaining are quite similar, considering that it is the setting of the market itself which is responsible for the interactants' preference to remain strangers. Normally, both the buyer and the seller involved in market bargaining only focus on the transaction, remaining in their buyer and seller roles by default. As the present analysis will demonstrate, however, this does not mean that their interaction is 'robotic': through the rite of bargaining, which unfolds after the Opening Phase, the participants often engage in intensive interaction and the role of the Opening is to lead them to this active (Core) Phase of the encounter.

When examining the corpus, the team of researchers with whom I conducted this research categorised those utterances that occur at the beginning of the encounter as part of Opening, in which, categorically, no bargaining takes place. The analysis revealed three types of structure for the Opening Phase of Chinese market bargaining, although it is worth noting that these structures are essentially variations of each other.

Opening Structures

The Chinese market encounters in the data often begin when the buyer Initiates the encounter with the substantive speech act of a Request (for information). A distinction is made here between Requests for information and Requests for goods and services ('Request to-do-x'), following Edmondson and House (1981). The following extract provides a typical example of this Opening structure:

Example 11.1

1. 买家1：虾爬子怎么卖的?
2. 商家：虾爬子28,
   给你27。

1. B1:	How much is the mantis shrimp?	1. Request (for information) (Initiate)
2. S:	28 yuan,	2. Tell (Satisfy)
	27 for you.	3. Willing (Initiate)

Normally, when the encounter is Initiated with a Request (for information), it is Satisfied with the speech act of Tell. While this speech act is relatively straightforward (see also Chapter 10), I provide a brief definition here:

The Tell we might call the most "neutral" information illocution. . . . Tells . . . commonly Satisfy Requests for Tells, and appear in highly simplistic Initiate–Satisfy exchange structures (Edmondson & House 1981: 177–178)

What Example 11.1 reveals is that Tell is not necessarily a 'standalone' speech act: in the context of market bargaining, it may lead directly into the Core Phase of the encounter. For example, here the Tell is immediately followed by a Willing. In Example 11.1, the Willing definitely fulfills the function of an 'offer' – the latter is not a speech act category in the typology of speech acts used in the present framework. It is worth noting that while Willing is included in the analysis of the Opening here, this speech act as an Initiate represents a transition to the Core Phase of the ritual of bargaining, and therefore in the data analysis it has been categorised as part of the Core Phase.

In Example 11.1, the Tell which Satisfies the Request directly follows the Request. However, as Example 11.2 shows, it is also possible to insert other speech acts before realising the Satisfying Tell. The goal of such speech acts is to prepare the grounds for the ritual of bargaining:

Example 11.2

1. 买家：这个背心儿多钱?
2. 商家：你真有眼力!
   这是今年最流行的款式, 98

1. B:	How much is the vest?	1. Request for information (Initiate)
2. S:	You have a keen eye!	2. Remark
	This is the latest fashion, 98 *yuan*.	Opine, Tell (Satisfy)

In this example, the seller first realises the speech act of Remark, which in the present system encompasses 'compliment' (see e.g., Wolfson & Manes 1980). The utterance 'You have a keen eye' represents a typical positive Remark in the speech act typology used in the present study, as the seller positively comments on the buyer for having chosen that particular vest out of all the products on display. In this interaction, both Remark and the subsequent Opine prepare the grounds for bargaining, and they are finally followed by the requested Tell ('90 *yuan*').

The Openings in Examples 11.1 and 11.2 represent cases in which it is the buyer who Initiates the interaction. In the data, an alternative Opening pattern can also be observed: the seller may also Initiate an exchange, as Example 11.3 illustrates:

Example 11.3

1.	商家：	这花也好看，卖滴好。
2.	买家：	多钱？
3.		便宜点？20块钱还行。

1.	S:	The flowers [on the sheets] are very beautiful. The bestselling one.	1. Opine (Initiate)
2.	B:	How much?	2. Request (for information) (Satisfy)
3.		[Can they be sold] cheaper? 20 *yuan* would be okay.	3. Request (Initiate), Willing (Initiate)

In Example 11.3 the interaction starts with the speech act Opine, as the seller addresses the silent customer by praising the bedsheets on sale. This Initiate is Satisfied by the buyer as she realises a Request (for information), hence fulfilling the goal of the Initiate in this particular market context: in a market environment, an Opine is hardly 'innocent'. After realising the Request (for information), the buyer immediately Initiates the Core Phase of the interaction, by realising a Request and then a Willing.

Thus far, the analysis has highlighted the main patterns by which the Opening Phase operates in the corpus under investigation. In all these patterns the Opening is realised through non-Ritual types of speech act (see Figure 10.1), which reveals that Opening is not part of the ritual. All the above examples have illustrated that the transition between the Opening and Core Phases tends to be fluid. This is logical if one considers that the Opening Phase itself is not ritual in market bargaining. The transition between the Opening and Core Phases can be so fluid that, in some cases, it was difficult for the team of researchers involved in this case study to decide whether a particular utterance belonged to the Opening Phase or the Core Phase, as in the case of the following example:

Example 11.4

1. 买家：　这两个一样滴？
2. 商家：　一样滴。
3. 买家：　能不能照23？

1.	B:	Are those two the same?	1. Request for information (Initiate)
2.	S:	Yes, the same.	2. Tell (Satisfy)
3.	B:	Can you sell them at 23?	3. Request (to-do-x) (Initiate)

The interaction in Example 11.4 occurs after an initial Initiate–Satisfy pair. In this case the buyer realises a Request (for information), which indicates what we may call an 'expression of interest'. This expression of interest indicates that the buyer is going to bargain and, indeed, after the seller Satisfies the Request with a Tell, bargaining kicks off with a Request made by the buyer, hence Initiating the bargaining Phase.

11.4.2   Core (and Closing)

Before venturing into an analysis of the pragmatic patterns of the Core Phase in the corpus, it is important to explain why in the above heading 'Core (and Closing)' has been placed in brackets. In Chinese market bargaining it is the Core Phase that is ritual, and the Closing, like (or even more than) the Opening, appears to be marginal. As the analysis below will illustrate, bargaining very often ends rather 'abruptly' irrespective of whether the transaction is successful or unsuccessful. Therefore, the participants rarely (if at all) realise the speech act Leave-Take that is typical of a Closing in other interactional settings.

In this section, I will first discuss certain 'strategies' through which the Core Phase of bargaining is conducted in the ritual frame of the interaction. Following this, I will examine the role of complex participation (Goffman 1981) in ritual bargaining. Finally, I will briefly look at those cases when the bargaining is unsuccessful, in order to provide a more comprehensive view of the possible pragmatic dynamics of Chinese market bargaining in the data.

The notion of a conventionalised 'strategy' is important in the analysis because it reveals that ritual bargaining in Chinese markets is a typical every-day non-ceremonial ritual (see Kádár 2017), in the respect that few Ritual speech act types are used in this practice. The Core Phase is equally devoid of ceremonial Ritual speech acts and the interactional ritual is realised through conventionalised strategies.

Strategies of Chinese Market Bargaining

Bargaining essentially represents a conflict of interest since, in a sense, the seller has to make a decision on whether to give in to the buyer's request to provide the requested goods at a lower price, and the buyer generally deploys various strategies to persuade the seller to give in to his request. These strategies can only unfold if the seller is willing to engage in the ritual of bargaining: as the analysis of unsuccessful transactions below will illustrate, sometimes the seller does not allow the ritual to unfold. The strategies of bargaining in Chinese markets which have been identified in the analysis represent ritual aggression. The reason why such aggression is defined as 'ritual' accords with what has already been discussed in detail in Chapter 3: as part of the ritual frame of the interaction, aggression and related face threat are kept within certain boundaries. Furthermore, from the data, it transpires that the participants tend to be familiar with the conventions of the ritual game, and so they did not take the aggression seriously (see also Kádár 2017). As the analysis will demonstrate, there is often a sense of overlap between the various strategies identified in this study. The reason for establishing these strategies is that they help the analyst to systematise the phenomenon under investigation.

Strategy 1: Pressuring the Seller to Lower the Price

A key strategy for persuading the seller to lower the price of the requested product is to exert pressure on her in the form of a ritual threat. Such ritual threats tend to be realised in the form of the speech act Request (to-do-x), followed by a Grounder. The Request tends to be direct (see Blum-Kulka et al. 1989), hence emphasising the buyer's determination to terminate the transaction if the seller does not give in. The operation of this strategy is illustrated by Example 11.5:

Example 11.5

1.	买家：	能便宜不?
2.	卖家：	7块5进的。
3.	买家：	8块我就买,
		不给就走了。
4.	卖家：	那行,卖你吧。算我开个张吧, 图
		个吉利数。

1.	B:	Would you sell it cheaper?	1. Request (to-do-x) (Initiate)
2.	S:	The purchase price is 7.5 *yuan*.	2. Tell (Counter)
3.	B:	8 *yuan*,	3. Request (to-do-x) (Counter)
		or I'll leave.	Grounder
4.	S:	All right take it then. This is my first	4. Willing (Satisfy) Grounder
		transaction today and the price is the	
		lucky number.[2]	

Following the initial request in line 1, the buyer realises a direct Request in line 3, which can be defined as 'mood derivable' (see Blum-Kulka et al. 1989), followed by a Grounder ('or I'll leave'). This very direct Request conveys a sense of aggression. In many other contexts in both Chinese and other linguacultures, such a direct realisation of a Request would be unacceptable in a business setting.

However, since in this case the aggression and the related face threat are of a ritual nature and are part of the expected ritual frame, the seller not only gives in but also elaborates his Willing, which Satisfies the Request. Interestingly, the Grounder that follows the Willing in line 4 is also a ritual in the popular sense of the word: the seller indicates that he is giving in to the pressure being exerted by the buyer because selling the product for eight *yuan* will bring him good luck (eight is considered to be the most important lucky number in China).

Strategy 2: Belittling the Seller's Business Methods or His Shop

A frequently used strategy in the data includes cases in which the buyer criticises the methods used by the seller to persuade him to sell the goods at a lower price. Example (11.6) illustrates the operation of this strategy:

Example 11.6

1.	买家：	这是啥肉的？
2.	卖家：	羊腿肉的。
3.	买家：	怎么卖这个？
4.	卖家：	42 一斤。
5.	买家：	这么贵？
6.	卖家：	给你串好了还贵呀?多省事！
7.	买家：	你已经串上了还怎么卖呀？
		也 …这么称呀？
8.	卖家：	对呀。签子也一起称。
9.	买家：	那签子也42一斤呀？
10.	卖家：	串多费劲呢!只能给你抹零。
11.	买家：	那先来20串尝尝吧。
12.	卖家：	32块8, 32。

1.	B:	What meat is this?	1. Request for information (Initiate)
2.	S:	Lamb leg.	2. Tell (Satisfy)
3.	B:	How much is it?	3. Request for information (Initiate)
4.	S:	42 yuan per *jin*.	4. Tell (Satisfy)
5.	B:	So expensive?	5. Opine (Initiate)
6.	S:	Is it expensive when I sell ready-made skewers?	6. Opine (Counter)
		This saves you a lot of trouble!	Opine (Counter)
7.	B:	If you've made the skewers already how will you sell them?	7. Opine (Counter)
		Then … Weigh them in total?	Request for information (Initiate)
8.	S:	Yes. The skewers will be weighed together.	8. Tell (Satisfy)
9.	B:	So, skewers are also sold at 42 yuan per *jin*?	9. Request for information (Initiate)
10.	S:	It takes time to put muttons on skewers.	10. Opine (Counter)
		I can only give you a little discount.	Suggest (Satisfy)
11.	B:	I'll take 20 skewers first.	11. Request (to-do-x) (Initiate)
12.	S:	32.8 *yuan*. 32 *yuan* then.	12. Tell (Satisfy), Willing

As the dynamics of this interaction reveal, a key speech act category through which aggression is realised is Opine. In Example 11.6, the first Opine is realised by the buyer in line 5 when he asks 'So expensive?'. This Initiating Opine is Countered by the Opines realised by the seller, which function as Counters. The buyer, in turn, deploys another Opine in line 7, Countering the seller's Counters. The Opines, particularly the Opines realised by the buyer, are only aggressive to a certain degree, hence their ritual nature, i.e., the ritual cancels out fully-fledged aggression and related face-threat. The data shows that belittling the seller's methods (and the product on sale, see more below) showcases a sense of interest in the product, and so aggression in the ritual frame boosts rather than complicates the success of the transaction.

The next Example 11.7 is similar to Example 11.6, although in this case it is both the shop itself and the method of the seller that the buyer degrades:

Example 11.7

1.	买家:	便宜点?总在你家买。
2.	卖家:	不便宜了,你和商场比比,原价358的,最多打9折。
3.	买家:	这不来你家嘛,不去商场,再便宜点儿?
4.	卖家:	(摇头)
5.	买家:	我买2双。
6.	卖家:	那天一老太太也给孩子买,买2双,我也没打折。
7.	买家:	我不常来嘛。你看,孩子现在穿的鞋就是你家巴布豆的。
8.	卖家:	你买这个便宜,100,还白色,孩子幼儿园一定要。
9.	买家:	有了,上次买了。上次都买2双了,都便宜了。
10.	卖家:	(略显犹豫)2双,去个零。
11.	买家:	就6块呀,大老板。
12.	卖家:	疫情,今年生意不好做……
13.	买家:	再便宜点儿,再便宜点儿。
14.	卖家:	凑个整。微信呀,扫这个。(交钱)
15.	买家:	下次还来。

1.	B:	Can you give me a cheaper price? I'm a regular customer here.	1. Request (to-do-x) (Initiate) Grounder
2.	S:	It's not possible. You can compare it with the price in department stores. The original price is 358 *yuan*, while the maximum discount is 10 per cent.	2. Resolve (Counter) Grounder Grounder
3.	B:	Am I not in your shop now? This is not a department store. So, would you give it to me any cheaper?	3. Request (for information) (Counter) Opine (Counter) Request (to-do-x) (Initiate)
4.	S:	(shaking his head)	4. [nonverbal Contra]
5.	B:	I'll take two pairs.	5. Suggest (Initiate)
6.	S:	An old lady bought two pairs for her grandchild the other day, but I did not give her any discount.	6. Tell (Counter)
7.	B:	I always come here. Look, my grandchild is wearing shoes from your store.	7. Tell (Initiate) Grounder
8.	S:	This pair is cheaper, just 100 *yuan*, and is white. Kindergartens always require white shoes.	8. Suggest (Initiate) Grounder
9.	B:	We have, last time, we've already bought one pair. Last time we bought two pairs here, and we got a discount.	9. Tell (Counter) Grounder
10.	S:	(slightly hesitant) Two pairs, I'll give you a small discount.	10. Resolve (Satisfy)
11.	B:	Only 6 *yuan* cheaper?! Boss!	11. Request (for information) (Counter) Grounder
12.	S:	It's the pandemic, you know, business this year has not been as good as before...	12. Tell (Counter) Grounder
13.	B:	Make it cheaper, make it cheaper.	13. Request (to-do-x) (Counter)
14.	S:	Let's just round it up. WeChat? Scan this. (pays for the shoes)	14. Resolve (Satisfy) Request (for information) Request (to-do-x)
15.	B:	I'll come to your store next time.	15. Willing (Initiate)

The bargaining in Example 11.7 starts when the buyer realises a Request (to-do-x) and boosts it with a Grounder. Initially, the seller Counters the Request with the speech act of Resolve, which as an illocution essentially concerns the *speaker's* actions and interests, and is made as a response to a Request or a Suggest (see Edmondson & House 1981: 142). Importantly, the seller's Resolve functions here as a Counter rather than a Contra, and so the ritual of bargaining can unfold. In response, the buyer deploys the strategy of belittling the shop. First, he makes a Request (for information) by uttering 'Am I not in your shop', followed by an Opine. This Request is not 'innocent': since it is clear that he *is* in a low-cost shop in a marketplace, the question realises a sense of ritual aggression and serves as a lead-in for the ensuing bargaining. The bargaining process continues as the buyer re-Initiates it through a Request (to-do-x) which the seller declines through a non-verbal Contra, followed by a Suggest to re-Initiate the bargaining, which is Countered with a Tell. The buyer's repetition of the Requests is also a form of aggression: he keeps putting pressure on the seller. As part of the bargaining process, the buyer makes an appeal for a special discount through a Tell in line 7, and in line 8 the seller indicates his intention to reach a deal by Suggesting an alternative option. In line 9 the buyer belittles the seller's methods, by claiming that the seller is being inconsistent in his selling methods. In response, in line 10 the seller gives in by offering some minimal discount. In line 11, the buyer again uses a 'non-innocent' Request (for information), uttering 'Only 6 *yuan* cheaper?!', and he supports this Request by adding the term of address 'Boss!' in a slightly tongue-in-cheek manner. In line 12, the seller tries to reduce the intensity of the bargaining, by reminding the buyer that currently there is a pandemic (in reference to COVID-19). In lines 13 and 14, the bargaining ritual reaches a conclusion. Finally, in line 15 the satisfied buyer Initiates a Willing to come back to the store – this Willing represents a transition from the Core Phase to a proper Closing Phase, which is relatively rare in the data studied in this case study.

Strategy 3: Belittling the Product

Another basic strategy found in the data includes attempts made by the buyer to persuade the seller to sell the product for a cheaper price by belittling the product. Example 11.8 illustrates the operation of this strategy:

Example 11.8
1. 买家： 好贵啊!50块能卖么?
2. 商家： 这个价不能卖。你再添点,
             合适的话我就当给你捎
             儿了。
3. 买家： 老板,这背心儿虽然全
             棉的,
             但好像没有经过处理,一洗
             就变形,也就值50。
4. 商家： 你放心吧!不会变形的。
5. 买家： 还花里胡哨的!
6. 商家： 在家穿怕啥?你再添点儿!
7. 买家： 最多给你55。
8. 商家： 真能讲!这都赔钱!就当给
             你捎了!

1.	B:	It costs too much! Can you sell it for 50 *yuan*?	1.	Opine (Counter) Request (to-do-x)
2.	S:	No, not at that price. Add a bit more: I'll sell it to you at the wholesale price.	2.	Resolve (Counter) Suggest (Initiate)
3.	B:	Boss, although this vest is made of 100 per cent cotton, it doesn't seem to have been produced with special technology. It may deform after washing. It is only worth 50 *yuan*.	3.	Opine (Counter)
4.	S:	Don't worry! It won't deform.	4.	Opine (Counter)
5.	B:	It's also too fancy!	5.	Opine (Counter)
6.	S:	It's for home wear! Does it matter? Pay more.	6.	Opine (Counter) Request (to-do-x) (Counter)
7.	B:	I'll pay 55 *yuan* at most.	7.	Resolve (Satisfy)
8.	S:	You are really good at bargaining! I'll lose money this time! No profit at all!	8.	Remark (Satisfy) Opine (Satisfy) Tell (Satisfy)

In line 1, the buyer Initiates the Core Phase by Countering the seller's Tell, which occurred in the Opening Phase, which is not featured in the transcript. The buyer's Request (to-do-x) is Countered by the seller who, in line 2, first declines the Request through a Resolve and then re-Initiates the ritual of bargaining by realising a Suggest. In line 3, the buyer belittles the product through an elaborate Opine, Countering the seller's Suggest. This Opine is followed by a sequence of Opines in lines 4–6. Ultimately, in line 8 the bargaining succeeds, and the seller makes a noteworthy metapragmatic reference to the ritual of bargaining, by realising a complimenting Remark and adding an Opine which claims that he is the 'loser' of the ritual game.

The strategy of aggressively belittling a product can be very intensive. For example, in Example 11.9, the buyer belittles the product while at the same time putting pressure on the seller by referring to time:

Example 11.9

1.	买家：	3 块5吧!
2.	商家：	还抹我?
3.	买家：	哎呀，你那都半拉的。
4.	商家：	哪半拉的?就是个儿小。要不能这么便宜?
5.	买家：	一共给你4块钱，你这玩意也就是扔的玩意。
6.	商家：	你这不是6块钱嘛，你给我5块钱不就得了吗? 还在那犟啥呀?

7.	买家:	我说给你4块钱, 你这玩意也就是扔的玩意。
8.	商家:	那你给我多钱一个呀?一块、两块、三块、四块, 你给我5毛钱一个?
9.	买家:	快快快!拿袋儿来, 我要走了, 孩子在外面等我呢!
10.	商家:	一共给我5块钱。
11.	买家:	孩子在外面等我呢!给我拿袋儿来!太糙了, 下回再来买你的得了呗。
12.	商家:	不用你买了!你给我5块钱。
13.	买家:	你不用我买用谁买呀?你瞅你这都瘪啥样了。
14.	商家:	要不能这么卖吗?
15.	买家2:	那人家好的也是这价!
16.	商家:	你再给1块!给你抹1块就行了!
17.	买家2:	你咋给我抹1块了呢?你抹啥了抹?

1.	B:	3.5 *yuan*!	1.	Request (to-do-x) (Initiate)
2.	S:	Why are your bargaining?	2.	Request (for information) (Counter)
3.	B:	Well, the corns are half.	3.	Opine (Satisfy)
4.	S:	Half?	4.	Request (for information) (Counter)
		They are just small. That's why the price is low!		Opine Grounder
5.	B:	4 *yuan* in total.	5.	Request (to-do-x) (Counter)
		Your corns are not full.		Grounder Opine
		They would be thrown away otherwise [if I don't buy them].		
6.	S:	You should give me 6 *yuan*.	6.	Request (to-do-x) (Counter)
		But I'm only asking for 5 *yuan*.		Resolve Request (for information)
		Why are you being so obstinate?		
7.	B:	I said I will only give you 4 *yuan*.	7.	Resolve (Counter)
		They are not good enough.		Grounder
		They will be thrown away if I don't buy them.		Grounder
8.	S:	Then how much will you pay for each one?	8.	Request (for information) (Initiate)
		One, two, three, four [counts corns], you'll give me 50 cents for each?		Resolve
9.	B:	Hurry up! Hurry up! Give me a plastic bag.	9.	Request (to-do-x) (Initiate),
		I have to go. My child is waiting for me outside!		Request (to-do-x), Grounder Grounder
10.	S:	5 *yuan* in total.	10.	Resolve (Initiate)
11.	B:	My son is waiting for me outside!	11.	Tell (Initiate)
		Give me a bag!		Request (to-do-x)
		They [the corns] are not good.		Opine Suggest
		I will come here again!		
12.	S:	Don't come here again!	12.	Request (not-to-do-x) (Counter)
		You give me 5 *yuan*.		Request (to-do-x)
13.	B:	Who will buy your corns except me?	13.	Request (for information) (Counter)
		They are shriveled.		Grounder
14.	S:	That's why they are so cheap!	14.	Opine (Counter)
15.	B:	I've seen other better ones at the same price!	15.	Opine (Counter)
16.	S:	You have to pay me 1 *yuan* more!	16.	Request (to-do-x) (Counter)
		I've already given you discount of 1 *yuan*!		Grounder
17.	B:	Did you give me discount of 1 *yuan*?	17.	Request (for information) (Counter)
		I don't see it!		Grounder
		[the transaction successfully concludes as the buyer pays]		

In line 1, the buyer Initiates the ritual of bargaining by realising a very direct Request (see Blum-Kulka et al. 1989). In line 2, the seller makes a 'non-innocent' Request for information as a Counter, by ritually criticising the buyer for trying to bargain. In line 3, the buyer makes a Satisfying Opine. This marks the start of the strategy of belittling the product, and this strategy spans across all the ensuing interaction. In lines 4–8 the bargaining continues. In line 9, the factor of time is introduced into the interaction, in order to put greater pressure on the seller. In line 9, the buyer reiterates the strategy of using time pressure, and in line 11 she realises a Suggest, promising the buyer that she will be a returning customer. The seller Counters this in line 12 by uttering the ritually rude Request (not-to-do-x) ('Don't come here again'). The fact that the transaction succeeds despite the various forms of aggression involved showcases the operation of the ritual frame underlying the interaction. For example, in line 13 the buyer utters 'Who will buy your corns except me?', followed by an Opine and another series of Counters. If no ritual frame were in operation here, allowing the interactants to interpret criticism as part of the ritual game, the interaction would very likely turn out to be unsuccessful.

11.4.3   Unsuccessful Bargaining

Thus far this case study has focused on cases in which bargaining results in a successful outcome, i.e., the seller and the buyer agree on a price for the goods being sold. In order to provide a more comprehensive view of the ritual of bargaining in Chinese markets, it is worth considering cases in which the bargaining process is not successful. Examples 11.10 and 11.11 illustrate such cases:

Example 11.10

1. 买家：这个多钱？
2. 卖家：50。
3. 买家：能便宜点不？
4. 卖家：我家不讲价，
        谁来都这个价位。

1. B:	How much is it?	1. Request (for information) (Initiate)
2. S:	50.	2. Tell (Satisfy)
3. B:	Can you make it cheaper?	3. Request (to-do-x) (Initiate)
4. S:	This shop doesn't do bargaining. We have only one price.	4. Resolve (Contra) Grounder

Example 11.11

1. 买家： 能便宜点儿不?
2. 卖家： 200 以上9毛;超过200, 9毛;不
   超过200就是1块钱1个。
3. 买家： 再便宜点儿呗?
4. 卖家： 最低价了,这不能便宜,我这批
   发价。

1. B:	Can you make it cheaper?	1. Request (to-do-x) (Initiate)
2. S:	200 or more than 200, 0.9 yuan for each.	2. Resolve (Counter)
	No more than 200, 1 yuan for each.	
3. B:	A bit cheaper?	3. Request (to-do-x) (Counter)
4. S:	This is the lowest price. I cannot make any further reduction.	4. Resolve (Contra) Grounder
	It is the wholesale price.	Grounder

In Example 11.10, the buyer's Request (to-do-x) after the Opening Phase – which in other cases would Initiate bargaining in the Core Phase – is rebuked by the seller. This rebuke is a Contra rather than a Counter, and it ends the interaction: the buyer simply leaves the stall. In Example 11.11 the buyer is more persistent: in line 3 she continues to bargain after the seller's initial Counter in line 2, by repeating her Request for a cheaper price, hence Countering the seller's price offer. In line 4, the seller Contras this repeated Request, which terminates the interaction.

11.5   Conclusion and Summary of Part III

This chapter has discussed how the second methodological take on ritual can be used to study a context and a related ritual frame which trigger conventionalised ritual behaviour but cannot be subsumed under a single ritual heading from the pragmatician's point of view. Market bargaining is a typical manifestation of such a ritual: while both lay and academic observers would agree that it is ritual, for the pragmatician such a general observation is only valid if one is able to pin it down in a replicable way, by using pragmatic units of analysis. The approach proposed in the chapter uses the foundations of the model proposed in the previous Chapter 10. However, it is of a discourse-analytic scope and focuses on language use in one particular ritual frame.

As the case study of Chinese market bargaining has shown, the framework allows us to systematically describe complex interactions such as bargaining in which ritual plays a particularly important role. The analysis has demonstrated that while interactions between sellers and buyers in Chinese markets surprisingly lack ritual Opening and Closing Phases and the related ritual speech act categories – which characterise Opening and Closing Talk in daily interaction – the Core Phase of Chinese market interactions tends to be realised through conventional ritual strategies whenever a bargaining process unfolds. The system of speech acts in interactional slots and the notion of ritual frame provided a replicable framework for capturing the ritual phenomenon under investigation.

The case study has focused on the interactional use of speech acts, considering that the finite, replicable and interactionally defined set of speech acts is in the centre of the model used in both Chapters 10 and 11. However, it is relevant to note the analysis presented here could be complemented with the study of ritual frame indicating expressions (RFIEs) discussed in various previous chapters. As the team of researchers involved in the present study observed, participants of Chinese market bargaining tend to use conventionalised RFIEs to indicate that the aggression is unfolding in a ritual frame, hence deindividuating the aggression involved in the ritual of market bargaining.

The present chapter has once again shown the analytic power of the ritual perspective. In the ritual frame of Chinese market bargaining, the interactants use many forms of language behaviour which would qualify as aggressive and 'impolite' in other (non-ritual) contexts of language use. However, provided that their use does not saliently trespass what the ritual frame tolerates they are regarded as acceptable and even expected parts of the ritual of bargaining.

In summary, Part III of this book has covered two major methodological routes through which ritual can be studied in pragmatics, including approaches which depart from interpreting ritual as a form, and others which take ritual as a context as their departure point. I argued that the choice of a particular methodology largely depends on the choice of analytic unit through which a particular inquiry proceeds. What brings all these methodological considerations together is that they all operate with the three core units of pragmatic research – i.e., expressions, speech acts and discourse – with speech acts being at the centre of analytic foci.

After having discussed methodological issues in the pragmatic study of ritual, the following and final Chapter 12 concludes this book and discusses various areas of future research.

11.6   Recommended Reading

Edmondson, W., House J., Kádár, D. (2023) *Expressions, Speech Acts and Discourse: A Pedagogic Interactional Grammar of English*. Cambridge: Cambridge University Press.

The analytic framework of the second part of Part III builds heavily on the seminal work of Edmondson and House, which is now available in an updated and extended format in the above book. The following excerpt is from this book, where the authors discuss various principles of using the typology of speech acts also adopted in the represent book in data analysis:

A remark is due about using this typology to 'code' data. This system is essentially interactional, meaning that in interpreting speech acts and coding them according to our typology one should avoid trying to 'interpret' the speaker's intention, especially in naturally occurring data. Speech acts should be coded first according to their formal realisation rather than the alleged intention of the speaker. As a second step, one needs to interpret the interactionally situated function of a speech act, which may be different from the formal realisation. Consider the following:

—What the heck are you doing

On the formal level, a Wh-question like this is a Request-for-information . . ., and, as such, should be coded accordingly. However, as part of this coding procedure, the analyst should also make it clear that the interactional function of this utterance is Complain.

. . . let us here revisit why this typology is advantageous for the study of real-life data in English and beyond, including typologically distant languages such as Chinese. The number of speech acts, in theory, could be infinite. But this leads to questions: What would be the point of such an infiniteness? If one invents a new speech act to fit one's analysis, would such a speech act be comparable across linguacultures? Our typology proposes a finite system of empirically derived categories of illocutionary acts which fill slots in an interactional system. (Edmondson et al. 2023: 104)

12   Conclusion

12.1   Retrospect

In the following, I provide short synopses of the chapters of this book:
- Chapter 1: Provided an introduction, including its objectives and the concept of the ritual perspective, as well as the conventions used in this book.
- Chapter 2: Positioned interaction ritual in the field of pragmatics and defined its key features, hence providing a framework to be used in the present book.
- Chapter 3: Discussed why and how the ritual perspective can help us to understand and replicably analyse seemingly *ad hoc* and erratic events, such as mediatised rites of aggression.
- Chapter 4: Considered why and how the ritual perspective can help us to understand and analyse social protocols in public discourse, representing seemingly redundant language use.
- Chapter 5: Explored the phenomenon of mimesis, which is a typical aspect of ritual behaviour, from a pragmatic point of view.
- Chapter 6: Explored the phenomenon of (self-)displaying behaviour, which is another typical aspect of ritual behaviour.
- Chapter 7: Examined liminality, yet another typical aspect of ritual behaviour.
- Chapter 8: Discussed the relationship between expressions, the smallest unit of pragmatic analysis, and ritual, by proposing a bottom–up, corpus-based and replicable approach.
- Chapter 9: Examined how speech acts associated with ritual can be studied without creating 'new' speech acts *ad libitum*.
- Chapter 10: Explored how complex ritual behaviour spanning across many different contexts can be described with the aid of corpora, in a bottom–up and replicable way.
- Chapter 11: Discussed how complex ritual behaviour in one particular ritual frame can be described with a discourse-analytic and pragmatically anchored methodology.

12.2   Prospect

As the present book has shown, ritual is a fundamental aspect of language use, which needs to be considered if we aim to understand why people use language in the way they do across linguacultures. Clearly, a single book can simply not capture all the fascinating facets of interaction ritual, and it is hoped that future research will witness more interest in various areas of the pragmatic study of ritual, including cross-cultural and intercultural, historical and second-language pragmatic investigations.

As regards the cross-cultural and intercultural study of ritual, various chapters like Chapter 8 have shown that it is worth comparing ritual language use across linguacultures, especially in typologically distant linguacultures. However, to date little contrastive pragmatic work has been done with an explicit ritual focus, and the linguacultures involved in this book have also been limited simply because I had to operate with languages I know. It would be fundamental for future research to fill this knowledge gap, all the more so because the contrastive pragmatic study of ritual would allow us to study 'ritual-rich' linguacultures, such as Japanese and Arabic on a par with their 'Western' counterparts, without falling into the trap of the so-called 'East–West dichotomy'. Similarly, the intercultural pragmatic study of ritual would provide new insights into intercultural pragmatics. As the present book has shown, ritual is so much present in our daily language use that often one does not notice that one is interacting in a ritual frame until the frame is breached. Some other rituals, such as market bargaining, require strong competence and understanding of linguaculturally embedded pragmatic conventions. It would be important for future research to consider intercultural encounters by focusing on how language users reinforce and breach ritual frames, and subsequent linguaculturally situated reactions to such behaviours.

The importance of ritual for historical pragmatic research perhaps goes without saying because historical pragmaticians have had a vested interest in ritual for a long time. The present book has also used historical data in various chapters because such data provides intriguing and rich examples of ritual language use for the scholar to consider. Future historical pragmatic research on ritual should ideally include a contrastive take, in particular because historical pragmatics currently heavily focuses on English and other mainstream 'Western' linguacultures. A major strength of the ritual perspective is that the key features of interaction ritual discussed in this book exist in every linguaculture, even though their importance may vary in degree. Contrastive pragmatic research comparing culturally embedded historical ritual data could provide new insights into many important questions, such as how historical events and changes influenced the importance of a certain features of ritual – like (self-)displaying behaviour – in social ceremonies and other facets of ritual interaction.

It may be less self-explanatory how second-language pragmatics could benefit from the study of ritual, and it is worth here referring to research I have recently conducted with my colleagues on this area.[1] In these studies, we have found that non-quotidian rituals, like expressing congratulations for someone's eightieth birthday, are more important than would normally be assumed. While the learner of a foreign language may not have many opportunities to participate at ritual events in her target country, in daily interaction there are many scenarios in which one needs to use such rituals. For example, while a foreigner in China may rarely be invited for someone's eightieth birthday party, in one's daily interaction in workplaces and other 'mundane' settings it is very easy to encounter situations where one nevertheless needs to express congratulation for such an event, e.g., when someone's friend mentions that his grandfather just turned eighty. Thus, more research needs to be devoted to the role of pragmatic competence in ritual language use in foreign-language learning.

The existence of these many areas where more research is due shows that the language of ritual is a fascinating phenomenon, which will hopefully trigger further interest in the years to come!

Notes

1   Introduction

1. See Austin (1962); Searle (1969).
2. See e.g., Verhoeven (2011).
3. See Bloch (1989).
4. See Austin (1962).
5. See e.g., Bax (2003b).
6. See e.g., Kádár (2013).
7. Goffman (1967).
8. See e.g., Bax (2010).
9. The concept of the 'communal orientation' of ritual in this book is therefore not related to the so-called 'individual–communal dialectic' (see e.g., Katriel 1991: 4).
10. See an overview of the phenomenon of the function of ritual in social reproduction in Kelly and Kaplan (1990).
11. In this book, I use the term 'sociopragmatics' by following Leech's (1983) definition.
12. See e.g., Lee (2013).
13. See e.g., Ridealgh (2020).
14. See e.g., Collins (2004); Kádár (2017); Garcia (1993).
15. See e.g., Robbins (2015).
16. Readers with an interest in the ethical procedures of pragmatics are advised to consult Locher and Bolander (2019).
17. Here I use 'ad hoc' to distinguish unceremonious and/or non-scripted rituals – often rites of aggression – from ceremonial and scripted ones. For example, while trash talk studied in Chapter 3 has its own conventions, it is typically *ad hoc*. Being *ad hoc* is of course a matter of degree, e.g. goading in ancient societies (see e.g., Tolmie 2003), which can be called an 'ancestor' of trash talk was arguably less *ad hoc* than present-day trash talk.
18. For an overview, see Lorenz's ([1967] 2021) classic. For a more recent discussion on this area, see e.g., Kádár et al. (2019).
19. On 'temporal' versus 'permanent' liminality, see e.g., Karioris (2016).

2   Interaction Ritual: The Basics

1. See e.g., Luger (1983); Alexander (2004).
2. See e.g., Culpeper (1996); Kádár and Márquez-Reiter (2015).
3. See e.g., Ide (1998); Haugh (2004).

4. For a general overview and definition of politeness, see Kádár and Haugh (2013).
5. See an excellent overview in Kopytko (2007).
6. See an overview in Verhoeven (1993); and more recently Lunt (2020).
7. For example, Brown and Levinson (1987) who were cited previously in this chapter and who start their book with a quote from Durkheim, defined ritual largely in Goffman's sense. For instance, they mention the following: 'The "ritual" character of politeness has been much stressed by Goffman and others. One diagnostic of ritual is often held to be repetitive or prepatterned behaviour. Although our theory plays down the importance of politeness routines by stressing the "generative" production of linguistic politeness, polite formulae clearly form an important focal element in folk notions and in the distinction between "personal" tact and "positional" politeness . . ., where the latter is associated with formulaic decorum (Coulmas 1979, 1981).' (see Brown and Levinson 1987: 43).
8. It can be argued that, in pragmatics, moral order has been understood in two different ways (see also Kádár 2017). First, the seminal work of Garfinkel (1964) influenced researchers such as Haugh (2013a, 2015) who pinned down the moral order through interactional notions like adjacency pairs and preference organisation. Second, the sociological framework of Wuthnow (1987) and Douglas (1999) influenced researchers such as Kádár (2017), Parvaresh & Tayebi (2018) and Márquez-Reiter (2022), who interpreted moral order in a discourse-analytic sense. The present book aims to contribute to this second body of research.
9. In this book I largely avoid using the technical terms '(im)politeness' and 'im/politeness' and – unless specified otherwise – use 'politeness' in a general sense to describe both the polite and impolite aspects of language behaviour.
10. This argument also accords with Brown's (2009) argument, i.e., that public settings trigger deferential negative politeness, i.e., strategies of avoiding impeding on the other.
11. Readers with interest in the prosody of politeness are advised to consult the authoritative work of Brown and Prieto (2017).
12. What is argued here is also valid for the concept of 'speech event'. While scholars such as Ilieva (2003) used the category of 'ritual speech events', ritual has many pragmatic characteristics which bind together ritual behaviour across many different speech events, and so I do not adopt the notion of 'speech event' in the present book.
13. Various scholars have used the notions of 'politeness formulas' and 'polite speech acts' (e.g., Held 1996; Taavitsainen & Jucker 2010; Tantucci & Wang 2018), primarily to distinguish certain forms of language use with relevance to politeness and impoliteness from others. While I agree with Eelen (2001) and others that associating forms of language use with politeness is wrong, it might be acceptable to make such an association for typological reasons, provided that the association only serves a practical purpose. See more details in Chapter 8 regarding the problem of associating forms of language use with politeness.
14. It is also worth referring here to Culpeper's (2011) study: Culpeper referred to the conventionalised use of impoliteness between a mother and her child to demonstrate that impoliteness behaviour can become a form of endearment.

15. See relevant overviews in Dégh and Vázsonyi (1983), Ellis (1989) and Németh T. (2008).
16. These include personal rituals and hidden rituals; however, the study of such rituals is normally beyond the scope of pragmatic inquiries. It is worth noting that the pragmatic typological considerations presented in this book are very different from anthropological typologies, which often distinguish rituals according to their situated goals, formal features and effect on the participants. For instance, Victor Turner (1969), whose typology is used in a simplified way in this book, distinguishes ritual types like 'rites of affliction', which in my view are difficult to operationalise in pragmatic inquiries.

3   Order in the Extraordinary: More on the Ritual Perspective

1. Readers with interest in this area are advised to consult Thomassen (2014).
2. See also Kennedy (1966).
3. See www.independent.ie/sport/other-sports/he-talked-about-my-religion-my-country-and-my-father-nurmagomedov-explains-why-he-attacked-mcgregor-team/37392589.html.
4. It is worth noting the way in which various datatypes summarised in Table 3.1 do not fully accord with the order in which they are featured in the analysis of Chapter 3.
5. Importantly, Justify can also be understood as a speech act for its own sake (see Edmondson & House 1981). However, since the present incident centres on a perceived speech act Apologise, it is reasonable here to interpret justification as a realisation type of Apologise.

4   'Politeness' in the Realm of the Overly Ordinary: Concluding Notes on the Ritual Perspective

1. As an example of extreme escalation of aggression in the seemingly 'civil' and institutionalised context of the British parliament, one may refer to the ninety-minute 'shouting match' that the late Prime Minister Liz Truss had with Suella Braverman in October 2022 (see e.g.: https://metro.co.uk/2022/10/20/liz-truss-had-90-minute-shouting-match-with-suella-braverman-before-departure-17599931/ [last accessed 6 June 2023]).
2. I use 'merely' in this sentence because ultimately one may never precisely tell whether an utterance in public political discourse only effects a politician as a person or also the face of the group he is affiliated to. Such a question belongs to the realm of psychology and is not considered in this book.
3. One, for instance, has no way of witnessing autonomous communicative actions at the city level, not mentioning conflict between various administrative levels.
4. Various expressions in the first part of the text which are relevant to the analysis are featured in boxes in the Chinese original and are underlined in the English gloss.
5. Although in Pan & Kádár (2011) I argued that in modern Chinese language use many traditional honorifics are no longer in use, several of the deferential expressions in the corpus of this case study are archaic and follow the format of 'four characters' set phrases (sizi-shuyu 四字熟语). This formal style may also increase the alignment-triggering

function of such texts, as in the wake of a national social crisis it implies that the
authorities are handling the situation professionally and with a sense of gravity.
6. One could argue that 'face' has also not-individual manifestations, such as 'national
face' (Kádár et al. 2013). However, from a pragmatic point of view, communal
manifestations of face also come into existence strictly on the individual level.

5 Mimesis

1. The mimetic notion of conversational convergence (Dragojevic et al. 2016; Giles
2016) has been broadly studied in the field of language and social psychology,
particularly in the context of accommodation theory. Similar to pragmatic research
on 'reciprocation', social psychologists focusing on accommodation pursued interest
in mimesis in everyday conversation where mimesis is not only occasional but is also
preferentially manifested in particular phases of an interaction. For instance, as van
Baaren et al. (2009: 2382) argue, 'Research revealed we don't imitate everyone all
the time. Our tendency to unconsciously mimic is moderated by both enduring and
temporary characteristics of the mimicker and the mimickee.'
2. A small body of historical pragmatic research on ritual has pointed to the importance
of performative mimesis in ceremonial settings – key research in this area was
conducted by Bax (2000, 2003, 2011). Yet, such research did not attempt to
differentiate performative mimesis from its interpersonal counterpart.
3. See also Culpeper et al. (2003).
4. For an overview of the pragmatic repetition, see Johnstone (1994).
5. In Chinese, questions are typically formed with the help of 'questioning' particles
and tag question in sentence-final position.

6 (Self-)Display

1. This corpus of sixty letters is available in a bilingual (Classical Chinese–English)
form in the monograph *Model Letters in Late Imperial China* (see Kádár 2009).
2. Historical Chinese epistolary collections, unlike their European counterparts (e.g.,
Fitzmaurice 2002), usually do not include subscriptions (nor superscriptions), and
so it is usually difficult to date them.
3. See Cole (1980); Zhu and Li (2008).
4. The section *zuo wo chunfeng* 坐我春風, translated as 'you instructed me with noble
words', literally reads 'seating me and [giving me] wise instruction'. *Chunfeng* 春風
(lit. 'spring wind', i.e., '[instructive words that are as pleasant as the] spring breeze')
is an indirect other-elevating expression that refers to the recipient's words.
5. The deferential structure *gan ... miyin* 感 ... 彌殷 ('the gratitude ... for the
abundance [of the other's kindness]', translated as 'I am imbued with the greatest
gratitude') is an honorific expression of gratitude.
6. In the present context *shuyi* 戚誼 (lit. 'ties/emotions between relatives', translated
as 'your kindness') functions as an expression of gratitude by implicitly comparing
the recipient's kindness for the author to that of relatives.
7. The author uses the 'honorific prefix' *zhuo* 拙 (lit. 'clumsy', translated as
'worthless') in order to refer to his own poem, as *zhuoshi* 拙詩 (translated as

'worthless poem'). In historical Chinese deferential communication *zhuo* is a self-denigrating honorific prefix, which can modify nouns that refer to one's own works.

8. *Fengjiao* 奉教 (lit. 'to accept with both hands [the recipient's] teaching', translated as 'beg your esteemed opinion') is an honorific other-elevating verbal form, which refers to the author's symbolical request for the recipient to evaluate his work.

9. In the original text it is evident from the author's reference to the story of the Western Shi and the Eastern Shi hat he applies this anecdote to deferentially diminish the recipient's appraisal. Therefore, in the English translation 'I wonder whether you did not appraise the work mistakenly' is adopted for the sake of clarity.

10. Here the author refers to Fan Li 范蠡 (517–448 BC). Fan was a famous minister of the ancient Wu 吳 State.

11. Here the author refers to the story of the Western and the Eastern Shi (*Zhuangzi*, *Waipian* 外篇, *Tianyun* 天運 [*The Revolution of Heaven*] Chapter, Section 4) and the alleged love between the Western Shi and Fan Li. The author uses this anecdote in order to diminish the recipient's appraisal by drawing an analogy between the recipient and Fan Li, as well as the Eastern Shi and himself.

12. Jingzhou 荊州 is the name of a prefecture in Hubei Province. In the original text the author uses the abbreviated form Jing 荊; in the English translation, for the sake of clarity, Jingzhou occurs in its full form. Xiangzhou 襄州 is the name of a prefecture in Hubei Province. In the original text the author uses the abbreviated form Xiang 襄; in the English translation, for the sake of clarity, Xiangzhou occurs in its full form.

13. *Lianhua-luo* 蓮花落 (lit. 'the falling flowers of the lotus', translated as 'the beggars' song') is the designation of a Chinese dramatic genre of Song Dynasty (960–1279) origin. It was originally performed by blind beggars, and thus the author uses it to symbolically describe his miserable status as an office assistant.

14. The author cites the words *yan jiu-rou* 饜酒肉 ('consume wine and flesh') from *Mencius*'s (*Lilou xia* 離婁下 Chapter, Section 61; *Mencius* 4B-33) anecdote of the boasting person of Qi Kingdom (see above). The source contains the following line: 齊人有一妻一妾而處室者。其良人出，則必饜酒肉而後反 ('A man of Qi had a wife and a concubine and lived with them in his house. When the man went out, he would get himself well filled with wine and flesh, and then return … '). Thus, through this reference the author reinforces the symbolic analogy between office assistants and beggars.

15. It is worth noting that, while biographic information on Zhou Jieyan can only be retrieved from various Shaoxing letter corpora, according to this scarce information he was holder of an official post and a person whom Shaoxing clerks respected. This is further confirmed by the fact that the honorific forms used in the letter show that he was higher ranking than Gong. For example, Gong refers to the recipient by using the other-elevating form of address *lianhua-mu* 蓮花幕, in reference to his office. In the *Xuehongxuan* corpus it is used towards addressees who either serve as magistrates or are at least higher in the office hierarchy than the author (see Kádár 2009).

16. Due to the geographical distances within the Chinese empire and linguistic/dialectal differences, this was often the only way in which elite writers could interact with each other from afar.

17. Note that this is not a speculative claim, in that I have run this term through a corpus of vernacular Chinese (*jindai-Hanyu*) texts to confirm that it occurs in novels and other colloquial sources.

18. *Nuoguan* 搦管 (lit. 'grasping the stalk [of the writing brush]', translated as 'take up my brush and write') is a literary synonym for 'writing correspondence'.

19. Although in the original text it is evident from the context that the author uses the allegory of cut plants (see the next footnote) in order to express his intention to avoid neglecting his correspondence with the recipient, this is not explicitly mentioned, while in the English translation the section 'I shall not neglect our correspondence' is adopted for the sake of clarity.

20. In the present letter the idiom *chang-suo-yuyan* 暢所欲言 (lit. '[speaking] freely what one wants to say', translated as 'narrating one's feelings with artless words') is used in a positive sense.

21. *Hongpian-duanzhi* 鴻篇短製 (lit. 'wild geese essay, short product', translated as 'outstanding letters of various length') is an indirect honorific recipient-elevating form of address, which refers to the correspondence of the recipient. It should be noted that *hongpian-duanzhi* is a modified form of the honorific expression *hongpian-juzhi* 鴻篇巨製 ('wild geese essay, outstanding product', i.e., 'one's masterpiece'). In historical Chinese letter writing *hong* 鴻 ('wild goose') is often used in honorific expressions, as a synonym for 'greatness'; this implication of *hong* originates in the association of wild goose with physical largeness, i.e., a goose is a large (and so great) bird.

22. In the original text the author does not specify the contextual meaning of 'admirers' (*aizhe* 愛者). In the English translation the circumspect section 'by others who also admire your work' is adopted for the sake of clarity.

23. The expression *siliu* 四六 (lit. 'four-six') refers here to the rhythm of parallel prose in Classical Chinese.

24. *Meiyu* 美玉 (lit. 'fine jade', translated as 'refined works') is an indirect recipient-elevating form of address, which refers to the works of the recipient (by using this expression the author deferentially emphasises the contrast between the recipient's and his own works).

25. Although in the original text the author makes an implicit reference to the recipient's works and only refers to them as 'shiny jades', he deferentially avoids directly mentioning them in this request. Therefore, the section 'I would like to ask you, sir, to lend me your works and let them illuminate my worthless collection' is only adopted in the English translation for the sake of clarity.

26. *Wenzi-zhi-jiao* 文字之交 (lit. 'friendship of writing', translated as 'friendship of men of letters') is a traditional Chinese synonym for 'friendship between educated personae'.

27. Although in the original text it is evident from the context that the author differentiates his friendship with the recipient from negative examples, it is not made clear whether *shili-jiao* 勢利交 ('snobbish and greedy connection') refers to a certain negative example or it describes foul relationships in general. In the English translation the general form 'of some of the literati' is adopted after 'snobbish and greedy connection' for stylistic reasons.

28. The idiom *shijia-zhi-pi* 嗜痂之癖 (lit. 'depraved taste of eating scab', translated as 'eccentric taste') is applied in order to deferentially denigrate the quality of the author's

works. Although in the original text it is evident from the context that this idiom denigrates the author's work, its reference is not specified, while in the English translation 'badly written work' is adopted for the sake of clarity.

29. *Fenggao* 奉告 (lit. 'informing deferentially with two hands', translated as 'humbly inform you about this matter') is an honorific recipient-elevating verbal form, which refers to the author's announcement of a certain matter to the recipient.

30. *Rong* 容 ('allow me') often functions as a deferential verbal form in historical Chinese letters.

31. *Qing-jiaoxue* 請教削 (lit. 'asking teaching and cutting [errors]', translated as '[fulfil] my humble request by correcting it') is an honorific recipient-elevating verbal structure, which conveys the author's wish that the recipient critically review his work.

32. It is nevertheless worth bearing in mind that being skilled in etiquette represented a sense of social competiton: in pre-modern and early modern times etiquette was often considered as a 'property' of the elite (see e.g., Watts 1999).

7   Liminality

1. The reader might have noted that here I do not capitalise 'apology'. This is because public apologies mostly manifest themselves as interactional phenomena realised by various speech acts rather than a single speech act.

2. For a general overview of metapragmatics, see Lucy (1993), and Kádár and Haugh (2013).

3. Readers with an interest in the relationship between norms and breaches of the ritual frame are advised to consult Kádár (2020).

4. It would be interesting to consider whether there is any variation between the interpretation of dignity across relatively 'close' linguacultures such as the United Kingdom versus the United States because of differences in employment law.

5. Interestingly, these positive comments appear to reflect 'trolling attempts', that is, it is unclear whether they reflect 'sincere' evaluations (see Hopkinson 2013 on sincerity and trolling).

6. Unlike in Chapter 4, in the current inquiry 'alignment' involves a choice between actors with whom one can align oneself. However, due to the way in which media constructs messages, such a choice is usually not 'objective' as the present case study also shows.

7. These illustrative evaluations are cited from the same website as Example 7.12: www.mirror.co.uk/news/uk-news/boss-justifies-sacking-shocked-staff-11833113 [last accessed 7 June 2023].

8   Methodological Take-1A: The Relationship Between Expressions and Ritual

1. I use 'Apologise' instead of apology, following the convention of the speech act typology proposed by Edmondson and House (1981).

2. Note that 'politeness marker' and 'politeness formula' are not identical: the former is a broader categorisation which includes the grammaticalised expressions by means of which speech acts are realised, honorifics, forms of address and so on, while the latter refers to the stereotypical ways of expressing politeness. Here I only use the term 'politeness marker' to avoid the proliferation of technical terms.

9   Methodological Take-1B: The Relationship Between Speech Acts and Ritual

1. An exception to this is the category of structurally ritual speech acts (see also Chapter 8). However, as was noted, such speech acts are 'ritual' simply because they tend to occur in those parts of an interaction which trigger ritual behaviour. Also, this set of structurally ritual speech acts includes a small number of such speech acts which can be realised in any interaction, including mundane ones.
2. Even though there are of course extended speech acts as well, see e.g., Kádár et al.'s (2018) study of ritual public apologies.
3. Master Yan is a deferential reference to Yan Ying, the author of the *Annals of Master Yan*.
4. King Wu was a highly respected ancient ruler.
5. All translations in this chapter are mine.
6. In pragmatic theory, although Japanese and Korean are usually referred to as the main 'honorific languages' (see e.g., Ide 1989), historical Chinese is also considered to be an 'honorific-rich' linguaculture (Pan & Kádár 2011). For an overview of addressing phenomenon in Chinese, see He and Ren (2016).
7. King Wen, a mythical king, was highly respected in Chinese culture.
8. King Chuling ruled the ancient Kingdom of Chu between 540 and 529 BC.
9. Wu Yun (526–484 BC) was a general and politician in the ancient Kingdom of Wu.
10. Here the adviser – Zhongsun Qiu 仲孫湫 (ca. fifth century BC) – refers to the fact that the Kingdom of Lu, unlike other kingdoms, continued to use the sacred source *Zhouli* 周禮 (*The Rites of Zhou*) in matters of daily governance.
11. Duke Huan ruled the Kingdom of Qi between 685 and 643 BC.
12. The mythical king, King Jie – along with other kings mentioned at this section – was regarded as an archetype of a bad ruler in historical Chinese texts.
13. Shun and Yu, mentioned in this section, were sacred mythical rulers.
14. Guan Jingzhong or Guan Zhong (d. 645 BC) was a philosopher and politician.
15. *Kanggao* is a chapter of *The Book of Documents*.

10   Methodological Take-2A: Capturing Ritual Practices

1. Importantly, this is only a popular association: as historical pragmaticians such as Held (2005) have pointed out, self-denigration can also be found in historical European sources.
2. Notably, Pomerantz used the concept 'self-denigration' outside of the Chinese context as early as 1984.

3. It is worth noting that a key difference between Japanese/Korean and Chinese is that many honorifics in the former are morphemes, while Chinese only has lexemes as honorifics.

4. Readers with an interest in the relationship between ritual and strategy are advised to consult Tuchman (1972).

5. For instance, in terms of the present framework, the label 'refusal' involves any speech act through which a particular move is countered in interaction. This wide use of refusing in interaction implies that it is actually unproductive to define it as a speech act. The same applies to label 'agree': interactants tend to agree with each other by using many different speech acts, and also by supporting each other in many ways in interaction, and so it is simply not productive to narrow down agreement to one particular speech act.

6. This typology of speech acts is also interactional because it approaches speech act categories with relation to one another within Types of Talk (see House & Kádár 2023).

7. The word 'by default' should be emphasised here. The reader may recall the hypothetical example of an angry hiker mentioned in Chapter 6 who shouts an angry Greet at fellow hikers who fail to notice him in a narrow mountain path. In such a case, Greet clearly does have a pragmatic agenda!

8. This novel is attributed to Shi Nai'an 施耐庵 (1333–1368), and so various sources argue that it is a fourteenth-century rather than sixteenth-century novel. However, the first available edition of this source is from the sixteenth century.

9. All translations are mine.

10. As was already noted in Chapter 6, Opine is an Informative illocution which is rather similar to the speech act Tell. However, while in a Tell the speaker states what she or he believes is a fact, through an Opine the speaker states her or his opinion.

11. The term 'Business Talk' is intended to have a rather more general implication than what is normally called 'business'. A business is involved in a pragmatic sense whenever a talk is geared towards an outcome which has practical consequences for one or more of the interactants.

12. In the speech act typology of Edmondson and House (1981), Willing includes both Offer and Promise.

13. Considering that the data here is quasi-authentic, I do not intend to make any grand claim about whether greeting expressions were used in historical Chinese or not. The goal of this investigation is simply to consider what the data reveals about the use of self-denigrating expressions themselves.

11   Methodological Take-2B: Describing Ritual Contexts

1. Focusing on such realisation patterns provides an insight into variations in the pragmatic conventions of bargaining, as witnessed by studies such as Arent (1998), Kharakki (2001), Becker (2002), Chakrani (2007), Winke and Teng (2010), Cohen (2016) and Placencia (2019). For example, Placencia (2019) provides a systematic analysis of bargaining in online settings, Cohen (2016) explores bargaining in L2 settings, while Kharakki (2001) examines bargaining on the macro-cultural level by comparing the bargaining practices of Arabs with their 'Western' counterparts.

2. The seller refers here to the fact that eight is a lucky number in the Chinese linguaculture, and by completing a successful first transaction, the seller believes it has made his day.

12   Conclusion

1. See House and Kádár (2023).

References

Agha, **A.** (1998) Stereotypes and registers of honorific language. *Language in Society* **27**(2), 151–193. https://doi.org/10.1017/S0047404500019849

Agha, **A.** (2005) Voice, footing, enregisterment. *Journal of Linguistic Anthropology* **15** (1), 38–59. https://doi.org/10.1525/jlin.2005.15.1.38

Aijmer, **K.** (2009) *Please*: A politeness formula viewed in a translation perspective. *Brno Studies in English* **35**(2), 63–77.

Ainsworth, **J.** (1993) In a different register: The pragmatics of powerlessness in police interrogation. *The Yale Law Journal* **103**(2), 259–322. https://doi.org/10.2307/797097.

Alexander, **J.** (2004) Cultural pragmatics: Social performance between ritual and strategy. *Sociological Theory* **22**(4), 527–573. https://doi.org/10.1111/j.0735–2751.2004.00233.x

Alexander, J., **Giesen, B.**, **Mast, J.** (eds. 2006) *Social Performance: Symbolic Action, Cultural Pragmatics, and Ritual*. Cambridge: Cambridge University Press. https://doi.org/10.1017/CBO9780511616839

Arent, **R.** (1998) The Pragmatics of Cross-Cultural Bargaining in an Ammani Suq: An Exploration of Language Choice, Discourse Structure and Pragmatic Failure in Discourse Involving Arab and Non-Arab Participants. PhD dissertation, University of Minnesota.

Arizavi, S., **Choubsaz, Y.** (2018) To use or not use the shorter forms: A corpus-based analysis of the apologetic expressions "Sorry and I'm sorry" in American spoken English discourse. *Corpus Pragmatics* **3**(1), 21–47. https://doi.org/10.1007/s41701-018–0045-z

Arnovick, **L.** (1984) *Diachronic Pragmatics: Seven Case Studies in English Illocutionary Development*. Amsterdam: John Benjamins. https://doi.org/10.1075/pbns.68

Austin, **J.** (1962) *How to Do Things with Words*. Oxford: Clarendon Press.

Balteiro, **I.** (2019) The emotional content of English swearwords in football chatspeak: *WTF* and other pragmatic devices. In Calles, M., Levin, M. (eds.), *Corpus Approaches to the Language of Sports: Texts, Media, Modalities*. London: Bloomsbury, 139–160. https://doi.org/10.5040/9781350088238.ch-007

Bargiela-Chiappini, **F.** (2003) Face and politeness: new (insights) for old (concepts). *Journal of Pragmatics* **35**(10/11), 1453–1469. https://doi.org/10.1016/S0378-2166(02)00173-X

Barsalou, **L.** (1992) Frames, concepts and conceptual fields. In Lehrer, A., Feder Kittay, E. (eds.), *Frames, Fields and Contrasts*. Hillsdale, NJ: Erlbaum, 21–74.

Baumgarten, N., House, J., Du Bois, I. (eds.) (2012) *Subjectivity in Language and in Discourse*. Bingley: Emerald.

Bax, M. (1981) Rules for ritual challenges: A speech convention among medieval knights. *Journal of Pragmatics* **5**(5), 423–444. https://doi.org/10.1016/0378–2166 (81)90027–8

Bax, M. (1999) Ritual levelling: The balance between the eristic and contractual motive in hostile verbal encounters in medieval romance and early modern drama. In Jucker, A., Fritz, G., Lebsanft, F. (eds.), *Historical Dialogue Analysis*. Amsterdam: John Benjamins, 35–80. https://doi.org/10.1075/pbns.66.03bax

Bax, M. (2001) Historical frame analysis: Hoaxing and make-believe in a seventeenth-century Dutch play. *Journal of Historical Pragmatics* **2**(1), 33–67. https://doi.org/10.1075/jhp.2.1.03bax

Bax, M. (ed.) (2003a) Ritual language behaviour: Special issue of *Journal of Historical Pragmatics* **4**(2). https://doi.org/10.1075/jhp.4.2

Bax, M. (2003b) Ritual modes, ritual minds: Introduction to the special issue on ritual language behaviour. *Journal of Historical Pragmatics* **4**(2), 159–170. https://doi.org/10.1075/jhp.4.2.02bax

Bax, M. (2010) Epistolary presentation rituals: Face-work, politeness, and ritual display in early-modern Dutch letter writing. In Culpeper, J., Kádár, D. (eds.), *Historical (Im)Politeness*. Bern: Peter Lang, 37–86.

Bednarek, M. (2005) Frames revisited: The coherence-inducing function of frames. *Journal of Pragmatics* **37**, 685–705. https://doi.org/10.1016/j.pragma.2004.09.007

Becker, M. (2002) "Yf ye wyll bergayne wullen cloth or othir marchandise…": Bargaining in early modern language teaching textbooks. *Journal of Historical Pragmatics* **3**(2), 273–297. https://doi.org/10.1075/jhp.3.2.06bec

Bendazzoli, C. (2023 ahead of print) Breaching protocol and flouting norms on the European Parliament floor reactions from a micro- and macro-context perspective in 22 languages. *Contrastive Pragmatics* **4**(1), 64–87. https://doi.org/10.1163/2666039 3-bja10072

Berkowitz, L. (1994) On the escalation of aggression. In Potegal, M., Kutzon, J. (eds.), *The Dynamics of Aggression: Biological and Social Processes in Dyads and Groups*. New York, NY: Lawrence Erlbaum Associates, Inc., 33–41.

Billig, M. (2005) *Laughter and Ridicule: Towards a Social Critique of Humour*. Thousand Oaks, CA: Sage. https://doi.org/10.4135/9781446211779

Blackwell, S. (2010) Evaluation as a pragmatic act in Spanish film narratives. *Journal of Pragmatics* **42**(11), 2945–2963. https://doi.org/10.1016/j.pragma.2010.06.018

Bloch, M. (1989) *Ritual, History and Power: Selected Papers in Anthropology*. London: Routledge.

Blum-Kulka, S. (1987) Indirectness and politeness in requests: Same or different?. *Journal of Pragmatics* **11**(2), 131–146. https://doi.org/10.1016/0378–2166(87)9019 2–5

Blum-Kulka, S. (1990) You don't touch lettuce with your fingers: Parental politeness in family discourse. *Journal of Pragmatics* **14**(2), 259–288. https://doi.org/10.1016/03 78–2166(90)90083-P

Blum-Kulka, S., House, J., Kasper, G. (eds.) (1989) *Cross-Cultural Pragmatics: Requests and Apologies*. Norwood, NJ: Ablex.

Boxer, **D.**, **Cortés-Conde F.** (1997) From bonding to biting: Conversational joking and identity display. *Journal of Pragmatics* **27**(3), 275–294. https://doi.org/10.1016/S03 78-2166(96)00031–8

Brinton, **L.** (2001) Historical discourse analysis. In Schriffin, D., Tannen, D., Hamilton, H. (eds.), *The Handbook of Discourse Analysis*. Oxford: Blackwell, 138–160. https://doi.org/10.1002/9781118584194.ch10

Brown, **L.**, **Prieto**, **P.** (2017) (Im)politeness: Prosody and gesture. In Culpeper, J., Haugh, M., Kádár, D. (eds.), *The Palgrave Handbook of Linguistic (Im)politeness*. Basingstoke: Palgrave Macmillan, 357–379. https://doi.org/10.1057/978–1-137–37 508-7_14

Brown, **P.** (2009) Gender, politeness, and confrontation in Tenejapa. *Discourse Processes* **13**(1), 123–141. https://doi.org/10.1080/01638539009544749

Brown, **P.**, **Levinson**, **S. J.** (1987) *Politeness: Some Universals of Language Usage*. Cambridge: Cambridge University Press.

Bruti, **S.** (2018) (Im)politeness rituals in The Young Pope and teaching pragmatics. In Werner, W. (ed.), *The Language of Pop Culture*. New York, NY: Routledge, 230–251. https://doi.org/10.4324/9781315168210

Bryant, **G. A.**, **Fox Tree**, **J. E.** (2005) Is there an ironic tone of voice? *Language and Speech* **48**(3), 257–277. https://doi.org/10.1177/00238309050480030101

Bull, **P.**, **Fetzer**, **A.**, **Kádár, D**. (2020) The strategic use of ritual references to the Speaker of the UK House of Commons. *Pragmatics* **30**(1), 64–87. https://doi.org/10 .1075/prag.19020.bul

Byon, **A.** (2003) Language socialisation and Korean as a heritage language: A study of Hawaiian classrooms. *Language, Culture and Curriculum* **16**(3), 269–283. https://doi .org/10.1080/07908310308666674

Cai, **M**. (2009) Mingdai guanyuan jinjian moshi ji qi tedian (The key features of admonishments in the Ming Dynasty). *Beijing Lianhe Daxue Xuebao* (Journal of Beijing United University) **7**(4), 62–68.

Chafe, **W.** (1994) *Discourse, Consciousness and Time*. Chicago, IL: University of Chicago Press.

Chakrani, **B.** (2007) Cultural context and speech act theory: A socio-pragmatic analysis of bargaining exchanges in Morocco. *Texas Linguistics Forum* **51**, 43–53.

Chen, **K.** (2017) The Book of Odes: A case study of the Chinese hermeneutic tradition. In Tu, I. (ed.), *Interpretation and Intellectual Change: Chinese Hermeneutics in Historical Perspective*. New York, NY: Routledge, 47–62. https://doi.org/10.4324 /9780203788288

Chen, **R.** (1993) Responding to compliments: A contrastive study of politeness strategies between American English and Chinese speakers. *Journal of Pragmatics* **20**(1), 49–75. https://doi.org/10.1016/0378–2166(93)90106-Y

Chen, **R.** (2001) Self-politeness: A proposal. *Journal of Pragmatics* **33**, 87–106. https:// doi.org/10.1016/S0378-2166(99)00124–1

Chen, **R.** (2010) Pragmatics east and west: Similar or different. In Trosborg, A. (ed.), *Pragmatics across Languages and Cultures*. Berlin: Mouton de Gruyter, 167–187. https://doi.org/10.1515/9783110214444.1.167

Chen, **R.** (2020) Single author self-reference: Identity construction and pragmatic competence. *Journal of English for Academic Purposes* **45**, 203–214. https://doi .org/10.1016/j.jeap.2020.100856

Chen, W. (2011) *Richang hanyu guiquan yanyu xingwei ji celüeyanjiu* (On admonishing speech acts and strategies adopted in daily Chinese communication). *Jixi Daxue Xuebao* (Journal of Jixi University) **11**(2), 130–133.

Chen, X. (2019) 'Family-culture' and Chinese politeness: An emancipatory pragmatic account. *Acta Linguistica Academica* **66**(2), 251–270. https://doi.org/10.1556/2062 .2019.66.2.6

Chen, X., Yao, Y. (2015) Yi jisuanji weimeijie de hanyufuwu jiechuyulei yanjiu (A study on the genre of Chinese service encounter mediated by computer). *Xi'an Waiguoyu Daxue Xuebao* (Journal of Xi' an International Studies University) **23**(2), 43–47.

Cohen, A. (2008) Teaching and assessing L2 pragmatics: What can we expect from learners? *Language Teaching* **41**(2), 213–235. https://doi.org/10.1017 /S0261444807004880

Cohen, A. (2016) The teaching of pragmatics by native and nonnative language teachers: What they know and what they report doing. *Studies in Second Language Learning and Teaching* **6**(4), 561–585. https://doi.org/10.14746/ssllt.2016.6.4.2

Cole, J. (1980) The Shaoxing connection: A vertical administrative clique in late Qing China. *Modern China* **6**(3), 317–326. https://doi.org/10.1177/009770048000600

Collins, R. (2004) *Interaction Ritual Chains*. Princeton, NJ: Princeton University Press. https://doi.org/10.1515/9781400851744

Cook, H. (1998) Situational meanings of Japanese social deixis: The mixed use of the masu and plain forms. *Journal of Linguistic Anthropology* **8**(1), 87–110. https://doi .org/10.1525/jlin.1998.8.1.87

Cook, H. (2005) Reanalysis of discernment from a social constructivist perspective: Academic consultation sessions in Japanese universities (Research note #42). University of Hawaii, National Foreign Language Resource Center, Honolulu.

Coulmas, F. (1979) On the sociolinguistic relevance of routine formulae. *Journal of Pragmatics* **3**(3/4), 239–266. https://doi.org/10.1016/0378-2166(79)90033-X

Coulmas, F. (1981) Conversational routine. In Coulmas, F. (ed.), *Conversational Routine: Explorations in Standardized Communication Situations and Prepatterned Speech*. Berlin: Mouton de Gruyter, 1–18.

Culpeper, J. (1996) Towards an anatomy of impoliteness. *Journal of Pragmatics* **15**(3), 349–367. https://doi.org/10.1016/0378–2166(95)00014–3

Culpeper, J. (2005) Impoliteness and entertainment in the television quiz show: The Weakest Link. *Journal of Politeness Research* **1**(1), 35–72. https://doi.org/10.1515/ jplr.2005.1.1.35

Culpeper, J. (2011) *Impoliteness: Using Language to Cause Offence*. Cambridge: Cambridge University Press. https://doi.org/10.1017/CBO9780511975752

Culpeper, J., Bousfield, D., Wichmann. A. (2003) Impoliteness revisited: With special reference to dynamic and prosodic aspects. *Journal of Pragmatics* **35**(10/11), 1545–1579. https://doi.org/10.1016/S0378-2166(02)00118-2

Culpeper, J., Demmen, J. (2011) Nineteenth-century English politeness: Negative politeness, conventional indirect requests and the rise of the individual self. *Journal of Historical Pragmatics* **12**(1/2), 49–81. https://doi.org/10.1075/jhp.12.1–2.03cul

Culpeper, J., Kádár, D. (eds.) (2010) *Historical (Im)Politeness*. Bern: Peter Lang. https://doi.org/10.3726/978–3–0351–0025-9

Culpeper, J., Terkourafi, M. (2017) Pragmatic approaches (im)politeness. In Culpeper, J., Haugh, M., Kádár, D. (eds.), *The Palgrave Handbook of Linguistic*

(Im)Politeness. Basingstoke: Palgrave Macmillan, 11–39. https://doi.org/10.1057/9 78–1-137–37508-7_2

Dadlez, **E.** (2011) Truly funny: Humor, irony, and satire as moral criticism. *The Journal of Aesthetic Education* **45**(1), 1–17. https://doi.org/10.5406/jaesteduc.45.1.0001

Dauphinais, **M.**, **Levering**, **M.** (2005) *Holy People, Holy Land: A Theological Introduction to the Bible*. New York, NY: Baker Books.

Dégh, **L.**, **Vázsonyi**, **A.** (1983) Does the word "dog" bite? Ostensive action: A means of legend-telling. *Journal of Folklore Research* **20**(1), 5–34.

Dobs, **A.**, **Garcés-Conejos Blitvich**, **P.** (2013) Impoliteness in polylogal interaction: Accounting for face threat witnesses' responses. *Journal of Pragmatics* **52**, 112–130. https://doi.org/10.1016/j.pragma.2013.05.002

Donald, **M.** (2013) Mimesis theory re-examined, twenty years after the fact. In Hatfield, G., Pittman, H. (eds.), *Evolution of Mind, Brain and Culture*. Philadelphia, PA: University of Pennsylvania Press, 169–192.

Dou, **W.**, **Zhang**, **X.** (2007) Cross-cultural pragmatic analysis of evasion strategy at Chinese and American regular press conferences – with special reference to the North Korean nuclear issue. *Caligrama (São Paulo. Online)* **3**(2). https://doi.org/10.11606 /issn.1808–0820.cali.2007.65490

Douglas, **M.** (1999) *Implicit Meanings: Selected Essays in Anthropology*. London: Routledge. https://doi.org/10.4324/9780203029909

Dragojevic, **M.**, **Gasiorek**, **J.**, **Giles**, **H.** (2016) Accommodative strategies as core of the theory. In Giles, H. (ed.), *Communication Accommodation Theory: Negotiating Personal Relationships and Social Identities across Contexts*. Cambridge: Cambridge University Press, 36–59. https://doi.org/10.1017/CBO9781316226537 .003

Drew, **P.** (2013) Conversation analysis and social action. *Journal of Foreign Languages* **37**(3), 2–19.

Drew, **P.**, **Walker**, **T.** (2010). Citizens' emergency calls requesting assistance in calls to the police. In Coulthard M., Johnson A. (eds.), *The Routledge Handbook of Forensic Linguistics*. London: Routledge, 96–110. https://doi.org/10.4324/9780203855607– 18

DuBois, **J.** (2002) Adolf Reinach: Metaethics and the philosophy of law. *Phenomenological Approaches to Moral Philosophy* **47**, 327–346. https://doi.org/10 .1007/978–94-015–9924-5_17

Durkheim, **É.** (1912 [1954/2001]) *The Elementary Forms of Religious Life*, translated by Cosman, C. Oxford: Oxford University Press.

Dynel, **M.**, **Poppi**, **F.** (2019) Risum teneatis, amici?*: The socio-pragmatics of RoastMe humour. *Journal of Pragmatics* **139**, 1–21. https://doi.org/10.1016/j.pragma.2018.10 .010

Edmondson, **W.** (1981) *Spoken Discourse: A Model for Analysis*. London: Longman

Edmondson, **W.**, **House**, **J.** (1981) *Let's Talk and Talk About It: A Pedagogic Interactional Grammar of English*. Münich: Urban & Schwarzenberg.

Edmondson, **W.**, **House**, **J.** (2011) *Einführung in die Sprachlehrforschung*, 4th ed. Tübingen: Narr.

Edmondson, **W.**, **House**, **J.**, **Kádár**, **D.** (2023) *Expressions, Speech Acts and Discourse: A Pedagogic Interactional Grammar of English*. Cambridge: Cambridge University Press.

Edwards, E. (1948) A classified guide to the Thirteen Classes of Chinese Prose. *Bulletin of the School of Oriental and African Studies* **12**(3/4), 770–788. https://doi .org/10.1017/S0041977X0008335X

Eelen, G. (2001) *A Critique of Politeness Theories*. Manchester: St. Jerome.

Ellis, B. (1989) Death by folklore: Ostension, contemporary legend, and murder. *Western Folklore* **48**(3), 201–220. https://doi.org/10.2307/1499739

Escandell-Vidal, V. (1996) Towards a cognitive approach to politeness. *Language Sciences* **18**(3/4), 629–650. https://doi.org/10.1016/S0388-0001(96)00039-3

Felson, R. (1982) Impression management and the escalation of aggression and violence. *Social Psychology Quarterly* **45**(4), 245–254. https://doi.org/10.2307 /3033920

Ferguson, C. (1976) The structure and use of politeness formulas. *Language in Society* **5**(2), 137–151. https://doi.org/10.1017/S0047404500006989

Fillmore, C. (1980) Remarks on contrastive pragmatics. In Fisiak, J. (ed.), *Contrastive Linguistics: Prospects and Problems*. Berlin: Mouton de Gruyter, 119–141

Fillmore, C. (1982) Frame semantics. In Linguistic Society of Korea (ed.), *Linguistics in the Morning Calm*. Seoul: Hanshin, 111–137.

Fitzmaurice, S. (2002) *The Familiar Letter in Early Modern English: A Pragmatic Approach*. Amsterdam: John Benjamins. https://doi.org/10.1075/pbns.95

Fraser, B. (1990) Perspectives on politeness. *Journal of Pragmatics* **14**(2), 219–236. https://doi.org/10.1016/0378–2166(90)90081-N

Fraser, B., Nolen, W. (1981) The association of deference with linguistic form. *International Journal of the Sociology of Language* **27**, 93–109. https://doi.org/10 .1515/ijsl.1981.27.93

Frick, R. W. (1986) The prosodic expression of anger: Differentiating threat and frustration. *Aggressive Behaviour* **12**(2), 121–128. https://doi.org/10.1002/1098-23 37(1986)12:2<121::AID-AB2480120206>3.0.CO;2-F

Fuchs-Burnett, T. (2002) Mass public corporate apology. *Dispute Resolution Journal* **57**(2), 26–32.

Galvany, A. (2012) Sly mouths and silver tongues: The dynamics of psychological persuasion in ancient China. *Extreme-Orient* **34**, 15–40. https://doi.org/10.4000/extre meorient.250

Garcés-Conejos Blitvich, P. (2010) A genre approach to the study of im-politeness. *International Review of Pragmatics* **2**(1), 46–94. https://doi.org/10.1163 /187731010X491747

Garcés-Conejos Blitvich, P. (2015) Setting the linguistics research agenda for the r-service encounters genre: Natively digital versus digitized perspectives. In de la O Hernández-López, M., Fernández Amaya, L. (eds.), *A Multidisciplinary Approach to Service Encounters*. Leiden: Brill, 13–36. https://doi.org/10.1163/9789004260160_003

Garcia, C. (1993) Making a request and responding to it: A case study of Peruvian Spanish speakers. *Journal of Pragmatics* **19**(2), 127–152. https://doi.org/10.1016/0 378–2166(93)90085–4

Garfinkel, H. (1964) Studies of the routine grounds of everyday activities. *Social Problems* **11**(3), 225–250.

Georgakopolou, A. (1997) *Narrative Performances: A Study of Modern Greek Storytelling*. Amsterdam: John Benjamins. https://doi.org/10.1075/pbns.46

Ghezzi, C., Molinelli, P. (2019) Italian *scusa* from politeness to mock politeness. *Journal of Pragmatics* **142**, 245–257. https://doi.org/10.1016/j.pragma.2018.10.018

Giles, H. (2016) The social origins of CAT. In Giles, H. (ed.), *Communication Accommodation Theory: Negotiating Personal Relationships and Social Identities across Contexts*. Cambridge: Cambridge University Press, 1–12. https://doi.org/10.1017/CBO9781316226537.001

Gleason, J., Pearlmann, R., Greif, E. (1984) What's the magic word: Learning language through politeness routines. *Discourse Processes* **7**(4), 493–502. https://doi.org/10.1080/01638538409544603

Goffman, E. (1955) On face-work: An analysis of ritual elements in social interaction. *Psychiatry* **18**(3), 213–231. https://doi.org/10.1080/00332747.1955.11023008

Goffman, E. (1959) *The Presentation of Self in Everyday Life*. Garden City, NY: Doubleday.

Goffman, E. (1963) *Behavior in Public Places: Notes on the Social Organization of Gatherings*. New Brunswick, NJ: Transaction Publishers.

Goffman, E. (1967) *Interaction Ritual. Essays on Face-to-Face Behavior.* Garden City, NY: Doubleday.

Goffman, E. (1974) *Frame Analysis: An Essay on the Organization of Experience*. Cambridge, MA: Harvard University Press.

Goffman, E. (1976) Gender display. In Goffman, E. (ed.), *Gender Advertisements. Communications and Culture*. Basingstoke: Palgrave, 10–23. https://doi.org/10.1007/978–1–349–16079–2_1

Goffman, E. (1979) Footing. *Semiotica* **25**(1/2), 1–30. https://doi.org/10.1515/semi.1979.25.1–2.1

Goffman, E. (1981) *Forms of Talk*. Philadelphia, PA: University of Pennsylvania Press.

Goffman, E. (1983) The interaction order. *American Sociological Review* **48**(1), 1–17. https://doi.org/10.2307/2095141

Green, E. (1995) On syntactic and pragmatic features of speech acts in Wulfstan's Homilies. In Rauch, I., Carr, G. (eds.), *Insights in Germanic Linguistics I: Methodology in Transition*. Berlin: Mouten de Gruyter, 109–126.

Gu, Y. (1990) Politeness phenomena in modern Chinese. *Journal of Pragmatics* **14**(2), 237–257. https://doi.org/10.1016/0378–2166(90)90082-O

Haidt, J., Joseph, C. (2007) The moral mind: How five sets of innate intuitions guide the development of many culture-specific virtues, and perhaps even modules. In Carruthers, P., Laurence, S., Stich, S. (eds.), *The Innate Mind, Vol. 3*. Oxford: Oxford University Press, 367–391. https://doi.org/10.1093/acprof:oso/9780195332834.003.0019

Han, G. (2018) Chunqiu 'Lizhi' yu 'Jingguo-zhi-wen' de shengcheng – Yi zhenglun, jianci, wendui santi wei hexin ('Lizhi' in the Spring and Autumn Period and the creation of 'Jingguo Zhiwen': Examining political commentary, admonishment rhetoric and question-answers). *Wen-Shi-Zhe* (Literature, History and Philosophy) **364**(1): 70–88.

Harris, S., Grainger, K., Mullany, L. (2006) The pragmatics of political apologies. *Discourse and Society* **17**(6), 715–737. https://doi.org/10.1177/0957926506068429

Hartley, J. (2013) *Understanding News*. London: Routledge. https://doi.org/10.4324/9781315002378

Haugh, **M.** (2004) Revisiting the conceptualisation of politeness in English and Japanese. *Multilingua* **23**(1/2): 85–109. https://doi.org/10.1515/mult.2004.009

Haugh, **M.** (2013) Disentangling face, facework and im/politeness. *Pragmática Sociocultural / Sociocultural Pragmatics* **1**(1), 46–73. https://doi.org/10.1515/soprag-2012–0005

Haugh, **M.B** (2013a) Im/politeness, social practice and the participation order. *Journal of Pragmatics* **58**, 52–72. https://doi.org/10.1016/j.pragma.2013.07.003

Haugh, **M.** (2015) *Im/Politeness Implicatures*. Berlin: Mouton De Gruyter.

He, **T.** (2003) 'Zuozhuan' jianshuo yingdui-de celüe yishu (The art of persuasion tactics Zuozhuan). *Xibei Nonglin Keji Daxue Xuebao* (Journal of Northeast A&F University) **3**(5): 134–137.

He, **X.**, **Sheng**, **X.** (2014) BingYiFa xinxiu yu gaoxiao guofang jiaoyu chuangxin fazhan (Revision of conscription law and innovation and development of university defense education). *Hunan Shifan Daxue Shehui Kexue Xuebao* (Journal of Social Science of Hunan Normal University) **1**, 135–140.

He, **Z.**, **Ren**, **W.** (2016) Current address behaviour in China. *East Asian Pragmatics* **1** (2), 163–180. https://doi.org/10.1558/eap.v1i2.29537

Held, **G.** (1992) Politeness in linguistic research. In Watts, R., Ide, S., Ehlich, K. (eds.), *Politeness in Language: Studies in its History, Theory and Practice*. Berlin: Mouton de Gruyter, 131–154. https://doi.org/10.1515/9783110886542–008

Held, **G.** (1996) Two polite speech acts in contrastive view: Aspects of the realization of requesting and thanking in French and Italian. In Ammon, U. (ed.), *Contrastive Sociolinguistics*. Berlin: Mouton de Gruyter, 363–384. https://doi.org/10.1515/9783110811551.363

Held, **G.** (2005) Politeness in linguistic research. In Watts, R., Ide, S., Ehlich, K. (eds.), *Politeness in Language Studies in its History, Theory and Practice*. Berlin: Mouton, 131–154.

Held, **G.** (2010) Supplica la mia parvidade . . . : Petitions in medieval society – a matter of ritualised or first reflexive politeness? *Journal of Historical Pragmatics* **11**(2), 194–218. https://doi.org/10.1075/jhp.11.2.02hel

Heverkate, **H.** (1988) Toward a typology of politeness strategies in communicative interaction. *Multilingua* **7**(4), 385–410. https://doi.org/10.1515/mult.1988.7.4.385

Ho, **D.** (1976) On the concept of face. *American Journal of Sociology* **81**(4), 867–884. https://doi.org/10.1086/226145

Hollywood, **A.** (2002) Performativity, citationality, ritualization. *History of Religions* **42**(2), 93–115. https://doi.org/10.1086/463699

Holzinger, **K.** (2004) Bargaining through arguing: An empirical analysis based on speech act theory. *Political Communication* **21**(2), 195–222. https://doi.org/10.1080/10584600490443886

Hopkinson, **C.** (2013) Trolling in online discussions: From provocation to community-building. *Brno Studies in English* **39**(1), 5–25.

Horgan, **M.** (2019) Everyday incivility and the urban interaction order: Theorizing moral affordances in ritualized interaction. *Journal of Language Aggression and Conflict* **7**(1), 32–55. https://doi.org/10.1075/jlac.00018.hor

Horgan, **M.** (2020) Urban interaction ritual: Strangership, civil inattention and everyday incivilities in public space. *Pragmatics* **30**(1), 116–141. https://doi.org/10.1075/prag.19022.hor

Hostetler, M. (2012) The politeness of a disciplining text: Ideal readers in Ancrene Wisse. *Journal of Historical Pragmatics* **13**(1): 29–49. https://doi.org/10.1075/jhp.13.1.02hos

House, J. (1989) Politeness in English and German: The functions of Please and Bitte. In Blum-Kulka, S., House, J, Kasper, G. (eds.), *Cross-Cultural Pragmatics: Requests and Apologies*. Norwood, NJ: Ablex, 96–119.

House, J., Kádár, D. (2020) T/V pronouns in global communication practices: The case of IKEA catalogues across linguacultures. *Journal of Pragmatics* **161**, 1–15. https://doi.org/10.1016/j.pragma.2020.03.001

House, J., Kádár, D. (2021a) *Cross-Cultural Pragmatics*. Cambridge: Cambridge University Press. https://doi.org/10.1017/9781108954587

House, J., Kádár, D. (2021b) German and Japanese war crime apologies: A contrastive pragmatic study. *Journal of Pragmatics* **177**, 109–121. https://doi.org/10.1016/j.pragma.2021.02.001

House, J., Kádár, D. (2023 ahead of print) Speech acts and interaction in second language pragmatics: A position paper. *Language Teaching*, 1–12. https://doi.org/10.1017/S0261444822000477

House, J., Kádár, D. (2023) *Contrastive Pragmatics and Foreign Language Learning*. Edinburgh: Edinburgh University Press.

House, J., Kádár, D. (in press) Learning Chinese in a study abroad context – The case of ritual congratulating. *International Journal of Applied Linguistics*.

House, J., Kádár, D., Liu, F., Liu, S. (2022) Greeting in English as a foreign language: A problem for speakers of Chinese. *Applied Linguistics* **44**(2), 189–216. https://doi.org/10.1093/applin/amac031

House, J., Kádár, D., Liu, F., Song, Y. (2023 ahead of print) Aggression in diplomatic notes – a pragmatic analysis of a Chinese-American conflict in times of colonisation. *Text & Talk*. https://doi.org/10.1515/text-2021–0036

Houston, W. (1993) What did the prophets think they were doing? Speech acts and prophetic discourse in the Old Testament. *Biblical Interpretation* **1**(2), 167–188. https://doi.org/10.1163/156851593X00043

Houston, B., Hansen, G., Nisbett, G. (2011) Influence of user comments on perceptions of media bias and third-person effect in online news. *Electronic News* **5**(2), 79–92. https://doi.org/10.1177/193124311140

Huang, Y. (2008) Politeness principle in cross-culture communication. *English Language Teaching* **1**(1), 96–101.

Hultgren, C. (2017) Vocatives as rationalized politeness: Theoretical insights from emerging norms in call centre service encounters. *Journal of Sociolinguistics* **21**(1), 90–111. https://doi.org/10.1111/josl.12224

Hutchins, B., Rowe, D. (2012) *Sport Beyond Television: The Internet, Digital Media and the Rise of Networked Media Sport*. London: Routledge.

Ide, R. (1998) 'Sorry for your kindness': Japanese interactional ritual in public discourse. *Journal of Pragmatics* **29**(5), 509–529. doi.org/10.1016/S0378-2166(98)80006–4

Ide, S. (1989) Formal forms and discernment: Two neglected aspects of universals of linguistic politeness. *Multilingua* **8**(2/3), 223–248. https://doi.org/10.1515/mult.1989.8.2–3.223

Ide, S. (2005) How and why honorifics can signify dignity and elegance: The indexicality and reflexivity of linguistic rituals. In Lakoff, R., Ide, S. (eds.), *Broadening the Horizon of Linguistic Politeness.* Amsterdam: John Benjamins, 45–64. https://doi.org /10.1075/pbns.139.06ide

Ilieva, G. (2003) The Rg Vedic hymn as a ritual speech event: About some grammatical-rhetorical features of 10.39 from a pragmatic perspective. *Journal of Historical Pragmatics* **4**(2), 171–193. https://doi.org/10.1075/jhp.4.2.03ili

Itakura, H., Tsui, A. (2011) Evaluation in academic discourse: Managing criticism in Japanese and English book reviews. *Journal of Pragmatics* **45**(5), 1366–1379. https:// doi.org/10.1016/j.pragma.2010.10.023

Iyer, G, Villas-Boas, M. (2003) A bargaining theory of distribution channels. *Journal of Marketing Research* **40**(1), 80–100. https://doi.org/10.1509/jmkr.40.1.80.1913

Jacobs, A., Jucker, A. (1995) The historical perspective in pragmatics. In Jucker, A. (ed.), *Historical Pragmatics: Pragmatic Developments in The History of English.* Amsterdam: John Benjamins, 3–33.

Jaffe, A. (ed.) (2009) *Stance: Sociolinguistic Perspectives.* Oxford: Oxford University Press. https://doi.org/10.1093/acprof:oso/9780195331646.001.0001

Jalilifar, N., Mayahi, A. (2022) Self-denigration in academic discourse: The case of the Iranian doctoral defense. *Functions of Language* **29**(3), 300–327. https://doi.org/10 .1075/fol.22021.may

Jay, W. (2000) *Why We Curse: A Neuro-psycho-social Theory of Speech.* Philadelphia, PA and Amsterdam: John Benjamins. https://doi.org/10.1075/z.91

Jiang, X. (2006) Cross-cultural pragmatic differences in US and Chinese press conferences: The case of the North Korea Nuclear crisis. *Discourse & Society* **17**(2), 237–257. https://doi.org/10.1177/0957926506060

Johnstone, B. (1994) *Repetition in Discourse: Interdisciplinary Perspectives. 2 Vols.* Norwood, NJ: Ablex.

Kádár, D. (2007) *Terms of (Im)Politeness: On the Communicational Properties of Traditional Chinese Terms of Address.* Budapest: Eötvös Loránd University Press.

Kádár, D. (2009) *Model Letters in Late Imperial China – 60 Selected Epistles from 'Letters from Snow Swan Retreat'.* Munich: Lincom.

Kádár, D. (2010) Exploring the historical Chinese denigration/elevation phenomenon. In Culpeper, J., Kádár, D. (eds.), *Historical (Im)Politeness.* Bern: Peter Lang, 117–145.

Kádár, D. (2011) *Historical Chinese Letter Writing.* London: Bloomsbury.

Kádár, D. (2012) Historical Chinese politeness and rhetoric. A case study of epistolary refusals. *Journal of Politeness Research* **8**(1), 93–110. https://doi.org/10.1515/pr-20 12–0006

Kádár, D. (2013) *Relational Rituals and Communication: Ritual Interaction in Groups.* Basingstoke: Palgrave Macmillan. https://doi.org/10.1057/9780230393059

Kádár, D. (2014) Heckling – A mimetic-interpersonal perspective. *Journal of Language Aggression and Conflict* **2**(1), 1–35. https://doi.org/10.1075/jlac.2.1 .01kad

Kádár, D. (2017) *Politeness, Impoliteness and Ritual: Maintaining the Moral Order in Interpersonal Interaction.* Cambridge: Cambridge University Press. https://doi.org/ 10.1017/9781107280465

Kádár, D. (2020) Capturing injunctive norm in pragmatics: Meta-reflective evaluations and the moral order. *Lingua* **237**(10/11). https://doi.org/10.1016/j.lingua.2020.102814

Kádár, D., Bax, M. (2013) In-group ritual and relational work. *Journal of Pragmatics* **58**, 73–86. https://doi.org/10.1016/j.pragma.2013.03.011

Kádár, D., Culpeper, J. (2010) Historical (im)politeness: An introduction. In Culpeper, J., Kádár, D. (eds.), *Historical (Im)Politeness*. Bern: Peter Lang, 9–36.

Kádár, D., Haugh, M. (2013) *Understanding Politeness*. Cambridge: Cambridge University Press. https://doi.org/10.1017/CBO9781139382717

Kádár, D., Haugh, M., Chang, M. (2013) Aggression and perceived national face threats in Mainland Chinese and Taiwanese CMC discussion boards. *Multilingua* **32** (3), 343–372. https://doi.org/10.1515/multi-2013–0016

Kádár, D., House, J. (2020a) 'Politeness markers' revisited – A contrastive pragmatic perspective. *Journal of Politeness Research* **17**(1), 79–109. https://doi.org/10.1515/pr-2020–0029

Kádár, D., House, J. (2020b) Revisiting the duality of convention and ritual: A contrastive pragmatic inquiry. *Poznan Studies in Contemporary Linguistics* **56** (1), 83–111. https://doi.org/10.1515/psicl-2020–0003

Kádár, D., House, J., Liu, F., Shi, W. (2023). Historical language use in Europe from a contrastive pragmatic perspective: An exploratory case study of letter closings. *Journal of Historical Pragmatics* **24**(1), 143–159. https://doi.org/10.1075/jhp.00068.kad

Kádár, D., Márquez-Reiter, R. (2015) (Im)politeness and (im)morality: Insights from intervention. *Journal of Politeness Research* **11**(2), 239–260. https://doi.org/10.1515/pr-2015–0010

Kádár, D., Mills, S. (2011) Politeness and culture. In Kádár, D., Mills, S. (eds.), *Politeness in East Asia*. Cambridge: Cambridge University Press, 21–44. https://doi.org/10.1017/CBO9780511977886.004

Kádár, D., Ning, P., Ran, Y. (2018) Public ritual apology: A case study of Chinese. *Discourse, Context and Media* **26**, 21–31. https://doi.org/10.1016/j.dcm.2018.01.003

Kádár, D. Z., Parvaresh, V., Ning, P. (2019) Morality, moral order, and language conflict and aggression: A position paper. *Journal of Language Aggression and Conflict* **7**(1), 6–31.

Kádár, D., Paternoster, A. (2015) Historicity in metapragmatics: A study on 'discernment' in Italian metadiscourse. *Pragmatics* **25**(3), 369–391. https://doi.org/10.1075/prag.25.3.03kad

Kádár, D., Parvaresh, V., Ning, P. (2018) Morality, moral order, and language conflict and aggression: A position paper. *Journal of Language Aggression and Conflict* **7**(1), 6–31. https://doi.org/10.1075/jlac.00017.kad

Kádár, D., Robinson-Davies, S. (2015) Ritual, aggression, and participatory ambiguity: A case study of heckling. *Journal of Language Aggression and Conflict* **4**(2), 202–233. https://doi.org/10.1075/jlac.4.2.03kad

Kádár, D., Szalai, A. (2020) The socialisation of interactional rituals: A case study of ritual cursing as a form of teasing in Romani. *Pragmatics* **30**(1), 15–39. https://doi.org/10.1075/prag.19017.kad

Kádár, **D.**, **Zhang**, **S.** (2019) (Im)politeness and alignment: A case study of public political monologues. *Acta Linguistica Academica* **66**(2), 229–249. https://doi.org/10.1556/2062.2019.66.2.5

Kallia, **A.** (2005) Directness as a source of misunderstanding: The case of requests and suggestions. In Lakoff, R., Ide, S. (eds.), *Broadening the Horizon of Linguistic Politeness*. Amsterdam: John Benjamins, 217–234.

Karioris, **F.** (2016) Temporally adrift and permanently liminal: Relations, sistalgia and a U.S. university as site of transition and frontier. *Culture Unbound* **8**, 88–103. https://doi.org/10.3384/cu.2000.1525.168188

Katriel, **T.** (1991) *Communal Webs: Communication and Culture in Contemporary Israel*. New York, NY: State University of New York Press.

Ke, **Z.** (2012) Xian-Qin jian-tiwen ji qi wenhua yiyun (Admonishing literary pieces and their cultural impact in Pre-Qin China). *Wenyi Pinglun* (Literature and Art Criticism) **10**, 4–7.

Kelly, **J.**, **Kaplan**, **M.** (1990) History, structure and ritual. *Annual Review of Anthropology* **19**, 119–150. https://doi.org/10.1146/annurev.an.19.100190.001003

Kennedy, **J.** (1966) Pleasant society and the image of limited good: A critique. *American Anthropologist* **68**(5), 1212–1225. https://doi.org/10.1525/aa.1966.68.5.02a00080

Kerbrat-Orecchioni, **C.** (2011) From good manners to facework: Politeness variations and constants in France, from the classic age to today. *Journal of Historical Pragmatics* **12**(1/2), 133–155. https://doi.org/10.1075/jhp.12.1–2.06ker

Kerbrat-Orecchioni, **C.** (2006) Politeness in small shops in France. *Journal of Politeness Research* **2**(1), 79–103. https://doi.org/10.1515/PR.2006.005

Keshavarz, **M.**, **Eslami**, **Z.**, **Ghahreman**, **V.** (2006) Pragmatic transfer and Iranian EFL refusals: A cross-cultural perspective of Persian and English. In Bardovi-Harlig, K., Felix-Brasdefer, C., Saleh Omar, A. (eds.), *Pragmatics & Language Learning, Volume 11*. Honolulu: The University of Hawai'i Press, 359–401.

Kharakki, **A.** (2001) Moroccan sex-based linguistic difference in bargaining. *Discourse & Society* **12**(5), 615–632. https://doi.org/10.1177/0957926501012005003

Kitao, **S.**, **Kitao**, **K.** (2013). Apology, apology strategies, and apology forms for non-apologies in a spoken corpus. *Journal of Culture and Information Science* **8** (2), 1–13.

Knoblauch H. (2014) Benedict in Berlin: The mediatization of religion. In Hepp A., Krotz F. (eds.), *Mediatized Worlds*. London: Palgrave Macmillan, 143–158. https://doi.org/10.1057/97811373003559

Kopytko, **R.** (2007) Philosophy and pragmatics: A language-game with Ludwig Wittgenstein. *Journal of Pragmatics* **39**(5), 792–812. https://doi.org/10.1016/j.pragma.2006.04.011

Koster, **J.** (2003) Ritual performance and the politics of identity: On the functions and uses of ritual. *Journal of Historical Pragmatics* **4**(2), 211–248. https://doi.org/10.1075/jhp.4.2.05kos

Koutlaki, **S.** (2020) "By the elders' leave, I do": Rituals, ostensivity and perceptions of the moral order in Iranian Tehrani marriage ceremonies. *Pragmatics* **30**(1), 88–115. https://doi.org/10.1075/prag.19021.kou

Labov, **W.** (1972) Rules for ritual insults. In Labov, W. (ed.), *Language in The Inner City: Studies in Black English Vernacular*. Oxford: Blackwell, 297–353.

Lebow, R. (1996) *The Art of Bargaining*. Baltimore, MD: John Hopkins University Press.

Lee, J. (2013) Diplomatic ritual as a power resource: The politics of asymmetry in early modern Chinese-Korean relations. *Journal of East Asian Studies* **13**(2), 309–336. https://doi.org/10.1017/S1598240800003957

Leech, G. (1983) *Principles of Pragmatics*. London: Longman.

Leech, G. (2005) Politeness: Is there an East-West divide? *Journal of Foreign Languages* **6**, 3–31.

Leech, G. (2007) Politeness: Is there an East-West divide?. *Journal of Politeness Research* **3**(2), 167–206. https://doi.org/10.1515/PR.2007.009

Leech, G. (2008) *Language in Literature: Style and Foregrounding*. London: Pearson Longman.

Levinson, S. (1979) Activity types and language. *Linguistics* **17**(5/6), 365–400. https://doi.org/10.1515/ling.1979.17.5–6.365

Li, H. (2022) Keqi (客气) in historical Chinese: Evidence from metapragmatic comments. *Journal of Politeness Research* **18**(2), 403–422. https://doi.org/10.1515/pr-2019–0045

Lichtheim, M. (1976) *Ancient Egyptian Literature: A Book of Readings*. Berkeley, CA: University of California Press.

Locher, M., Bolander, B. (2019) Ethics in pragmatics. *Journal of Pragmatics* **145**, 83–90. https://doi.org/10.1016/j.pragma.2019.01.011

Lorenz, K. ([1967] 2021) *On Aggression*. London: Routledge. https://doi.org/10.4324/9781003209249

Lucy, J. (ed.) (1993) *Reflexive Language: Reported Speech and Metapragmatics*. Cambridge: Cambridge University Press. https://doi.org/10.1017/CBO9780511621031

Lunt, P. (2020) Beyond Bourdieu: The interactionist foundations of media practice theory. *International Journal of Communication* **14**, 2946–2963.

Lüger, H. (1983) Some aspects of ritual communication. *Journal of Pragmatics* **7**(6), 695–711. https://doi.org/10.1016/0378–2166(83)90091–7

Ma, L. (2005) Urban administrative restructuring, changing scale relations and local economic development in China. *Political Geography* **24**(4), 477–497. https://doi.org/10.1016/j.polgeo.2004.10.005

Mahmood, S. (2001) Rehearsed spontaneity and the conventionality of ritual: Disciplines of "Şalāt". *American Ethnologist* **28**(4), 827–853. https://doi.org/10.1525/ae.2001.28.4.827

Mai, S., Zong, S., He, Z. (2021) Hanyu zibian de yuyong yanjiu (Self-denigrating expressions in Chinese). *Waiyu Jiaoxue* (Foreign Language Teaching) **42**(1), 71–76.

Mair, V. (1978) Scroll presentation in the T'ang Dynasty. *Harvard Journal of Asiatic Studies* **38**(1), 35–60. https://doi.org/10.2307/2718932

Mair, V. (1984) Li Po's letters in pursuit of political patronage. *Harvard Journal of Asiatic Studies* **44**, 123–153. https://doi.org/10.2307/2719096

Malinowski, B. (2002 [1935]) *Coral Gardens and Their Magic: A Study of the Methods of Tilling the Soil and of Agricultural Rites in the Trobriand Islands*. London: Routledge.

Mao, Z., Hou, J. (2007) Gudai jinjian gongwen de shuofu xiuci (On persuasive rhetoric in ancient admonishment sources). *Xiuci Xuexi* (Rhetoric Study) **144**(6), 76–78.

Marmor, **A.** (2009) Chapter Five: Conventions of language: Pragmatics. In Marmor, A. (ed.), *Social Conventions*. Princeton, NJ: Princeton University Press, 106–130. https://doi.org/10.1515/9781400831654.106

Márquez-Reiter, **R.** (2022) Translocalisation of values, relationality and offence. *Language & Communication* **84**, 20–32.

Mayahi, **A.**, **Jalilifar**, **N.** (2022) Referral for re-submission: Scholarly expectations of EFL applied linguistics doctoral defense sessions. *European Journal of Applied Linguistics* **11**(1), 160–189. https://doi.org/10.1515/eujal-2021–0009

McCabe, **D.** (2008) How to Kill Things with Words: Ananias and Sapphira Under the Apostolic-Prophetic Speech-Act of Divine Judgment (Acts 4:32–5:11). PhD dissertation, The University of Edinburgh.

McConarchy, **T.** (2019) L2 pragmatics as 'intercultural pragmatics: Probing sociopragmatic aspects of pragmatic awareness. *Journal of Pragmatics* **151**, 167–176. https://doi.org/10.1016/j.pragma.2019.02.014

Mills, **S.** (2003) *Gender and Politeness*. Cambridge: Cambridge University Press. https://doi.org/10.1017/CBO9780511615238

Muir, **E.** (2005) *Ritual in Early Modern Europe*. Cambridge: Cambridge University Press.

Muthoo, **A.** (1999) *Bargaining Theory with Applications*. Cambridge: Cambridge University Press. https://doi.org/10.1017/CBO9780511607950

Németh T., **E.** (2008) Verbal information transmission without communicative intention. *Intercultural Pragmatics* **5**(2), 153–176. https://doi.org/10.1515/IP.2008.009

Nilsson, **J.**, **Norrby**, **C.**, **Bohman**, **L.**, **Skogmyr Marian**, **K.**, **Wide**, **C.**, **Lindströme**, **J.** (2020) What is in a greeting? The social meaning of greetings in Sweden-Swedish and Finland-Swedish service encounters. *Journal of Pragmatics* **168**, 1–15. https://doi.org/10.1016/j.pragma.2020.06.007

Ning, **D.** (2012) Xian-Qin tingzheng zhidu yu jianti wenxue de xingsheng (The hearing system of the Pre-Qin period and the development of the admonishment literature). *Xueshu Luntan* (Academic Forum) **6**(1), 158–162.

Nwoye, **O.** (1992) Linguistic politeness and socio-cultural variations of the notion of face. *Journal of Pragmatics* **18**(4), 309–328. https://doi.org/10.1016/0378–2166(92)90092-P

O'Driscoll, **J.** (1996) About face: A defence and elaboration of universal dualism. *Journal of Pragmatics* **25**(1), 1–32. https://doi.org/10.1016/0378–2166(94)00069-X

Ogiermann, **E.** (2009) Politeness and in-directness across cultures: A comparison of English, German, Polish and Russian requests. *Journal of Politeness Research* **5**(2), 189–216. https://doi.org/10.1515/JPLR.2009.011

Ohashi, **J.** (2008) Linguistic rituals for thanking in Japanese: Balancing obligations. *Journal of Pragmatics* **40**(12), 2150–2174. https://doi.org/10.1016/j.pragma.2008.04.001

Okamoto, **S.** (1999) Situated politeness: manipulating honorific and non-honorific expressions in Japanese conversations. *Pragmatics* **9**(1), 51–74. https://doi.org/10.1075/prag.9.1.05oka

Page, **R.** (2019) Self-denigration and the mixed messages of 'ugly' selfies in Instagram. *Internet Pragmatics* **2**(2), 173–205. https://doi.org/10.1075/ip.00035.pag

Pan, **Y.**, **Kádár**, **D.** (2011) *Politeness in Historical and Contemporary Chinese*. London: Bloomsbury.

Parvaresh, V., Tayebi, T. (2018) Impoliteness, aggression and the moral order. *Journal of Pragmatics* **132**, 91–107. https://doi.org/10.1016/j.pragma.2018.05.010

Paternoster, A. (2022) Blunders. In Paternoster, A. (ed.), *Historical Etiquette: Etiquette Books in Nineteenth-Century Western Cultures*. Basingstoke: Palgrave Macmillan, 235–280. https://doi.org/10.1007/978-3-031-07578-0_6

Peet, A. (2015) Testimony, pragmatics, and plausible deniability. *Episteme* **12**(1), 29–51. https://doi.org/10.1017/epi.2014.31

Perritt, H. (2006) *Employee Dismissal Law and Practice*. New York, NY: Kluwer.

Petersen, D. (2002) *The Prophetic Literature: An Introduction*. Westminster: John Know Press.

Pilegaard, M. (1997) Politeness in written business discourse: A textlinguistic perspective on requests. *Journal of Pragmatics* **28**(2), 223–244. https://doi.org/10.1016/S0 378-2166(96)00084-7

Pizziconi, B. (2003) Re-examining politeness, face and the Japanese language. *Journal of Pragmatics* **35**(10/11), 1471–1506. https://doi.org/10.1016/S0378-2166(02)0020 0-X

Pizziconi, B. (2011) Honorifics: The cultural specificity of a universal mechanism in Japanese. In Kádár, D., Mills, S. (eds.), *Politeness in East Asia*. Cambridge: Cambridge University Press, 45–71. https://doi.org/10.1017/CBO9780511977886 .005

Placencia, M. (2019) Responding to bargaining Moves in a digital era: Refusals of offers on Mercado Libre Ecuador. In Garcés-Conejos Blitvich, P., Fernández-Amaya, L., de la O Hernández-López, M. (eds.), *Technology Mediated Service Encounters*. Amsterdam: John Benjamins, 173–197. https://doi.org/10.1075/pbns .300.07pla

Pomerantz, A. (1984) Agreeing and disagreeing with assessments: Some features of preferred/dispreferred turn shapes. In Atkinson, M., Heritage, J. (eds.), *Structures of Social Action*. Cambridge: Cambridge University Press, 57–101. https://doi.org/10 .1017/CBO9780511665868.008

Rampton, B. (1995) Language crossing and the problematisation of ethnicity and socialization. *Pragmatics* **5**(4), 485–513. https://doi.org/10.1075/prag.5.4.04ram

Reichl, K. (2003) The search for origins: Ritual aspects of the performance of epic. *Journal of Historical Pragmatics* **4**(2), 249–267. https://doi.org/10.1075/jhp .4.2.06rei

Ren, W., Woodfield, H. (2016) Chinese females' date refusals in reality TV shows: Expressing involvement or independence? *Discourse, Context & Media* **13**, 89–97. https://doi.org/10.1016/j.dcm.2016.05.008

Richter, A. (2013) *Letters and Epistolary Culture in Early Medieval China*. Seattle, WA: University of Washington Press.

Ridealgh, K. (2020) Talking to God: Conceptualizing an alternative politeness approach for the human/divine relationship. *Journal of Politeness Research* **17**(1), 61–78. https://doi.org/10.1515/pr-2020–0027

Robbins, J. (2015) Ritual, value, and example: On the perfection of cultural representations. *Journal of Royal Anthropological Institute* **21**(51), 18–29. https://doi .org/10.1111/1467–9655.12163

Rota, **A.** (2022) (Re)connecting analytic philosophy and empirical research: The example of ritual speech acts and religious collectivities. *Sophia* **61**, 79–92. https://doi.org/10.1007/s11841-021–00899-5

Ruytenbeek, **N.** (2019) Indirect requests, relevance, and politeness. *Journal of Pragmatics* **142**, 78–89. https://doi.org/10.1016/j.pragma.2019.01.007

Sally, **D.** (2003) Risky speech: Behavioral game theory and pragmatics. *Journal of Pragmatics* **35**(8), 1223–1245. https://doi.org/10.1016/S0378-2166(02)00170–4

Schank, **R.**, **Abelson**, **R**. (1977) *Scripts, Plans, Goals and Understanding*. Hillsdale, NJ: Erlbaum.

Schlund, **K.** (2014) On form and function of politeness formulae. *Journal of Politeness Research* **10**(2), 271–296. https://doi.org/10.1515/pr-2014–0012

Searle, **J.** (1969) *Speech Acts: An Essay in the Philosophy of Language*. Cambridge: Cambridge University Press. https://doi.org/10.1017/CBO9781139173438

Senft, **G.**, **Basso**, **E.** (2009) *Ritual Communication*. Oxford: Berg Books. https://doi.org/10.4324/9781003086581

Shen, **X.**, **Chen**, **S.** (2019) Doing power threatening acts (PTAs) in ancient China: An empirical study of Chinese jian discourse. *Journal of Historical Pragmatics* **20**(1), 132–156. https://doi.org/10.1075/jhp.17002.she

Shields, **A.** (2015). *One Who Knows Me: Friendship and Literary Culture in Mid-Tang China*. Cambridge, MA: Harvard University Asia Center.

Sifianou, **M.** (1992) The use of diminutives in expressing politeness: Modern Greek versus English. *Journal of Pragmatics* **17**(2), 155–173. https://doi.org/10.1016/0378–2166(92)90038-D

Spencer-Oatey, **H.** (ed.) (2000) *Culturally Speaking*. London: Continuum. https://doi.org/10.5040/9781350934085

Staal, **F.** (1979) The meaninglessness of ritual. *Numen* **26**(1), 2–22. https://doi.org/10.1163/156852779X00244

Staal, **F.** (1982) Ritual, grammar, and the origins of science in India. *Journal of Indian Philosophy* **10**, 3–35. https://doi.org/10.1007/BF00200181

Stanley, **C.** (2004) *Arguing with Scripture: The Rhetoric of Quotations in the Letters of Paul*. London: Bloomsbury.

Swidler, **A.** (2001) What anchors cultural practices? In Schatzki, T., Knorr-Cetina, K., von Savigny, E. (eds.), *The Practice Turn In Contemporary Theory*. London: Routledge, 74–92. https://doi.org/10.4324/9780203977453

Taavitsainen, **I.**, **Jucker**, **A.** (2010) Expressive speech acts and politeness in eighteenth-century English. In Hickey, R. (ed.), *Eighteenth-Century English: Ideology and Change*. Cambridge: Cambridge University Press, 159–181. https://doi.org/10.1017/CBO9780511781643.010

Tang, **C.**, **Zhang**, **G.** (2009) A contrastive study of compliment responses among Australian English and Mandarin Chinese speakers. *Journal of Pragmatics* **41**(2), 325–345. https://doi.org/10.1016/j.pragma.2008.05.019

Tannen, **D.** (1979) What's in a frame? Service evidence for underlying expectations. In Friedl, R. (ed.), *New Directions in Discourse Processing*. Norwood, NJ: Ablex, 14–56.

Tantucci, **V.**, **Wang**, **A.** (2018) Illocutional concurrences: The case of evaluative speech acts and face-work in spoken Mandarin and American English. *Journal of Pragmatics* **138**, 60–67. https://doi.org/10.1016/j.pragma.2018.09.014

Tao, M. (2012) Tanpan yanyuxingwei yanjiu (The study of the speech act of negotiation). *Hunan Daxue Xuebao* (Journal of Hunan University) **16**(1), 53–57.

Tasca, L. (2004) *Galatei. Buone maniere e cultura borghese nell'Italia dell'Ottocento* [Etiquette. Good manners and bourgeois culture in nineteenth-century Italy] Florence: Le Lettere.

Terkourafi, M. (2001) Politeness in Cypriot Greek: A Frame-Based Approach. PhD dissertation, University of Cambridge, Cambridge.

Terkourafi, M. (2005) An argument for a frame-based approach to politeness: Evidence from the use of imperative in Cypriot Greek. In Lakoff, R., Ide, S. (eds.), *Broadening the Horizon of Linguistic Politeness*. Amsterdam: John Benjamins, 99–116. https://doi.org/10.1075/pbns.139.10ter

Terkourafi, M. (2011) The puzzle of indirect speech. *Journal of Pragmatics* **43**(11), 2861–2865. https://doi.org/10.1016/j.pragma.2011.05.003

Terkourafi, M., Kádár, D. (2017) Convention and ritual (im)politeness. In Culpeper, J., Haugh, J., Kádár, D. (eds.), *The Palgrave Handbook of Linguistic (Im)Politeness*. Basingstoke: Palgrave Macmillan, 171–195. https://doi.org/10.1057/978-1-137-37508-7_8

Thomassen, B. (2014) *Liminality and the Modern: Living Through the In-Between*. London: Routledge. https://doi.org/10.4324/9781315592435

Ting-Toomey, S., Kurogi, A. (1998) Facework competence in intercultural conflict: An updated face-negotiation theory. *International Journal of Intercultural Relations* **22** (2), 187–225. https://doi.org/10.1016/S0147-1767(98)00004-2

Tolmie, J. (2003) Goading, ritual discord and the deflection of blame. *Journal of Historical Pragmatics* **4**(2), 287–301. https://doi.org/10.1075/jhp.4.2.08tol

Traverso, V. (2006) Aspects of polite behaviour in French and Syrian service encounters: A data-based comparative study. *Journal of Politeness Research* **2**(1), 105–122. https://doi.org/10.1515/PR.2006.006

Tuchman, G. (1972) Objectivity as strategic ritual: An examination of newsmen's notions of objectivity. *American Journal of Sociology* **77**(4), 660–679. https://doi.org/10.1086/225193

Turner, V. (1969) *The Ritual Process: Structure and Anti-Structure*. Chicago, IL: Aldine Publishing.

Turner, V. (1974) Liminal to liminoid, in play, flow, and ritual: An essay in comparative symbology. *Mediações: Revista de Ciências Sociais* **17**(2), 214–257. https://doi.org/10.5433/2176-6665.2012v17n2p214

Turner, V. (1979) Frame, flow and reflection: Ritual and drama as public liminality. *Japanese Journal of Religious Studies* **6**(4), 465–449.

Turner, V. (1982) *From Ritual to Theatre: The Human Seriousness of Play*. New York, NY: PAJ Publications.

Usami, M. (2002) *Discourse Politeness in Japanese Conversation: Some Implications for a Universal Theory of Politeness*. Tokyo: Hituzi Shobo.

van Baaren, R., Janssen, L., Chartrand, T., Dijksterhuis, A. (2009) Where is the love? The social aspects of mimesis. *Philosophical Transactions of the Royal Society of London. Series B, Biological Sciences* **364**, 2381–2389. https://doi.org/10.1098/rstb.2009.0057

Van Gennep, A. (1960) *The Rites of Passage*. Chicago, IL: University of Chicago Press.

Van Mulken, **M.** (1996) Politeness markers in French and Dutch requests. *Language Sciences* **18**(3/4), 689–702. https://doi.org/10.1016/S0388-0001(96)00042-3

Verhoeven, **M.** (1993) An interview with Erving Goffman, 1980. *Research on Language and Social Interaction* **26**(3), 317–348. https://doi.org/10.1207/s15327973rlsi2603_

Verhoeven, **M.** (2011) The many dimensions of ritual. In Insoll, T. (ed.), *The Oxford Handbook of the Archaeology of Ritual and Religion*. Oxford: Oxford University Press, 115–132. https://doi.org/10.1093/oxfordhb/9780199232444.013.0010

Vladimirou, **D.**, **House**, **J.**, **Kádár**, **D.** (2021) Aggressive complaining on social media: The case of #MuckyMerton. *Journal of Pragmatics* **177**, 51–64. https://doi.org/10.1016/j.pragma.2021.01.017

Volkov, **S.** (1991) Die Erfindung einer Tradition. *Historische Zeitschrift* **253**, 603–628.

Vollmer, **H.**, **Olshtain**, **E.** (1989) Apologies in German. In Blum-Kulka, S., House, J., Kasper, G. (eds.), *Cross-Cultural Pragmatics: Requests and Apologies*. Norwood, NJ: Ablex, 197–220.

Walkinshaw, **I.**, **Mitchell**, **N.**, **Subhan**, **S.** (2019) Self-denigration as a relational strategy in lingua franca talk: Asian English speakers. *Journal of Pragmatics* **139**, 40–51. https://doi.org/10.1016/j.pragma.2018.10.013

Watts, **R.** (1999) Language and politeness in early eighteenth century Britain. *Pragmatics* **9**(1), 5–20. https://doi.org/10.1075/prag.9.1.02wat

Watts, **R.** (2003) *Politeness*. Cambridge: Cambridge University Press. https://doi.org/10.1017/CBO9780511615184

Weisser, **M.** (2014) Speech act annotation. In Aijmer, K., Rühlemann, C. (eds.), *Corpus Pragmatics: A Handbook*. Cambridge: Cambridge University Press, 84–114. https://doi.org/10.1017/CBO9781139057493.005

Wichmann, **A.** (2004) The intonation of please-requests: A corpus-based study. *Journal of Pragmatics* **36**(9), 1521–1549. https://doi.org/10.1016/j.pragma.2004.03.003

Winke, **P.**, **Teng**, **C.** (2010) Using task-based pragmatics tutorials while studying abroad in China. *Intercultural Pragmatics* **7**(2), 363–399. https://doi.org/10.1515/iprg.2010.016

Wolfson, **N.**, **Manes**, **J.** (1980) The compliment as a social strategy. *Paper in Linguistics* **13**(3), 391–410. https://doi.org/10.1080/08351818009370503

Wuthnow, **R.** (1987) *Meaning and Moral Order: Explorations in Cultural Analysis*. Berkeley, CA: University of California Press.

Xie, **Q.**, **Zhan**, **Y.** (2018) Guoji shangwutanpan huayuyanjiu huigui ji xinjinzhan: shangwu huayuyanjiu xilie zhisi (A review of business negotiation discourse study abroad) *Waiyu Xuekan* (Foreign Language Research) **205**(6), 68–73.

Xu, **H.** (2013) Gudai junzhu ziqian liubian kaozheng – Yi zhaoling wei kaocha duixiang (Studying the evolution of the self-denigrating expression of ancient monarchs – Taking imperial orders as a case study). *Jiangxi Shehui Kexue* [Jiangxi Social Sciences] **33**(12), 128–132.

Xygalatas, **D.** (2022) *Ritual: How Seemingly Senseless Acts Make Life Worth Living*. London: Profile Books.

Yang, **M.** (1997) Mass media and transnational subjectivity in Shanghai: Notes on (re)cosmopolitanism in a Chinese metropolis. In Ong, A., Nonini, D. (eds.), *Ungrounded Empires: The Cultural Politics of Modern Chinese Transnationalism*. New York, NY: Routledge, 287–321.

Yeung, L. (1997) Polite requests in English and Chinese business correspondence in Hong Kong. *Journal of Pragmatics* **27**(4), 505–522. https://doi.org/10.1016/0378-2 166(95)00050-X

Zeng, Q. (2019) Democracy Wisdom in Ancient China: Remonstrating with the Emperor. Paper presented at the RSU International Research Conference 2019. Retrieved from: https://rsucon.rsu.ac.th/files/proceedings/inter2019/IN19-202.pdf [last accessed 9 June 2023].

Zhao S. (1999) *Zhongguo chidu wenxue shi* (*The History of Chinese Epistolary Literature*). Shijiazhuang: Hebei renmin chubanshe.

Zhou, L. (2022) Self-denigration in Mandarin Chinese: An alternative account from sincerity. *Language & Communication* **87**, 1–10. https://doi.org/10.1016/j .langcom.2022.05.002

Zhu, Z., Li, Y. (2008) *Shaoxing shiye yu Zhonggzo mufu wenhua* (The Masters of Shaoxing and the Chinese Office Assistant Culture). Beijing: Renmin chubanshe.

Primary Sources

Cobbett's Parliamentary History of England, Volume 1: From the Norman Conquest, in 1066, to the Year, 1809. London: Curson Hansard.

Guanzi (*Master Guan*). 2016 Edition. Beijing: Zhonghua shuju.

Guoyu (*Discourses of the States*). 2016 Edition. Beijing: Zhonghua shuju.

Lüshi Chunqiu (*Master Lü's Spring and Autumn Annals*). 2011 Edition. Beijing: Zhonghua shuju.

Shiji (*Records of the Grand Historian*). 2011 Edition. Beijing: Zhonghua shuju.

Yanzi Chunqiu (*Annals of Master Yan*). 2015 Edition. Beijing: Zhonghua shuju.

Zhan Guo Ce (*Annals of the Warring States*). 2012 Edition. Beijing: Zhonghua shuju.

Zuozhuan (*The Commentary of Zuo*). 2016 Edition. Beijing: Zhonghua shuju.

Index

activity type, 23–24
addressivity, 48, 54, 63
admonishment, 166
aggression, 6–7, 13, 25, 31–33, 35, 37–40,
    42–45, 59, 61–62, 81, 83, 85, 92, 94, 119,
    196, 204, 206, 208, 211, 213
Agha, Asif, 160
Alexander, Jeffrey, 14, 18
alignment, 64
ambiguity, 39, 47–51, 54–55, 59, 63, 85
ambiguous addressivity, 48
anti-structure, 34, 40–44, 47–50, 52, 55–62, 67,
    73–74, 110–111, 196
Apologise (speech act), 5, 9–10, 24, 39, 46,
    49–50, 52–53, 56, 119, 132–133, 136,
    139–145, 147, 174, 178, 180–181, 185–190
Austin, John, 1, 14, 138, 184

bargaining, 10, 192, 194–204, 207,
    209–213, 216
Bax, Marcel, 2, 14, 17, 21, 33, 44, 81, 96–97,
    99, 108–110
Bendazzoli, Claudio, 62
Blum-Kulka, Shoshana, 19, 22, 84, 88, 91,
    119, 131, 134, 176, 195, 204, 211
Brown, Penelope, 3, 14, 16, 21, 25, 62, 100,
    108, 134, 156, 167, 171–172

ceremonies, 1, 8, 10, 13, 15, 18–19, 34, 79, 140,
    153, 155, 158, 168–169, 217
Chen, Rong, 28, 171
civility, 1, 7, 13, 15, 18, 24, 37, 40–41, 43, 59,
    61–62, 97–98, 125, 148
Collins, Randall, 19, 41, 44, 96, 103, 126
communal orientation, 1, 22–23, 27–28, 41–42,
    55, 59, 63, 73, 82, 85
communitas, 34, 39, 41–43, 46–48, 50–51,
    54–55, 57–59, 110
Complain (speech act), 178–181, 189, 214
Contra move, 194
contrastive pragmatics, 2, 9, 100, 107, 133,
    135–136, 138, 147, 197–198, 200, 216

convention, 1–3, 5, 8–9, 15, 17, 20, 22–30,
    34–36, 40–41, 60, 64, 79, 81, 83, 89, 93–94,
    98, 103–104, 133–134, 149, 156–157, 161,
    167, 172–174, 179, 192, 196, 197, 199, 203,
    212–213
Cook, Haruko, 173
Coulmas, Florian, 16, 25
Counter move, 194
crossing, 18, 32, 80, 157
Culpeper, Jonathan, 22–23, 44, 82, 108
cursing, 7, 15, 28, 30–33, 37

deference, 1, 20, 62, 64, 70, 72, 97–98, 100,
    103, 105, 107, 124, 170, 190
definitions of ritual in pragmatics, 15
Disclose (speech act), 50, 53, 178, 182, 189, 200
Donald, Merlin, 80, 94
Douglas, Mary, 32, 75
downgraders, 88, 92, 159–160
Durkheim, Émile, 14, 16, 19–20
Dynel, Marta, 44

Edmondson, Willis J., 5, 15–16, 22, 26–27, 32,
    35–36, 39, 46–47, 63, 79, 84, 88, 90, 103,
    112, 119, 131–132, 147, 150, 152, 159, 167,
    174, 182, 193–195, 198, 200–201, 207,
    213–214
Eelen, Gino, 19, 22, 25–26, 29, 62, 133
epistolary rituals, 108
escalation, 31–33, 39–40, 44, 47, 49, 59,
    73–74, 88
Excuse/Justify (speech act), 119, 180–181

face threat, 113, 156–157, 159, 162, 173,
    204–205
finiteness of speech acts, 150
Fraser, Bruce, 21, 133

Garcés-Conejos Blitvich, Pilar, 23, 159
Goffman, Erving, 1, 6, 14–15, 19–20, 24, 26,
    32, 35, 43, 48, 63–64, 72–75, 81–82, 96, 103,
    111–112, 137, 139, 193, 203

Milton Keynes UK
Ingram Content Group UK Ltd.
UKHW050957260324
439684UK00032B/486